ONLY THE BEST WILL DO!

By Herb Goldsmith

Published by
TriMark Press, Inc.
800-889-0693

LIBRARY OF CONGRESS CATALOGING-IN-PUBLICATION DATA

Only The Best Will Do!
Goldsmith, Herb

1. Autobiography 2. Business
P. CM.

ISBN: 978-0-9829702-9-4
A12
10 9 8 7 6 5 4 3 2 1
Printed and Bound in the United States of America.

publishing the written word

trimarkpress

A publication of TriMark Press, Inc.
368 South Military Trail
Deerfield Beach, FL 33442
800.889.0693
WWW.TRIMARKPRESS.COM

Dedication

I dedicate this book to the memory of my dear wife, Dolores. She was my companion, my lover, and my best friend. Her constant encouragement and unquestioning faith in me was the motivation for my success. Dolores's love

and devotion was my inspiration. Her pat on the back, her sensuous kiss, and her sumptuous home-cooked meals were my most important rewards in life.

I hope that reading this book will enable my three daughters, Gail, Michelle, and Ileen, and my grandchildren, Blayne, Eric, Sam, and Ivory, to better understand my life and accomplishments, and to appreciate the love and happiness that I enjoyed for 58 years.

Life is what you make it; all it takes is a strong enough belief in yourself. If you're as lucky as I was, you'll find that special person who will admire, motivate, and love you – no matter what your goals are. Evolution has already provided you with everything you'll need. Now go for it.

Set your objectives. Believe in yourself. Don't let everyday problems get in the way.

These were my *Ten Commandments* that I abided by in my career:

1. Believe in your own potential.
2. Be exciting and positive.
3. Look for new objectives.
4. Have pride in yourself and the company you work for.
5. Help others as others helped you.
6. Make time for your family.
7. Reward those who reward you.
8. Be open to new ideas.
9. Have fun in what you do.
10. Achieve your full potential... *and if you decide to sell to retailers add:*

11. NEVER TAKE BACK GOODS!

Chapter One

OH, I HAD TALENT ALL RIGHT. Not the kind of talent you would associate with Sinatra or the Barrymores. No, it was a talent that could identify trends and that allowed me to take advantage of situations in rapidly evolving environments. While we are all products of our time, it is to those who recognize and act on opportunities as they are presented that the future really belongs. While I remember very little about my childhood, I do know that I was born in the Bronx and that we moved to Brooklyn when I was nine years old. I spent my early adolescence in Brighton Beach and Manhattan Beach, and I attended Lincoln High School. Shortly thereafter, I encountered the first of many "coincidental" opportunities that would eventually propel me along the different paths my life would take. It was *where* I was that shaped my memories and caused me to become *who* I was. The Brighton Beach Baths. Coney Island. Nathan's. The Boardwalk, Lundy's, Sheepshead Bay, Dubrow's, Feltman's, Luna Park, Mrs. Stahl's Knishes . . . These were the landscapes of my world – a world that is gone and will never come again.

The first place I remember living in the 1930s was on Anderson Avenue in the Bronx: a four-story walk-up with no air conditioning (well, actually, *no one* had air conditioning). Anderson Avenue ran north and south on a cliff overlooking Jerome Avenue, where we did most of our shopping. I counted 120 steps from our house leading down a steep incline to Jerome

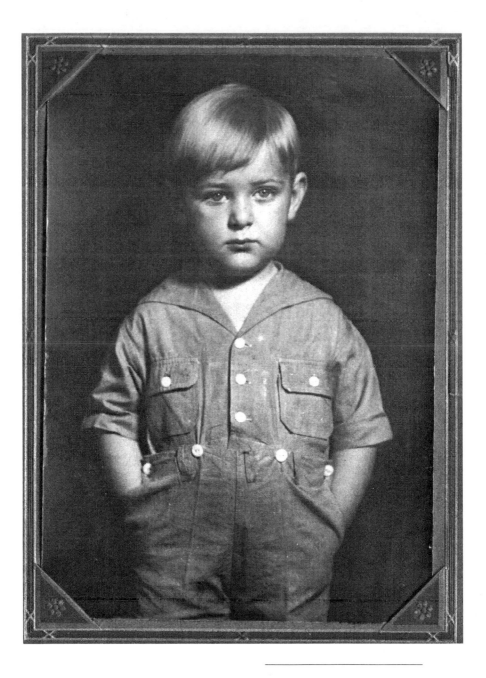

As a young boy
in the Bronx.

Avenue. The bedroom I shared with my brother Billy, who was six years younger, overlooked that seemingly vertical drop.

Since our building was within walking distance of Yankee Stadium, I was often able to get Yankee players to sign their autographs in my most precious possession – a speckled composition book. The book was a priceless treasure, with its autographs of Babe Ruth, Lou Gehrig, and other famous Yankees, as well as visiting team players. One day, when I was about nine years old, my brother Billy picked up his crayons and turned my autograph book into a coloring book. He made purple swirls around "Babe Ruth" and drew orange X's all over "Lou Gehrig." Some pages he just covered in black and green scribbles. I was furious as only a nine-year-old could be. As my three-year-old brother sat on the floor, with my treasured book on his lap and those crayons in his grubby little paws, I quickly picked him up by his ankles and dangled him outside the bedroom window. He screamed for dear life as he eyed the long, treacherous drop down to Jerome Avenue. I think I "scared him good" because he was never quite the same afterwards!

In those days, kids were basically "cut from the same cloth." We knew what our responsibilities were, and we knew what the week held in store for us: school, play, homework, family chores, dinner at home on a wood table, and quality time with the family. There were no fast food joints and no feeling of rush, rush. It was really quite tranquil – girls and boys just gathering together, with no real anxiety in the air, never once giving thought to break-ins or petty robberies. It was a great life.

Even within our small corner of the Bronx, there were distinct ethnic neighborhoods. You lived with your own kind, and everybody had so many relatives nearby that families formed their own "pocket ghettos." There were no school yards, and so from time to time we'd go to a park or a playground for a little excitement and maybe end up playing on some other kid's "turf." The Irish kids lived on Woodycrest Avenue, parallel to Anderson Avenue. In an empty corner lot between Woodycrest and Anderson, we played dueling games against kids with names like Paddy and Sean, with both "gangs" using swords made from orange crate slats and shields made from garbage can

*With my
younger brother Billy.*

covers. It may have been the very first time I considered that they, too, had a right to stand their ground, their turf.

I remember the call of the "I Cash Clothes" man; as housewives dropped their used clothing from fourth-story windows, he would catch the clothes, wrap coins in wads of newspaper, and then somehow toss the payments back up four stories. He hardly missed throwing, and somehow the women never missed catching.

Most of my entertainment came from listening to the radio: an Emerson plug-in that sat in the kitchen. Nobody sat in the living room; you weren't allowed. My shows were mostly serials like *Tom Mix, The Shadow, Little Orphan Annie,* and *The Green Hornet.* When those shows were over, I did my homework and my parents took over the radio, listening to *Fibber McGee and Molly,* something called *Mr. Keen, Tracer of Lost Persons,* and a mind-reading show from which I remember only the phrase: "Doctor Anthony, I have a contestant in the balcony...."

On weekends, of course, the family gathered together to listen to *Jack Benny, Fred Allen,* and *Major Bowes Amateur Hour.*

My maternal grandmother lived with us, and one Sunday, when I was about ten and my brother was four, my mother woke up late. (We were never allowed to disturb her while she was sleeping, especially not on Sundays.)

"Who was at the door earlier? I heard the bell," she said to my brother.

"Oh, that was the dry cleaner. He came to pick up your fur coat. I told him that you were sleeping and I said, 'I can't give it to you without her permission, so why don't you come back? Or I could give you my grandma's fur coat instead.'" And so he did. Innocently and unwittingly, he had given my grandmother's fur coat to a thief! I assumed that my brother's days were numbered – that my mother and grandmother would be absolutely *livid* – but shortly thereafter, we found them in the kitchen telling and retelling the story, and hysterically laughing!

There were very few "children's stores" when I was growing up, but in a family clothing store window one day, I saw a sweatshirt with Mickey Mouse printed on it. I'd never seen a shirt with something printed on it, and having one of my own became an obsession. The sweatshirt cost $2, and I asked my mother if she would buy it for me.

"You have to understand," she began, "that your father works hard and I have to run the house. We don't have money for expendables, things that aren't important. So if you really want that sweatshirt, why don't you go to the grocery store and see if you can get a job and earn the $2?"

So I did. I was seven. I delivered milk in our apartment building, carrying the bottles in a metal holder, four at a time, leaving the bottles outside the doors and collecting the empties. At 40 cents a week, it took five weeks to earn the $2. I was so proud.

"Okay mom, I got the money; can you buy the sweatshirt for me now?"

"Sit down," she said.

I sat.

"Now you're a working person and you're making a salary, so you'll have to pay rent."

How much was the rent? Can you guess? Right! Rent was $2. So I kept working until I cleared a $2 profit, and then I got that sweatshirt. To this day, I love Mickey Mouse.

My mother used that experience to teach me an important lesson about the value of money: things don't just come to you because you *want* them; you have to *do* something to get them.

At that time, there was a building boom going on in the Bronx and a lot of apartment houses were going up. Builders, eager to quickly fill the newly-built apartment houses, competed with landlords for their tenants. To encourage families to continue renting from *them*, landlords offered their tenants a new paint job. Builders, on the other hand, offered tenants not only their choice of paint colors, but also new appliances and free rent for six months – all for signing a two- or three-year lease!

So what did we do? We moved every two or three years to a brand new apartment house. Once, my father came home from selling on the road and couldn't find us; we'd moved. He had to call my Aunt Dottie to find out where we were. My mother, who was a great negotiator, had secured a new apartment for us, with eight months free rent. I was on my way to learning "The Art of the Deal" long before someone wrote a book about it.

Ethel, my mom, was born in the United States and had graduated from high school. She loved books, and a day didn't go by that she didn't read. She looked like your typical American girl: blond hair, blue eyes, perky nose, and a very good figure. She knew how to put it all together: perfectly dressed in the current style for our neighborhood. In order to design a personal wardrobe on a budget, she used a local dressmaker and was careful not to have the same styles in the same fabrics as her friends and neighbors. Sometimes she would buy fabric and a "pattern" from a magazine and have the dressmaker assemble it. She was always eager to show off her new clothes at the many dance halls scattered around the city, and she became an excellent dancer.

Irving, my dad, sold men's outerwear and rainwear to Army Navy stores throughout northern New York state and eastern Pennsylvania. He worked on commission, which meant that he was paid no salary, only a percentage of what he sold – and even then, not until the merchandise was shipped. He was a very well-groomed, dapper man. Much of his wardrobe was made to order, because looking successful implied to his clients that he was making a very good living, which meant that his merchandise had to be good. How he looked was critical in enabling him to impress clients with his "aura of confidence." Image was everything – it meant success! The importance of "image" was brought home to me at an early age, and it is a lesson that has remained with me throughout my career.

> THE IMPORTANCE OF "IMAGE" WAS BROUGHT HOME TO ME AT AN EARLY AGE.

Not everyone in the neighborhood owned a car, but my father needed a large car for business. It was a four-door black Buick, and my friends and I were often given the treat of washing that Goliath. Without thruways, interstate highways, or expressways, my father traveled weeks at a time over rural byways. He would lug his large, strapped-up valises of samples

This picture is of my father Irving and me.

My mother, Ethel.

from his car into the stores, write the orders, and then record his sales in a small, black leather notebook. That notebook represented more than an order book. It was like a diary of my father's life, neatly chronicling his life on the road. I still have one of those notebooks. Recently, I picked it up and turned to a page in the middle of the week. My father had written that he'd returned home that day. Why would he give up a sales day to come home? It was the day his mother had passed away. He had come home, sat *Shiva* for the required week, and gone back out on the road again the very next day, even writing some orders. Because motorist cabins (known today as motels) were few and far between, and were considered a "luxury," he would usually spend nights at customer's homes, once in a while leaving his car there and taking the train back home for the weekend.

Time with my father was precious, and the few things we did together really stand out. Like the time – one of the few times – I went on the road with him . . .

We arrive in a small town, maybe Schenectady, where no chain or department stores existed, only mom and pop stores that carried workmen's boots, sheepskin-lined coats, knives, and working men's clothes. Some were actually called Army Navy Stores.

"Wait in the car," he tells me.

Opening the door, he flicks his hat into the first store we come to. (In those days, men always had to wear hats, especially in the apparel business.) Inside the leather hatband of my father's hat were his initials: "I.G."

"This is my calling card," he says. "They'll know that I'm in town, and they'll be waiting for me to come back before they close. We'll probably be having dinner and sleeping over with these people."

We drive to the end of town, where he visits another store and gets an order, and then we come back. The owner has seen dad's calling card and knows "Goldsmith" is in town. While my father is writing in his order book, the owner (just as my father predicted) is calling his wife to tell her that there will be two more dinner and overnight guests. I realize that my father is more than just a salesman to the people in this small, rural upstate town. He supplies them goods; that's true. But he also supplies them *news*. News from the big city; news about what's happening in the retail business elsewhere. And that news is information they can use to help them grow their own businesses.

When my father did manage to come home for the weekend, it meant taking a day-long train ride on Friday, losing half a workday, and arriving home late Friday night in no condition to go out for dinner with my mother. Even though there were shipping clerks picking and shipping orders during the week, the following Saturday morning, he went to the company's business office and warehouse to make sure that all the orders he'd written had been shipped. (Remember, he only received his commission check after the orders were shipped to the customer.) Other salesmen working within 100 miles of New York City also went in on Saturday to "pick their orders." They walked along the rows of styles, colors, and sizes, picking and choosing and filling their customers' orders. Stragglers invariably arrived to find critical merchandise already gone and were forced to wait to collect their commissions. Insufficient stock to meet a customer's delivery requests were a constant headache. Several times, my father brought me along to guard the orders he had picked and placed on carts, keeping the other salesmen away. Arguments and threats were common.

Saturday night was mom and dad's night out. When he drove home, Sunday was "family day," which often meant going to Uncle Ben and Aunt Ray's house in Flushing, Queens. This is where I'd see my father's parents, Tillie and Max; my uncles, Leo and Ben, aunts Ray, Carleen, and Helen; and lots of cousins for a big cooking feast. If my father didn't make it home for the weekend, we'd spend time with my mother's side of the family: her brother Willie (who was also in the apparel industry and worked for the Adams Hat Corporation); Willie's wife, Dottie; and their three children, Myrna, Teddy, and Carol. We'd also visit Aunt Becky, whom I called *Tanta*. She lived in a walk-up apartment near the Brighton Beach train station and was married to a Communist (there were a lot of those in the 1930s, but all I really understood about Communists back then was that they were people who never seemed to be working but always seemed to be complaining about working conditions). At Aunt Becky's, I would see some of my other cousins: Ethel and Tootsie; Bernie (who ended up with a successful advertising agency); and Abe (who became a high school principal). Abe always wanted to write, and he said that when he got published he'd change his name from Abraham Zamichow to Al Zane. Right! His name is still Abraham Zamichow.

These family Sundays were all about great cooking and great traditional Jewish food. Grilling was not yet an art, so most of the main dishes were potted – like pot roast, or roasted turkey, or chicken. Broiled Rumanian steaks and boiled tongue, with lots of gravy, rounded out our traditional Eastern European feast. The cooking was very creative. It had to be, because we were using animal parts that didn't cost much, like *lungen* and *miltz* (lungs and intestines, made with mushrooms), *kasha varnishkes* (bow tie noodles with sautéed onions and buckwheat groats), *helzel* (stuffed derma), *kugel*, *latkes*, gefilte fish, stuffed cabbage, and *tsimmes*. We ate liver – chopped or broiled, chick peas (called *n'hit*), cooked, cooled, salted, and put in salads, usually with lots of garlic and paprika. Nobody offered a precise recipe for any of these delicacies – a *tzendel*, they'd say – a tooth of this or a *bissel* (bit) of that.

> SUNDAYS WERE ALL ABOUT GREAT COOKING AND GREAT TRADITIONAL JEWISH FOOD.

I remember that for those *special* celebrations, there would always be roast beef. A number one favorite of mine was chicken soup with matzo balls, and I'd always fight with my cousins over the cholesterol-laden unborn chicken eggs (*aelach*) you could sometimes find in the soup. No one drank beer, so we'd have seltzer, or Dr. Brown's cream soda, cherry soda, or celery tonic, and Fox's u-bet chocolate syrup, mixed with seltzer.

But by late Sunday afternoon or early Sunday evening, the celebration would come to an end, and my father would say his goodbyes, walk quietly to his car, and head back out on the road again.

Many of my childhood memories have stayed with me over the years, but one memory was particularly significant because of the impact it made on me. I was ten years old, and my friends and I had just found a bunch of cigarette butts in a grassy area behind our apartment house. Somebody got matches and we quickly lit up. The apartment windows offered a full view of us, and I continually looked up, nervously, until we finally moved to where we were hidden by clotheslines and hanging laundry. My mother, you should know, was a heavy smoker and was addicted to Camels. After dinner that night, she sat me down in the living room, took out a pack of Camels and handed it to me.

"Take one," she said casually. "Light up. If you want to smoke, smoke."

"Mom," I protested, "I'm only ten, I . . ."

"If you can do it in the back yard with your friends, you can smoke with your mother."

How did she know? I smoked until I threw up. After that, I never smoked a cigarette again.

The sounds and smells of the neighborhood left an indelible impression of their own: Kids playing, shouting, and laughing in the street; bells ringing on the Good Humor truck or the Bungalow Bar ice cream truck; young boys and girls running out with their pennies to get their favorite ice cream; children scurrying to catch the Dugan Bakery truck or Stumer's Pumpernickel truck, getting what their mothers had forgotten and, hopefully, getting a free cupcake, as well; aromas filling the streets from the local stores, restaurants, bakeries, and delis, or from the fresh fish truck that came by on Fridays and the fruit and vegetable trucks that offered daily fresh produce.

* * * * * * *

At P.S. 73, my elementary school, I developed a talent for sketching. Interestingly, it was through my "talent" that I discovered my "deficiency" – a deficiency that I was destined to carry with me for the rest of my life. For Thanksgiving, our class had made mural panels on brown wrapping paper. I drew Priscilla and John Alden on Plymouth Rock, while other kids drew the Indians. I drew the two figures first in pencil; the teacher approved. Then I made the same drawing with white chalk; more approval. But when I colored the sketch with pastel chalks, for the final phase, the teacher stopped me.

"Herbert, I want your mother to see me in school tomorrow."

At home, my mother asked, "What did you do now?"

I said, "I don't know. Maybe the teacher wanted to show you how well I was drawing?"

My mother arrived at school. She stared at the pastel sketch of Priscilla Alden. I had colored her lips blue, her hair green, and the water behind her red. My mother laughed hysterically. She said to the teacher, "Don't you know?" And that's how I discovered that I was color blind. (This would become important later on.)

My mother was a strict disciplinarian. She made sure that my brother and I made our beds each day and changed the bedding weekly. I had to wash the dishes after each meal, and sometimes my brother tried to dry them. She made out lists and gave me money to buy items at the local grocery store. She was a very good cook, always experimenting with new dishes and recipes.

It was hard for my father to get back home in the winter because the roads were often icy or made impassable by the snow. A few of those winters, my mother went to Florida by herself on the Silver Meteor train or by ship on the Clyde Mallory Line. My brother and I would stay with Aunt Dottie for weeks at a time. One year, my mother moved my brother and me to the Flamingo Park neighborhood in Miami Beach for the whole school year. Too young to question why she had taken us, we went and made the best of it. The school was made up of small buildings, like chicken coops, and we would trudge from coop to coop in 90-degree heat all day long. There were no air conditioners; all we had in those airless, stifling rooms was a fan or two to break the heat and dry the beads of sweat inching down our backs.

For summer vacations, we went to "the Catskills." This was a major undertaking that involved packing lots of clothes and bedding, as well as stuffing and re-stuffing the car. As my father drove north toward Wurtsboro

Hills and the Catskill Mountains, we would often pass disabled cars, with plumes of steam spewing from their overheated radiators. Remember, this was before there were thruways, and the road was packed with vacationers who had piled mattresses, chairs, and boxes atop their cars. Three hours out of New York, we'd start to feel hungry and uncomfortable. Anxiety would build until we saw the first sign of relief: "Red Apple Rest – Two Miles Ahead." We'd stop at the Red Apple Rest, the Orsek Boys, or the Four Aces to rest, wash, and eat. Then, we'd continue on to White Sulphur Springs – outside of Liberty, New York – where Abe, my mother's father, had a *cuchalane* (which literally means a "cook alone"). It was a bungalow colony where the same four families retreated every summer to escape the city heat, renew friendships, swim in the nearby lake, create their own entertainment, and forget the concrete for a couple of months.

My grandfather Abe built the bungalow colony with money he earned as a window cleaner – cleaning windows at the Empire State Building. He made good money, but it was a dangerous job. Suspended high above the city, a pail of water in one hand and a squeegee in the other, he washed windows with nothing more than a belt around his waist to hold him. At either end of the belt, there was a hook. To keep from falling, he would secure both hooks to the metal eyelets attached to the window frame. This hooked you in and kept you from falling.

Our cottage in Abe's colony had two rooms: a small sitting room and a bedroom. Although it supplied running water, there was neither a kitchen nor a toilet-only a communal outhouse in the back. The main house had two big wood-burning stoves and four ice boxes. There were no refrigerators; every family was allotted half an icebox, we always tried to get the top half because it was closer to the ice. All cooking and eating was done in the main house.

My grand Pa loved to fish. From time to time he let me go along. He had a small row boat that was moored on the shore of Swan Lake. Before climbing into the boat, we had to dig up worms which were used for bait. Our fishing poles were bamboo stick's without a fishing reel. When we hooked a fish we had to swing the entire rod around and unhook the fish. We always caught all kinds of small fish. For some reason he always threw them back into the lake, never bringing any home.

We swam in the lake, picked blueberries, and on weekends went to the nearby hotels, where we tried to sneak into their swimming pools. My mother convinced one of the hotel maids to keep an eye on my brother and me in the evening while she and dad went places like the Lesser Lodge and the Swan Lake Hotel.

Sometimes my father would leave us while we were all at the colony, to go to the office or to get orders from new customers. Many of the other men stayed in the city all week and joined their families on weekends. Aside from this cherished all-too-brief summer vacation, my father was constantly on the road, following his weekly routine.

Although he was starting to make more money, that didn't mean he was around more. Free time with my father was never something I could count on. He did make enough money, however, to enable us to eventually move to a house in Manhattan Beach, Brooklyn.

It was a single-family house on Dover Street, with lots of space, including a basement and a garden. Thanks to a referral from one of my father's Pennsylvania customers, we now had a maid: a farm girl, who removed the burden of housework from my mother's shoulders. Unlike the Bronx, this new neighborhood was primarily "residential," and you needed a bus or a car to get anywhere. It was hard for me to get to school, so sometimes – especially in bad weather – my mother would drive me there. Like the Florida school, this one was also a series of small wooden shacks. I was back to chicken-coop school. Dad had bought my mother a two-seater Ford with a rumble seat. One day, she had an accident right in front of the school, and wouldn't you know it, the car she hit was my *principal's* car! My mother got off easy by apologizing, but my humiliation lasted for the rest of the school year.

My mother was never comfortable in Manhattan Beach. Maybe it was too isolated . . . or maybe having a live-in maid was too intrusive on our personal lives . . . or maybe the house and garden were just too much to maintain. Although my father liked the place more than my mother did, when they heard that "new, modern apartment buildings with elevators" were going up right on the ocean in nearby Brighton Beach, they were ready to move again.

These modern apartments on Brighton Beach Avenue were called the Joseph P. Day apartments; they were a string of four apartment buildings on the beach, at the end of the boardwalk. Instead of the fire escape we'd had in the Bronx, we now had a real balcony. The elevator took you down to the basement, which had locker rooms for beach items and showers for rinsing off the beach sand, making it easier to keep the apartment clean. Included in the rent was a free membership to the private Brighton Beach Baths.

Brighton Beach Avenue was a wide street with room for two traffic lanes on each side. Stores lined one side of the street; apartment houses lined the other: the beach side. Starting at Brighton 16th Street, stores and restaurants – hundreds of them – marched up 20 continuous blocks, crossed Coney Island Avenue, and continued to Ocean Parkway. The BMT subway overhead trestle began over Brighton Beach Ave at 10th Street and ended at Coney Island, the last stop.

Next door to our new building was the celebrated private Brighton Beach Baths, renowned for its oceanfront location and boasting handball courts, basketball courts, heated pools, and sun decks. At night, besides its restaurants and snack bars, the Baths at the "Band Shell" offered musical entertainment – famous bands like Benny Goodman or Ina Rae Hutton and her "all girls band"– and comedians like Danny Kaye, Milton Berle, and Red Buttons. Because everything was outdoors and our apartment was right next door, we enjoyed free admission all summer until just before the Jewish holidays, when the place closed down for the winter.

"I'm going to the beach club tonight. Watch your brother."

My mother was in heaven, at the Brighton Beach Baths, where there were dance classes and dance instructors. When they had dance bands on the weekends and my father was out of town, she would dance with the instructors. Sometimes she went dancing at places like the Manhattan Beach Hotel (whose lobby had an immense plant hanging over a circular, red velvet couch) or at Oriental Beach to the east – where, like the Brighton Beach Baths, they also had bands, shows, and more comedians. Boy, my mother could dance . . . and she never gave it up!

Long after I had gotten married and my mother had moved to Miami Beach, she would come up to Brighton Beach for the summer, rent a room in a bungalow, and go into Manhattan with her lady friends. In Manhattan, they'd rent a rehearsal studio space near Broadway, hire a dance instructor, spend the afternoon doing the cha-cha or the mambo, and eat the lunches they had brought with them to the studio. At the end of the day, in fresh clothes (and, of course, repaired makeup), they would head off to Roseland to dance the night away.

If my father was around on Sundays, he would occasionally play handball at the Baths. He was good, and I can still see his worn-out leather glove and hear the crowds in the stands, watching the tournament and rooting for their favorite player. A lot of money changed hands during those tournaments; the betting was big and the winner could walk away with a hefty pot. But that year – the year of my Bar Mitzvah – my parents separated, and my father began to slowly fade from the family picture . . .

By the time I was in high school, I was working at a butcher shop on 11th Street. From 7:30 to 8:30 in the morning, I would empty kegs filled with iced, fresh-killed chickens. Turning my nose away and gingerly sticking my hands into the carcasses, I had to pull out the necks, gizzards, eggs, and livers, stack the trays with chickens, put them in the display windows and on the shop counters, wash my hands, and get to Lincoln High School before the morning bell rang.

I was a lousy student, sorely lacking in discipline and unable to hone in on my studies. I did silly, wise-guy things with my pals – like sneaking into the school building to steal the upcoming Regents exam that was stored in the principal's office. We were inside poking around when we heard footsteps; we stopped, held our breaths, and then hid under the desks. It turned out to be another bunch of wise guys, also hoping to steal the exam. We jumped up, scaring the hell out of them, and then both groups of wise guys fled in opposite directions, out of the building. We all had to take the Regents exam without any "advance preparation." Amazingly, I passed!

Some nights, after a long day at school, I would cook dinner. My mother was now working two days a week as a salesperson in a hat store – not because we needed the money, I don't think, but just to have something to do and people to talk to while my father was out of town. In those days most women wore a hat especially in the evening and no ensemble would be complete without a pair of gloves. She would come home from work at around 6:00 p.m., too late to start cooking the hot meal we had always enjoyed, and so it was up to me to cook. She instructed me in the "culinary arts," teaching me how to prepare dishes like pot roast, chicken fricassee, boiled fish, and vegetables. This newly acquired skill would stand me in good stead in the years to come.

My friends and I never thought of going into the city because everything we needed was within walking distance. Our entire universe existed within a three- or four-block radius. The beach and the beach club – which occupied everyone's time from May through October – were easily accessed from the basement of our apartment house. All day long, vendors on the public beach – typically kids working to make extra money – came by to sell knishes, ice cream, jelly apples, and soda. The beachgoers all had steady spots on the beach, and the vendors developed their own regular "clientele." They knew what you wanted even before you told them.

On the private side streets, we played stickball and stoop ball. We had "Spawldeens" (really "Spalding" rubber balls) and yo-yos (which were sold on the street by guys from Hawaii, who would carve your name on the yo-yo), and we played jai-alai games with a wooden paddle that was attached to a small rubber ball by an extra-long rubber band. Our yo-yo and jai-alai contests, held at the movie theater, always drew a big turnout.

Brighton Beach Avenue had elevated trains and the Lakeland Theatre, which was cooled on hot summer days by a big fan blowing air over ice. On Saturdays, you saw not only two movies, but also a serial (like Buck Rogers), cartoons, trailers, and a newsreel. The number on your theatre ticket was also your entry into a horse race, filmed at a track and shown in the theater, and you could win a prize if your ticket number's last digit matched the winning horse's number. The 35 cents that Mom gave me covered all of my expenses: a dime would get me into the movie, and a quarter would get me two franks, French fries, and a soft drink at the deli.

Later, the big Oceania Theatre opened across from the Brighton Beach Baths. It was air conditioned, with a large balcony that sure made it easy to fool around! Both the Paramount and the Roxy were just a subway ride away in Manhattan, but the truant officer liked to hang out at those theatres, so we usually avoided them. Once in a blue moon, we'd venture into the city to hear somebody like Frank Sinatra, and we'd look around, thinking, "Wow, look at this place!" as though we were foreign tourists.

Nobody in the neighborhood seemed to want for anything, and if someone did need help, people pitched in. All the stores were family operated, and if they needed extra workers from time to time – for simple chores, like unpacking cartons – the neighborhood kids would fill in for a few hours to make some extra money. There was entertainment everywhere and food all around – everything we needed seemed to be close at hand. There were countless specialty food stores, and stores that became after-hour restaurants (a store might sell woolen yarn during the regular workday and offer home-cooked meals in the back at nighttime).

Sometimes when my mom came home late from work, I *wouldn't* have to cook – we would all go to the local luncheonette instead. We sat at a big counter and watched the food being prepared. I remember the excitement when they got an electric broiler! It was amazing to watch food being cooked on a broiling grill with heating coils on top, and to realize how different broiled food tasted from food that was literally fried on a flat steel sheet, with burners underneath.

Our favorite restaurant was the famous Lundy's on Ocean Avenue in Sheepshead Bay. Behind Lundy's ran the trolley tracks and the trolley that would take us to Lincoln High School, when we didn't walk to school. Most of the waiters were elderly black men who wore white gloves and, at least in my memory, all had white hair. You always had the same waiter – families would come in and ask for their "usual waiter." We ate warm buttermilk muffins with a melting pat of butter on them, fish, lobsters, coconut custard pie, and key lime pie, which nobody had ever heard of. Sometimes on my way back from school, I'd go to the clam bar there, put my schoolbooks down, joke around with the guy shucking clams, and have a couple of clams. Half the time, I didn't have to pay for them, and the oyster crackers were free.

You could take the Ocean Avenue trolley to King's Highway and go to the most famous cafeteria in America, Dubrows, which took up half a city block. They offered every kind of food you could imagine, and my eyes were always bigger than my stomach. Just two stops and 10 cents away was Coney Island – the largest amusement area in the country, and the home of the Cyclone roller coaster, the Wonder Wheel, Nathan's Famous hot dogs, the longest board walk and Coney Island Beach.

This idyllic phase of my life ended when my parents separated. I wasn't aware of what had happened between them, but I assumed that Mom was unhappy with the fact that Dad was constantly traveling and away from home. He was handsome, made a good living, and was well-respected, but I think my mother was lonely. It's hard to remember . . . my parents were young, only in their thirties when they separated.

Seven years later, my mother married Harold, an accountant she'd met while dancing at Roseland. Harold was the opposite of my father: gentle, soft spoken, and a great dancer. My father would later re-marry as well, but all that comes later.

I went to Brooklyn's Lincoln High School, which was very sports oriented. Football was the big thing, but in addition to a football team, they also had a baseball team, a tennis team, and a swimming team. Lincoln had tennis courts, rare in the city then, and a large indoor pool. Not being terribly athletic, the only team that would have me was the swimming team, which practiced often and required a lot of "training time." I also spent Saturday mornings playing in a baseball league in Prospect Park, we wore official team uniforms. I had a pretty good curve ball and started out as a pitcher for the "Cobras." One day, the batter fouled a ball back behind him. It went over the fence, and a kid in the street picked it up.

"Is this yours?" he yelled.

"Yeah," I said. He threw it back to me.

I watched the ball sail back over the fence, not noticing that the umpire had thrown me a replacement ball. It went straight at my head; I went out like a light. When I came to, I had a swollen, bloody nose and bloodstains all over my brand new, official uniform; from then on, I played second base.

In the background, World War II was just beginning. I decided to do my part by joining the Civil Air Patrol at Lincoln High. Besides, what could be more exciting for a 16-year-old than learning to fly? Not many people had *cars*, and here I was going out to Teterboro Airfield in New Jersey with a dozen other kids, learning to fly a Piper Cub. After weeks of lessons, during which I became increasingly confident about my ability with the stick, I was ready for a solo flight. My parents had signed the release, and I was ready! Just before I entered the cockpit, the instructor showed me a page in a book – a page with different colored dots that appeared to form a number.

"Tell us what number you see in the middle," the instructor said.

"Six."

"Hey kid, you want to play games or you want to fly?"

He turned the page; this time I saw a 12. Four tries later, my flying career was over.

I was color blind, remember? I couldn't see the correct numbers on the pages, which meant that I wouldn't have been able to pick out the correct colored lights on a small landing strip from the air. To me, a red light looks orange and a green light looks white. I eventually learned to manage my "color ignorance." But at that moment, on Teterboro Airfield, I was crushed. They wouldn't let me fly, and even worse, the dreaded Army draft was looming in my future.

Meanwhile, I was still a kid in high school and life went on. The other students and I wrote our school's graduation show, *Class Night*, satirizing the teachers. The show was performed by students, Arnold and I were the MCs. It was my first bite of the theatrical apple, and boy did it taste great.

When football season came that year, I was announcing the home games. Speaking into a microphone and hearing my voice reverberating from the portable loudspeakers spread around the field was electrifying. Our football games were played on Saturdays, just like the college games. On Sunday, the radio stations and newspaper reported scores for all of the college games, but not for the high school games (which were ten times more important to me and to all of the other high school kids). Although some of the scores finally made it to the paper by mid-week, teams around the city wanted to know much sooner where they stood in the league standings and how their rivals were doing.

I have no idea how the notion came to me, but one day I found my fingers dialing the number for the local NYC radio station. When someone at the station answered, I asked him why they weren't reporting high school football scores, only college team scores. He had no idea what I was talking about. Didn't he know how many high schools there were in the area? Didn't he know how important high school football was?

"Want to come up to the station after school and talk to us about it?" he asked.

"Sure I would," I replied.

So off I went to the radio station to voice my complaints. When the guy at the station asked if I could get the weekly scores and call them in, I had the good sense to tell him that I was an experienced game announcer and that he should have me announce the scores on the air instead of calling them in. He agreed.

To start, I was given a fifteen-minute time slot early on Sunday mornings, during which I would announce the scores. I had a job with no salary, but it didn't matter – I was on the air. The studio light would go on and I'd give the scores, adding some highlights. Some friends at other schools, and their coaches, provided a smattering of other results. There was no way that I could get <u>all</u> of the scores from <u>all</u> of the schools (or even know who was playing), so I simply made up some of the scores.

Then the phone would start to ring: everyone wanted to talk to the guy who reported the scores. They'd complain about being left out, or they'd complain about my having given out the wrong scores. In response, I'd simply introduce myself and ask if they'd like to become my correspondent. Eventually, I had people all over the city feeding me not only high school football scores, but also the specific details of the game – passes thrown, yardage gained, number of interceptions... Mentioning the correspondents' names on the air made them happy and kept the information flowing.

By the end of the football season, my time slot had gotten longer, but it was my last year of high school and my radio career was over. I had loved every minute of it.

Chapter Two

IT WAS 1945, AND THE WAR in Europe was over, but not in the Pacific. My friends were getting drafted; hardly anyone went to college. I had already taken the ride on two trolleys to check out my draft board, where I had learned that you needed a physical disability in order to avoid the Army. I didn't have flat feet or poor vision, though I did have a tremendous aversion to bugs, jungles, and reptiles, which was what I imagined fighting for your country on one of those Pacific islands was all about. My fears alone wouldn't keep me out of the draft board's clutches.

As soon as I graduated from high school, I got the notice to report to the draft board.

"You're going in the army," they told me.

"What!" I said, thinking of the bugs and the jungles. "Are you guys kidding?"

Luckily, I had heard that if you worked in the Merchant Marine, or attended the Merchant Marine Academy and trained for a specific skill, you were exempted from being drafted into the Army. So, of course, I went to see the supervisor of the Brooklyn Merchant Marine Academy in Oriental Beach, east of Manhattan Beach and about three or four miles from my apartment house in Brighton Beach. By then, I had developed self-

Prepare in Duplicate

Local Board No. 144   23
Kings County   047

FEB 21 1946   144

1716-18 Voorhies Ave.
Brooklyn, New York

(LOCAL BOARD DATE STAMP WITH CODE)

February 21st 1946
(Date of mailing)

ORDER TO REPORT FOR INDUCTION

The President of the United States,

To   **Herbert**   **Martin**   **Goldsmith**
     (First name)   (Middle name)   (Last name)

Order No.   **12992-A**

GREETING:

Having submitted yourself to a local board composed of your neighbors for the purpose of determining your availability for training and service in the land or naval forces of the United States, you are hereby notified that you have now been selected for training and service therein.

LOCAL BOARD NO. 144
1716 - 1718 Voorhies Ave

You will, therefore, report to the local board named above at _____ **Brooklyn, N. Y.** _____
(Place of reporting)

at __ **8:15 A** __ m., on the _____ **4th** _____ day of _____ **March** _____, 19 **46**
(Hour of reporting)

    This local board will furnish transportation to an induction station. You will there be examined, and, if accepted for training and service, you will then be inducted into the land or naval forces.
    Persons reporting to the induction station in some instances may be rejected for physical or other reasons. It is well to keep this in mind in arranging your affairs, to prevent any undue hardship if you are rejected at the induction station. If you are employed, you should advise your employer of this notice and of the possibility that you may not be accepted at the induction station. Your employer can then be prepared to replace you if you are accepted, or to continue your employment if you are rejected.
    Willful failure to report promptly to this local board at the hour and on the day named in this notice is a violation of the Selective Training and Service Act of 1940, as amended, and subjects the violator to fine and imprisonment.
    If you are so far removed from your own local board that reporting in compliance with this order will be a serious hardship and you desire to report to a local board in the area of which you are now located, go immediately to that local board and make written request for transfer of your delivery for induction, taking this order with you.

Henry J Modell

D. S. S. Form 150
(Revised 1-15-48)

U. S. GOVERNMENT PRINTING OFFICE   16—18271-6

Member or clerk of the local board.

*My order papers to report
for Army induction -
February 21, 1946.*

confidence; I knew that if nothing else, I had a pleasing personality and that people liked me. So I gave him a song and dance about how the merchant marine had been a dream of mine since I was a little boy, and said that I was trying to better myself by launching a career with them. The supervisor let me into the Seaman's Class basic training course. When the class finished, I had not been assigned to an open position, and I was back to hanging around at home.

It didn't take the draft board long to remember me. To get a deferment from the Army, I had to be employed in the service of the Merchant Marine, which meant being on active duty aboard a ship or being an instructor at the Academy.

There just happened to be an opening for a swimming instructor. I had the right credentials and produced a recommendation from the swimming coach at Lincoln High. It was official – I was hired. For two hours a day, three days a week, I trained guys to swim; then I went home for four days. I was in the Merchant Marine . . . or so I thought!

The draft board wasn't satisfied; being a part-time instructor wasn't enough to get me a deferment. But I could still avoid the draft if I trained with a special arm of the Merchant Marine to become a radio operator, or an engineer, or . . . *a cook.*

Naturally, I jumped at the chance. I applied, was accepted, and started classes in the Merchant Marine Cook and Baker School. Remember, my mother had taught me how to cook, so I was able to pick things up quickly. Baking was a new experience, but it was easier than cooking. When I finished my training, the draft board was advised of my completion, but by now they were totally fed up with my stalling tactics. They threatened that unless I joined the Merchant Marine Union and applied for work as a cook/baker on a ship scheduled to leave New York within ten days, the United States Army would own my butt.

Luckily, the war was over in Europe and was winding down in the Pacific, but the Japanese had still not surrendered. I had run out of ideas and excuses, so I joined the union and requested duty on the earliest scheduled ship. I was assigned to the John Howland – a Liberty Ship that had been built especially for the war – and headed for Europe.

Liberty Ships were designed to carry cargo from the U.S. to our military bases overseas. The hull was fitted with enormous sections of cargo space. Sometimes, for ballast – to enable the ship to ride low in the water and avoid pitching and rolling, especially in rough seas – wheat grain would be pumped in; at the end of the journey, it would be pumped out. For this voyage, metal hooks and eyes had also been installed. They would hold the sleeping hammocks for the troops we would be bringing back from Europe. Food and water supplies for the troops and the ship's crew were to be brought on in France.

The John Howland looked like a giant bath tub and had six officers, with fewer than a dozen crew members. Its mission was to load up with wheat grain for ballast, sail to Le Havre in France, and bring back returning American troops. The day we were to ship out, a longshoremen strike, the first ever during wartime, hit the New York piers. The longshoremen wouldn't load the wheat. No one knew how long the strike would last. I think we waited only a few days before being told that we *had* to leave, with or without our ballast, because the army deployment bases in France were getting too crowded and were overflowing. We had to get them on a ship and get them home.

Finally, we shipped out. Because our cargo hold was empty, we bobbed around on the water like a cork. The second day at sea, we were hit by a storm so violent that our rudder kept riding out of the water. The boat rocked mercilessly and vibrated non-stop. All the glassware and dishes in the kitchen fell from their cabinets and broke. In the hold, eight freezers held two-hundred-pound animal carcasses on hooks – meat supply for the returning troops. As the ship rolled on the seas, these frozen carcasses slipped from their meat hooks, smashed against the freezer doors, and broke the doors open. Some of the carcasses ended up in the engine room, where they rotted; the carcasses created a stink you should never have to experience in your lifetime.

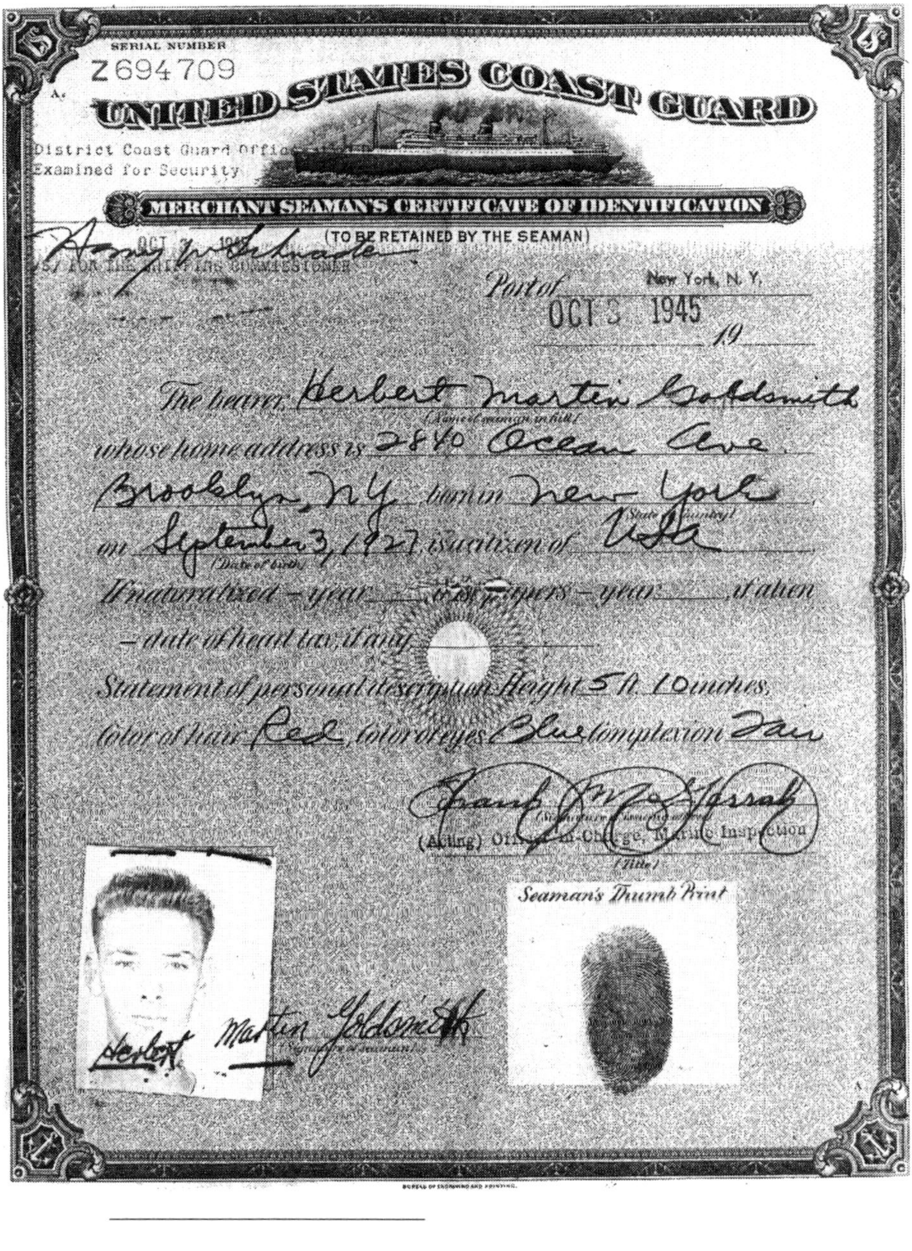

SERIAL NUMBER

Z694709

UNITED STATES COAST GUARD

District Coast Guard Offic
Examined for Security

MERCHANT SEAMAN'S CERTIFICATE OF IDENTIFICATION

(TO BE RETAINED BY THE SEAMAN)

OCT 3 194

Port of New York, N. Y.

OCT 3 1945 19

The bearer, Herbert Martin Goldsmith (Name of seaman in full)

whose home address is 2840 Ocean Ave

Brooklyn, N.Y. born in New York (State or country)

on September 3, 1927 (Date of birth) is a citizen of USA

If naturalized – year ___ 1st papers – year ___ if alien

– date of head tax, if any ___

Statement of personal description Height 5 ft 10 inches,

color of hair Red, color of eyes Blue complexion Fair

(Acting) Officer-in-Charge, Marine Inspection (Title)

Seaman's Thumb Print

Herbert Martin Goldsmith (Signature of seaman)

Merchant Seaman's certificate,
October 1945.

The other cook and I would normally take turns preparing meals, and all of this happened during my first turn at preparing the meals. Under the best of circumstances, I couldn't have cooked because of all the pitching and rolling. All we had were canned food and boxes of dry cereal and crackers, which we ate with water. The stoves couldn't hold the pots, so we couldn't even boil water.

It was a really bad day. Everybody was in their bunks when the ship's rudder snapped, forcing us to sail around in circles until the Coast Guard came and bolted the rudder back together. But we were still pitching and rolling.

After the fourth day of seasickness, I couldn't throw up any more. The crew took charge of my cure by holding my arms and legs down, pouring water down my throat, and stuffing crackers in my mouth. After that, I lived on mashed saltine crackers and Dole's pineapple juice until we landed in Le Havre, France. The crossing had been so bad that some of the crew cracked up; one of the seamen poured water over the captain's head, shouting, "Thou art baptized king of the sea." They put him in a padded cell on board, which I thought was an unusual thing to find on a simple freighter. I guess they had experience with that sort of thing.

As we neared the shores of France, I vowed that if getting home required getting back on this ship, I was staying in France.

When we docked, I couldn't run down the gangplank fast enough. But right in front of me, not ten feet from where I landed, was a steel fence; no one was allowed to leave the pier. Because of our late arrival, there was a lot of pressure to quickly load up and get those G.I.'s home; I couldn't even jump ship. I arrived in France but never got to see it, and my juice and cracker diet had cost me 14 pounds.

For the trip back, I was assigned to head the cooking staff below deck, feeding the soldiers by using the Army's personnel for all kitchen duties. Although I hadn't been in condition to even open a can on the trip over, I was now charged with producing three meals a day for 800 soldiers. The kitchen area had been fitted with several kerosene burners and enormous six-foot-tall pots. We had to stand on ladders to reach the top of the pots sitting high on top of the stoves, and we used an oar to mix the oatmeal, stews, and soups. We had ovens for broiling or roasting meats. It was like cooking for a giant party. I would mimeograph the menu every day but quickly learned to delegate all of the cooking to the Army cooks, making good use of soldiers with K.P. duty to peel potatoes, stir the pots, or slice the bread. I ate with the soldiers down below, in their mess area; they called me Goldie.

Our human cargo consisted of ambulatory soldiers from all over the States, with strange accents and different tastes – unlike any of the people I'd known, even at the Marine academy. They'd been through hell, killing on the battlefields, spending days on end in wet clothes, going without food and sleep; most of them didn't want to talk about the horrors they'd seen. But I noticed that many of them had brought back art treasures and that some had knapsacks full of cash, which they gambled on card games and crap games; a lot of money changed hands. They paid other soldiers $100 to be their bodyguards for the night so that they could get some sleep without worrying that the contents of their duffel bags would mysteriously disappear. When the card players and crap shooters would ask me during the late hours to bring them some sandwiches, I'd remind them that it was against the rules, but their generous tips quickly helped me to forget the rules. They took good care of me.

It was during this trip, while we were en route, that the war in the Pacific ended. After a few days at home, I went back to the draft board to check on my status. Surrender or no surrender, I would still have to spend several months in the Merchant Marine if I wanted to avoid the Army. On the other hand . . . if I let the Army draft me, I would be eligible for the G.I. Bill. The G.I. Bill would pay my college tuition, and I'd be eligible for the 52/50 Club, which would pay me $50 a week for twelve months each year until I graduated. Since the amount of time I had left in the Merchant

> IF I LET THE ARMY DRAFT ME, I WOULD BE ELIGIBLE FOR THE G.I. BILL.

Marine was equal to the amount of time I would have to serve in the Army, it was an easy choice.

"Alright, draft me."

Basic training was in Fayetteville, Arkansas, close to the University of Arkansas – where, coincidentally, three of my high school friends were in attendance. Sometime during my training, I went on a weekend furlough with my buddies. We took a hotel room, with two of us sleeping on the box springs and two sleeping on the mattresses we'd placed on the floor. I was never a *tummeler* (party guy) or a drinker. My pals were into boozing and were always on the make for women; I tried, but I was never convincing enough. In the middle of one of those nights, there was a loud banging on the door. Shortly thereafter, an M.P. came in to our room and arrested me. It turned out that one of my friends had put on my uniform while I was sleeping, and had gone out, hoping to pick up a girl. He had worn his own shoes (civilian shoes), and he had neither a hat nor dog tags. An M.P. saw him on the street and approached him.

"What's with the shoes?" he asked. "Where are your cap and dog tags?"

I was restricted to camp for the next weekend, for lending my uniform to a civilian.

When Basic Training ended, we were advised that we would be going back to New Jersey and then shipping out. We were all anxious to know where we were headed, but the answer was always: "We don't know. You'll find out when you get on the ship." We had an idea that if our destination was the Pacific, we would have been sent to California. From New Jersey, we assumed, we could be going to Europe.

This time, the ship was a converted trans-Atlantic liner with the usual large dining room and cocktail lounge. I was assigned lower level seven, two decks below the water line; no portholes, no cots. I had to climb a ladder to get to my hammock. I met two other guys from Brooklyn down there. We agreed that it was really claustrophobic – how could we sleep with hundreds of guys talking, snoring, and passing wind all night?

I said, "I can't go through this. Wait here. I'm gonna try something . . ."

I went up to the main deck and approached the sergeant standing at the gang plank, who was checking the I.D.s and papers of the soldiers as they boarded. I asked if he knew who the officer in charge was.

"Go up to the bridge . . ."

I must have looked puzzled.

"Where they steer the ship; he's probably up there."

The bridge was up several levels, but a sign indicated that there were elevators. As I walked toward them, I noticed large rooms that probably, in peacetime, served as the dining room, cocktail room, and card room; they were all entirely empty.

In front of the door to the bridge was a desk, where a sergeant was seated. I told him that I wanted to ask the officer in charge whether he could use some experienced show business professionals to help entertain the troops on this 11-day journey. He went inside; moments later, a major came out. I introduced myself and said, "In my civilian life (knowing there was no way he could check), I had an extensive background in show business and other forms of entertainment."

"Sir, are playing cards, games, and movies going to be available to the troops?" He didn't know. I suggested that perhaps the manifest of supplies would be helpful. I knew about manifests from the Merchant Marine. I told the sergeant that if there was a manifest, I would gladly go through it.

The sergeant said, "What's a manifest?"

The major smiled and assigned me to find it. "If entertainment items are listed, you organize and supervise these activities."

"You know, sir, you also have to think about news and sports; it's still baseball season. If I can get a hold of a mimeograph machine, we could give the guys scores every day; and sir, I could not possibly do all of this by myself. I happen to have two other men, buddies from New York, who I think I can convince to join the team. And one more thing, sir . . . we'll need an area where we can store the equipment, sort out each day's and evening's material, and secure it at the end of the day. My men need to type out each day's sports bulletin, mimeograph it, sort it, and get it distributed. We also have to set up for the day's movie – all this is a full day's responsibility. Sometimes we will need to work in shifts. Sir, I noticed that a few decks below, there are several unused large rooms. Signs on them say, 'Dining Room' or 'Cocktail Lounge.' We would need only the smaller room, and if you could arrange for three cots to be brought in, we could sleep there as well. It will be more than adequate and provide more security to the equipment."

He thought it was a great idea.

No more hammocks for me!

"Oh, by the way," said the Major. "How are you going to get the news and scores when we are out of range for the radio?"

"Don't worry about that," I said. "One of my guys knows Morse code. He'll go to the radio room and get the info at the convenience of the ship's operator."

The deal was set.

Of course, I had no way of knowing if either of the two guys waiting down below could take Morse code, or even if they could type. I didn't know them personally; I only knew that they were from New York City, and that was good enough for me.

I went below. There they were, waiting with baited breath. I told them the good news and gave them a blow-by-blow description of what was agreed. They thought I was out of my mind!

We proceeded to our new quarters – the cocktail lounge with "His" and "Hers" bathrooms – and found the part of the manifest that had what we were looking for: a film projector and films, a giant screen, playing cards, books, games, and even bingo cards.

By that time, I knew that the crossing would be to Livorno, Italy, via Marseilles, France.

My friend the major saw to it that we got cots delivered to our new accommodations – and because we were such busy workers, room service (when we needed it) was arranged.

We promised to write and print a daily newspaper. We interviewed people on the ship for features, but how would we do the news? Well, luckily Bernie knew Morse code, so in addition to what we could get on the wireless, we made up news every day – news and sports scores that were all bullshit.

Keeping hundreds of raw recruits busy for an eleven-day crossing of the Atlantic wasn't going to be easy. No television, no radio, no planned activities for hundreds of strangers thrown together from all over the States. Most spent a good deal of time throwing their guts up overboard because of seasickness. They tried to set up some impromptu singing groups or card games, but boredom would be their most constant companions. I had to put a stop to that.

Now, among all of the paraphernalia, remember the bingo cards? We set up games and sold the cards at two for a dollar. For every two cards, we put only 50 cents in the pot; everybody had a few dollar bills. Two days before we landed, the major found out what we were doing.

"Are you outta your mind? What are you guys, the Mafia?"

(I thought we should have been given medals.)

When we arrived in Livorno (Leghorn, today), the weather was nice and warm. A lot of the G.I.s and officers thanked us, and the major (despite the "bingo fiasco") shook my hand. On the pier, we all lined up in front of a desk where a sergeant checked our papers. Each G.I. carried his papers with him, which included date of birth, education, civilian and military occupations, and experience. As the sergeant handed me an envelope, I stared at the words written on the outside: 752 TANK BATTALION in Udine. A letter inside said that I was assigned as an Assistant Tank Driver; I panicked . . . here I go again.

I noticed an officer talking to the sergeant at the desk and asked to speak to him about a possible error in my assignment.

"What's your problem soldier?"

"Sir, there must be a mistake. I'm assigned as a tank driver; I can't even drive a car!"

He said he couldn't do anything about it since all assignments were done at 5th Army Headquarters in Rome. We were hundreds of miles from Rome; it might as well have been a thousand.

"Son, you will just have to sort it out with the officer in charge of the outfit you're going to. Sorry and good luck."

Now I was really depressed; I didn't work one of my miracles, and I couldn't find a bus with a 752 Tank sign. I did notice a Jeep with the 752 sign, and I told the driver about my assignment. He informed me that I was the only new guy assigned to the unit. I got in and we took off together. On the four-hour drive to Udine, which is in the northern part of Italy, near Trieste, the driver filled me in about this tank battalion. Even though the war was over, it seems that there was still unrest and serious fighting in Yugoslavia between the Partisans and the Chetnics, who had supported the Nazis. Because the U.S. didn't want these skirmishes to escalate, we had to maintain a presence and lend a hand if the Yugoslav government requested our help. A number of our tank companies were strategically positioned in several permanent camps on the border between Italy and Yugoslavia.

Because of minimum maneuverability and speed, the battalion was broken up into squads of 10-12 tanks each. Each had its own barracks, mess hall, repair shop, and social hall. The entire 752 tank group consisted of about eighty personnel. Already thinking about how to get a more suitable position, without getting assigned to do something I knew nothing about, I inquired about the cooking facilities and the mess hall. I was told that in order to keep half of the outfit on alert, there were two shifts for each meal. Each squad had two cooks, so they alternated days on and off – just like in the Merchant Marine. The kitchen staff consisted of several German prisoners of war and several Italian locals serving as kitchen help.

That's me in the driver's seat of
the tank on the right.

In the Army.

Sounds good to me! Now, how do I get myself into the kitchen and out of a tank?

We drove up to my assigned barrack; it had twenty beds – each with a partition for privacy – a small table and chair, and a private closet. I was given time to freshen up before seeing the captain. Seeing my papers in my hand, his assistant let me go right in. I saluted the captain and presented my papers. I noticed a West Point ring on his finger. He was tall, with typical straight-back West Point posture. It doesn't take long to identify the customary class distinctions in the Army.

After he had reviewed my papers, the captain asked if I had really trained as a cook and baker in the Merchant Marine. The "yes, sir" came out before I could even think it. He said that I would be of far greater value to the outfit as a cook than as a tank driver and asked if I would be terribly disappointed if I didn't get to drive a tank. The, "no, sir" was out before he could change his mind. We shook hands and he escorted me to the mess hall to meet Earl (the other cook) and the non-military personnel. The mess hall was small and well lit, but there was still plenty of room to maneuver. The kitchen was really up to date, with the same type of equipment used by the Merchant Marine Academy. I felt comfortable, and to my surprise, not nervous at all. I thought that this would be like cooking for a party: prepare eighty meals at a time and then serve half of them at one time. Actually, I found out that I didn't have to do any of the serving; no cafeteria style, we had civilians to do the serving, as well as to clean the equipment, clean the dinnerware, and scrub the entire mess hall.

After introductions, the captain left. I sensed that Earl wasn't too pleased to meet me. He had been in charge and didn't relish competition. When I told him that I had been a cook in the Merchant Marine, he made it a point to tell me that in the Army you cook to *Army* specs and that he cooked by the book – the Army book. He followed each recipe in the Army manual to a T, cooking them *exactly* as the recipe required. Two of the kitchen assistants were German POWs: the meat chef and the baker. The Italians helped clean the meats and washed the vegetables. Other locals cleaned the dishes, silverware, pots, and pans.

This cooking and baking assignment was going to be a piece of cake – cooks were on one day and off the other, just as they were in the Merchant Marines.

The next day, right after breakfast, Earl sent me into town with one of the POWs to barter for some local supplies, using flour, salt, and sugar requisitioned from the Army supply depot. The German POW got a jeep, which he was permitted to drive, and off we went. He spoke English pretty well and gave me a lesson in how things were done in town, but most of all, he told me what went on in the kitchen. He hated Earl and considered him totally incompetent. Earl didn't know beans about using the local spices, olive oils, and cheeses. The rolls he baked had no consistency. And although he had an allowance for supplies, Earl's idea of salad dressing was vinegar and pepper – a recipe *not* taken from the Army cookbook. When improvements were suggested, he simply ignored them, stating, "If it's not in the book, it's not in my kitchen." We returned in time to prepare lunch (which, in terms of culinary creativity, was no big deal).

Almost all of Earl's meals were smothered in ketchup (his idea of gravy), and the troops soon became so bored of his cooking that some spent their own money to eat in town. Nevertheless, I decided that it wasn't time to begin adding variety to the menu, and I continued to "cook by the book." Eventually, I would make the guys some *real* European food, like the dishes I had made at home: chicken fricassee with lots of chicken fat and garlic; beef pot roast with onions; fresh peas and carrots; even potato pancakes with apple sauce. But for now, I'd have to wait.

When I traveled to the town market to barter for local foodstuffs, I was usually accompanied by the two German POWs, Max and Hermann. POWs all wore uniforms exactly like the khakis that we wore, except that theirs had a large, round blue patch sewn on the left sleeve. It seemed odd to me that they were greeted fondly in the town market, but they did know the items to barter for. We could never understand why we weren't permitted to barter for the local fresh produce that was available in town. My opening presented itself when I learned that our captain's birthday was coming up the following weekend.

I checked with his aide to see whether our commanding officer would be on active duty that weekend because I wanted to plan a surprise for the captain. The aide should let the squad know that there was going to be a surprise party for the captain, with cake and all the trimmings, and that they had strict orders to show up.

We deliberately avoided telling Earl, who would be off for the weekend on a three-day leave. I agreed to cover for him on those days. After Earl left, I told Max and Hermann that we would make a special meal on the night of the captain's birthday, a meal to be remembered. We took our sugar, coffee, salt, etc., to the market to barter for fresh vegetables, olive oils, garlic, Italian cheeses, eggs, and spices. We were supplied from headquarters with all the meat we needed, but for this meal we needed special meat cuts and fresh fatty chickens only available from the local market.

Max, the meat chef, decided he would make a crown roast with roasted breaded artichokes. Hermann would make Italian pastries, including a very moist Ricotta cheesecake, in addition to a birthday cake in the shape of a tank. We bartered for Italian breads and rolls, as well. The Italian laborers volunteered to prepare platters of antipasto. To make sure we got the right meats, they gave us a list to bring to town including: cheeses, salamis, roasted peppers, and pickled vegetables.

I surprised Max and Hermann by announcing that my contribution would be to prepare my mother's specialties – potted chicken fricassee and beef-brisket pot roast, just as I had envisioned. For the chicken gravy, I used all the chicken fat I could find (together with the chicken livers, which Earl always threw away), plus fresh carrots, potatoes, and sweet onions – all simmered in olive oil, sweet peppers, my secret spices, and garlic. The brisket had to cook slowly in a sauce of fresh minced tomatoes, garlic, basil, oregano, a little olive oil, and other spices known only to me. To keep the food from getting dry and the sauce from evaporating, I waited until it was almost done and then put it in the oven to finish.

We were all laughing and patting each other on the backs, unconcerned that we had prepared a meal that wasn't official army mess! Throughout the meal, when the troops *weren't* eating, they were cheering; they didn't leave a single thing uneaten. After we sang "Happy Birthday," the captain stood up, made a complimentary speech, and saluted me and my staff. He was very appreciative of all the effort and thought that had gone into his special evening. The staff and I were very proud. After dinner, since nothing had been left, the staff and I had sandwiches, a cheese cake that we had forgotten to pull out of the fridge, and a few bottles of the local white (*friuli*) wine.

What we didn't realize was that we had unintentionally "spoiled" the squad. Now they wanted that kind of meal *every day*, and we were afraid to refuse. Even during lunch, we added three kinds of pasta dishes to the menu, along with various antipasto's. For dinner, I let Max and Hermann have full reign; two of the local Italian staff offered to cook, as well. It was a great three days of feasting, not just eating. WOW!

And then Earl came back. It was his day to cook, so he started early. Since it was my day off and I was kind of washed out, I got to the mess hall late for breakfast, after the troops had already left. Obviously, someone had told him about the feasts that were served while he was gone. I could see the rage in his face.

I said, "Hi, Earl, welcome back. I would . . ."

Before I could say another word, Earl grabbed a meat cleaver and came at me. I dodged him and grabbed a carving knife, cautioning him to calm down. "You probably didn't hear the whole, true story."

He kept coming . . . Our improvised clashing weapons sent sparks flying across the kitchen. It was like an Errol Flynn movie but with kitchen knives and cleavers instead of dueling swords. He wanted to kill me, screaming that I had insulted and made a fool of him. Who knows what he had been told about the surprise party and our weekend of fine dining.

The staff pulled us apart, but Earl never stopped cursing me. I could do nothing to calm him down. Someone must have run to the captain, because the Sergeant came in, grabbed my arm, and marched me down to the captain's office (just me, not Earl). When I entered, the captain thanked me again for his birthday dinner, as well as for the very enjoyable meals prior to that night. I learned that at breakfast Earl had been told about the "three days of great food" (apparently, the troops had warned him that if he didn't do what Goldie did, they wouldn't eat in the mess hall).

The captain told Earl that he'd have to find a way to resolve the situation. Fortunately, the captain had just that morning received a notice from Headquarters in Rome, advising that the Army was initiating purchases of products from local communities and that all cooking menus were to be changed to conform to that directive. He acknowledged that I was way ahead of them, and that I had helped to improve our relations with the townspeople. He was ordered to send one of the company cooks to Livorno to attend cooking school; as the new guy, and to keep the peace, I had been selected. I was to leave the next day. The captain wished me good luck and ordered that I always be true to the SEVEN-FIVE-TWO!

> THE CAPTAIN ORDERED THAT I ALWAYS BE TRUE TO THE SEVEN-FIVE-TWO!

The captain said that he would encourage Earl to give the staff a little leeway in their cooking. He stood up, shook my hand, and told me that he was proud of me and looked forward to my return. End of discussion. An order is an order, not an invitation to debate.

The next day, I packed my gear and was driven by jeep for four hours to the cooking school in Livorno, Italy.

Livorno is the second major port in Italy and, in peace time, is also a beach resort area. The Italians had surrendered to the Allies on April 29, 1945. By the time I arrived for Bakers and Cooks School in the late summer of 1946, the war had taken its toll on the beaches. Along the thousands of miles of coast, from Livorno to Rome, there were Army supplies in storage behind barbed wire fences, no longer required by the Armed Forces and scheduled to be shipped back to America.

After searching for some time, my driver finally found the gate where we were supposed to enter. On the building with a "B & C School" sign, I got out of the jeep. I handed the sergeant in charge my military file. I noticed the name plate on his desk: Sid Rappaport.

He looked up and asked what a Jewish kid from Brooklyn was doing here, going to a Bakers and Cooks School, no less. He was also from Brooklyn and had graduated from Madison High School, which had been Lincoln High School's arch rival in sports. He remarked about my time in the Merchant Marine as a cook and baker. Fortunately, the records didn't reflect how short a time I had actually cooked.

He scratched his head and said, "Can you really cook?"

"Of course," I said, and I proceeded to tell him about my experience at the 752 Tank Company.

"Listen, the course is four weeks, and really there's nothing dramatically new in cooking procedures; its mostly new menus. The most important change is that we want to use more local produce and cooking products. The Army is allowing purchases to be made in local currency, the *lire*. No need to barter."

"So, why do they need to have school for four weeks?" I asked. "Why not send all the outfits the new menus and the new directive regarding local purchases?"

"Listen, Herb, that's the way Headquarters wants it. Not all cooks can adapt quickly to new recipes and methods of cooking and, in some cases, new equipment. This class gives them time to experiment and get comfortable with it. At the end of the four weeks, a general will attend graduation and hand each guy a diploma and the new book of menus.

Since you know how to cook, you don't have to go to classes; you're staying with me at my villa. You'll love it; it's only a short walk to the beach.

I have a lot of buddies you'll like and, of course, lots of local beauties to make your stay comfortable. On graduation day, you'll show up, get your diploma, and off you'll go to your outfit. So relax, *Herbala*, and enjoy your month-long vacation on the Italian Riviera."

How is it, I wondered, that these unique events continue to happen to me?

Chapter Three

IT WAS LATE FRIDAY AFTERNOON. School didn't start until Monday, and I was the last to report. Sid closed the office and put my gear into his jeep, and off we went to the villa he shared with three other soldiers and quartermasters, none of whom were connected with the school. It was spacious: plenty of bedrooms, a very large patio, and a garden. They even had their own Italian cook, maid, and handy man. This was like a movie. I was a little apprehensive about all of these distractions and concerned about not being prepared for cooking school. Sid, noticing my concern, handed me the books for the full course, as well as the book of new menus. There wouldn't be a final test at the school, he told me, and if I was concerned about anything, a few days in class would bring me up to speed. "Meanwhile, Herb, enjoy and don't worry. I've got something special in mind for you."

My first night at the villa, we celebrated at a large restaurant, where we were greeted like royalty. We walked past a table with around a dozen trays of cold antipastos and breads. While a band played loudly, we made our way toward the back, outdoors to our table on a manicured lawn facing the Mediterranean. Local wine was poured so freely that it reminded me of New York waiters refilling our water glasses. We sampled the antipasto, three different pastas, two meat dishes, fresh-cooked vegetables, and especially the fried zucchini. We even made room for dessert; what amazing food. It was a night with the boys, enjoying food, wine, music, and laughs,

It was in the middle of my second night, around one or two in the morning, that I heard:

"Goldsmith, quick – get yourself up and keep quiet!"

"What? Who? . . ."

"Get dressed. Meet us outside."

Outside, in the chilly night, a truck was waiting – engine rumbling, smoke billowing from its exhaust. "Jump in," I was ordered. Six other guys were already inside.

We drove through the night until we came to what appeared to be a warehouse. Finding a break in the surrounding fence, we drove through and parked alongside a loading dock. Inside the warehouse were thousands of cartons containing all sorts of surplus army supplies.

"Don't touch anything but the cartons with blankets, and get them loaded into the truck."

Back on the road, we crept gingerly up steep hills following the coast line. I could hear waves pounding the shore. When we finally stopped, it was at an old two-story house. Its four bedrooms were crammed with bare Army cots; Sid has us put a blanket on each cot. Finished, we climbed back in the truck and returned to our villa. No one said a thing. I asked what the hell was going on but got no answer.

Every night after that, a similar routine: one night it was cartons of C-rations (water, tuna, and crackers), each bed getting a ration; the next night, more cots, clothes, shoes, and water. Then one night, we heard the sputtering and rattling of dilapidated old trucks and buses pulling to a stop outside the old house, just as we were carrying provisions inside. Children of all ages came out of the trucks and buses, lined up, and went inside the house, where each was told to stand in front of a cot. Many of the children were sobbing and crying. A few nights later we encountered men and

THE QUARTERMASTER
BAKERS AND COOKS SCHOOL
HEADQUARTERS, PBS
APO 782

Class No. 20

This is to certify that Pvt Herbert Goldsmith ASN 42275173

has demonstrated proficiency as a Cook

He is qualified to be a First Cook

Commandant

Quartermaster

Subjects Covered:
Baking
Preparation dehydrated foods
Preparation fresh and canned meats
Mess management
Mess sanitation

My Bakers and Cooks certificate.

Talking with the children.

women, also sobbing and wringing their hands. Once in a while, I heard the words "mein kindt" repeated.

Unable to contain my curiosity and concerned about what was going on, I asked Sid to fill me in. He told me to look out the wide-open bedroom window facing the sea. I noticed a rope ladder hanging from two hooks screwed into the window sill. The ladder fell down the cliff to the Mediterranean below, where a hulk of a rusty old ship was visible, bobbing precariously in the water.

"These children will go first, and the adults, some of whom are the parents, will go on a later ship." My friend explained: "They're attempting an exodus to Israel because although the British have blocked the Israeli ports, they have at times allowed ships carrying 'children only' to enter."

> THE CHILDREN WILL GO FIRST, AND THE ADULTS, SOME OF WHOM ARE THE PARENTS, WILL GO ON A LATER SHIP.

For months, Sid and his buddies had been secreting orphans, children, and parents through the mountains from various parts of Italy, evading the Italian police and local authorities ordered to keep these kids from reaching Israel.

"What about their parents?" I asked. Sid said that the British would only allow the children to enter, while the parents attempted to sneak through the blockade separately. In most cases, the parents never made it. With their ships destroyed, they were sent back to European refugee camps.

I couldn't find out more about the operation and who organized it because of the risk of our being caught. The less we knew, the better for the whole operation. These refugee programs seemed to be very organized, with participating activists in each country coordinating via clandestine radio. Our sorties were sporadic, but always at night. Every arriving group had a chaperon, usually a different one each time. I'm sure people behind the scenes donated handsomely for the ships, while others saw to it that ships were properly crewed and on time for their illicit rendezvous.

My four-week adventure at the villa ended none too soon for me. On graduation day at the Bakers and Cooks School, I dutifully marched up to some general who handed me my diploma and shook my hand, congratulating me on my fine achievements at the school. Then I was driven back to Udine. Fortunately, my arch-enemy Earl had been replaced by another cook.

"You're on duty the day after tomorrow, so take tomorrow off," the new guy said.

I spent the next day reacquainting with my crew and getting all the news. Earl had requested a transfer; that's why he was gone. I told them that we could now do more shopping in town, and that I had brought back some new recipes that I was sure they would enjoy trying. The night before my turn to cook, our outfit was ordered on maneuvers. We were being sent to rescue a band of Yugoslav partisans on the other side of the Yugo border. Not knowing that we would be camping in the mountains, I packed as if it were still summer and took only a light jacket, in the event that it got cool at night.

We left camp about 6:00 a.m. With tanks, you travel slowly; very slowly. I'm in a truck with my usual kitchen crew, nice and warm with the heater on, when two hours later we set camp and prepare for breakfast. I almost froze to death when I get out of the truck. There I was, just back from the Riviera, freezing in the mountains. Thinking fast, I tell my crew that for breakfast we would make French toast and that I'd do the cooking, hoping that being close to the stove would keep me warm.

On maneuvers, we used steel combat stoves, five feet tall and three feet wide and deep; my crew assembled two of them. One foot from the top, there was a slot and a track onto which you slid a tray with two kerosene burners built in. Above the burners, on the top of the stove, there was another track, where you slid in a 3 x 3 pan, about three inches deep. I had my crew beat the eggs with some milk, while I heated the lard in which we would fry the battered French toast. On another stove, we made hot oatmeal in a pot that sat at the top of the pan. I ladled the lard out of its can, into my top pan, and

My Army cook job.

then waited until it got hot enough to dip the battered bread. Boy, was I nice and warm.

I inserted the battered bread, piece by piece, onto the pan. I had half the pan full when it tipped. Not being level, the lard had poured off, scalding my arm. My arm began to swell; it was so painful that I wanted to die. My crew put me on the ground and tried to cut off the sleeve of my jacket, which was soaking up the boiling lard. The company medic finally applied salves and pricked the blisters, but to no avail. He had to give me a shot to kill the pain and to put me out.

After a few hours, he didn't like what he saw. "You gotta go back to headquarters and the hospital," he said.

Lying in my hospital bed in Udine, while they monitored me for possible infection and skin damage, I had a lot of time on my hands with nothing to do. I listened to Armed Forces radio, which played music all day or broadcast pre-recorded stateside shows like *Fibber McGee and Molly*, or *The Bob Hope Comedy Hour* and all the popular Big Band music.

> I HAD A LOT OF TIME ON MY HANDS WITH NOTHING TO DO. I LISTENED TO ARMED FORCES RADIO.

Listening to this repetitious, boring programming, I had an idea.

"Where is this originating," I asked one of the nurses. "Where's the radio station?"

She told me that it was in a town named *Gorizia* about 20 miles north of the hospital.

After a few days, I was able to walk around. Since my outfit would be gone for another four to five days, and I was in no condition to return to duty anyway, I asked if I could borrow a jeep to go visit the radio station. No problem.

The station was on a huge estate. The villa was situated behind twin giant metal gates, with a long stone wall securing the property. It looked like a small palace. I learned that it had previously been a nunnery; after the war the nuns stayed, being confined to the ground floor while the radio station took the second floor. I was impressed with the equipment that I saw. They had several glass-enclosed announcers' booths, each containing microphones, two record turntables, and control boards. Their library of recorded stateside programs was impressive.

I found a member of the staff and asked who was in charge. He led me to the office of Lieutenant Peters from Connecticut. I told the lieutenant about my accident and began to ask him questions about the station. Recalling my football-announcing show on WNYC, I asked why everything they played was recorded in the States. Didn't they localize anything? How about airing some of the exciting events taking place in each outfit, or having a call-in request show? Couldn't they broadcast the sporting events taking place between various Army units, like football games or boxing matches – sports that the soldiers had a chance to root for...? I was full of ideas.

"You think you can do it?" he asked. "Well, then why don't you go into that room and make a recording of what you're talking about. I'll play it for our production team and see what they have to say."

He took me into the booth and sat me down in front of a microphone. "All you have to do is push the button that says ON and when you're finished, press OFF. If you need music, the other turntable works the same way. There's also a volume control. You can even talk over the music or record without it."

The next day, I got some music records from their library and did my thing in the booth. I did an impression of someone announcing a football game, along with my unique version of a disc jockey playing requests from the listening audience, and mixed it in with some local happenings that I read from the Army paper, *Stars And Stripes*. For the next two days, I rehearsed over and over, recording for myself and making corrections until finally presenting my audition record to the lieutenant.

"You think you can get a transfer? We sure can use you," he informed me.

I told him that I would try my best. This was not going to be easy, but I had a feeling that if I presented the issue properly, there was a good chance of success.

A few days later, my unit returned to base. I immediately reported to the captain. He was aware of my injury and asked when I might be able to get back to work in the kitchen – he still remembered the great meal I had made for his birthday. I was sweating and my pulse was racing, but I got it out: "Sir, I respectfully request a transfer."

> "SIR, I RESPECTFULLY REQUEST A TRANSFER."

"I don't believe what I'm hearing," he roared. "You cooked all of three days, went to Bakers and Cooks School for four weeks, cooked twenty minutes on maneuver, went to Udine hospital for ten days, and now you want a transfer? What's wrong with you, Goldsmith?"

"It's like this," I told him. "The Army radio station wants me on the air to make the programming much more localized and interesting. I'd also be talking about our outfit, the SEVEN-FIVE-TWO and all the things we've accomplished in the course of our mission."

"Sir, isn't it true that the Army is always interested in furthering the careers of its men when they eventually enter into private life? And wouldn't it be great for the SEVEN-FIVE-TWO to have its own personal spokesman on the radio every day?"

With that, he literally jumped out of his chair, stood straight, and ordered me to stand at attention, to put my right hand over my heart, and to raise my left hand and swear, "I'll always be true to the SEVEN-FIVE-TWO!"

Being a good soldier, I followed his orders. He shook my hand and wished me good luck. The next day, with transfer papers in hand, I presented them at the station, as ordered.

Since the station was some twenty miles out of town, far from Army Headquarters, the atmosphere was so casual that nobody was required to wear uniforms. Sometimes we even worked in our bathrobes. We were provided with a maid named Emilia, who would wash our clothes and hang them outside to dry. On cold days, the clothes would freeze, sometimes taking a week to dry. Once, when it was particularly cold and raw, I developed a whopper of a cold. Emilia's cure for hangovers and illnesses was the same. She boiled white wine, made me drink it hot, and then sponged me down. This caused me to sweat as if I were in a *schvitz* (steam bath) until the bug was sweated out.

I worked at the station with Morty and Arnie (who eventually took over for me) and a chief engineer whose main responsibility was to make sure that our generator and tower were functioning properly. He lived by himself somewhere in town, with his dogs. We also had a pool of soldiers and locals. Some cooked our meals and some took care of maintaining the motor vehicles and radio equipment.

We used a truck that looked like a moving van, for remote broadcasts. It had all types of radio equipment, a small generator to transmit to our station's large transmitter, and a wire recorder that was so heavy it took two men to carry it (tape recorders hadn't been invented yet).

I started doing remote broadcasts, bringing the lifestyles of the Army and of the community to my listeners. We staged a "Battle of the Bands" on the air, broadcasting from each outfit's clubs. We got calls from every outfit in Northern Italy. Each had a club with a bar and a group of guys who played musical instruments and somehow found a way to form a band. They were allowed to have locals as guests in the club; dancing with the local gals was a must. Naturally, they were proud of their clubs. It took weeks to record all the bands. We formed a group of judges who selected a winner and a runner-up. *Stars and Stripes* wrote a story about them, and they played at special events.

The biggest hit of the station was my call-in request show, *The Night Watch*. I was the "Night Watchman," on the air from 10:00 p.m. until 11:00 p.m. I had a few telephones maintained during the day, accepting requests. My staff would write out the messages and prepare the records in the order that they were to be played. A typical one would be, "This is Frank

Staff at Armed Forces radio.

Enjoying a cigar in Italy.

dedicating 'I'll Always Have Eyes For You' to Sophia." Between playing the on-air requests, I mixed in local events and sport scores.

One guy called regularly, asking the Night Watchman to play the same song – for Maria. After his tenth call, I told my crew that when he called again I wanted to speak to him. When I got him on the phone, I asked him who he was and why he had requested the same song for Maria ten times, changing it only once.

It turned out that he was an army pilot, regularly flying a two-passenger Piper Cub to Venice, where the Army kept rooms in the Lido Hotel (and where, by chance, he had a girlfriend). Without telephones, how was he to let Maria know he was coming? Simple: he used my show. Dedicating a particular song signaled that he'd be seeing her; dedicating a different song meant that he wouldn't be able to make it. "We all do it," he said, pointing out to me how Joe was always dedicating song X to Lady Y and so forth.

"You think you're the king of radio," he said. "You're really just our mailbox."

That reinforced what I already knew at age nineteen: that everybody has an angle; everything is a deal. I was only a conduit. Nevertheless, the show was still popular with the Joes or Mikes or Jacks who didn't ask for dedicated requests but were just requesting their favorite songs, bringing back memories of home.

> THAT EVERYBODY HAS AN ANGLE; EVERYTHING IS A DEAL. I WAS ONLY CONDUIT.

I signed off each night with: "This is your Night Watchman, Herb Goldsmith, from the Seven-Five-Two." I kept my promise and was always true.

The Army pilot who used me as his mailbox now owed me one. I got him to fly me to Venice for a little R&R of my own. After landing, we took a motorized gondola to the Lido, the Army's official R&R hotel. One night, in the vicinity of St. Mark's Square, we met a few local girls at a bar. Well, one thing led to another and one of them took me to her place. She lived a 15-minute walk away, over four different canals and around too many turns to remember. Knowing that the last boat to leave St. Mark's Square to the Lido Hotel was at midnight, I made sure to leave her place with 30 minutes to get to the square.

After 15 minutes of wandering over too many canals, blind alleys, and dead-end streets, I was lost. Then, in the distance, I heard voices. As I approached, I saw two men; unfortunately, my Italian wasn't very good.

"Prego. Saint Marks?" No response. "Gondola?" Nothing.

Then one said to the other, *"Ich denk er ist ge shickeret."* They were speaking Yiddish; they thought I was drunk.

"Lantsmen," I said, *"Ich bin a yid und ich bin famisht."* (I'm Jewish and I'm mixed up.) *"Helfen mir tsu der grosse platz bairn der vasser."* (Please help me to get to the big square by the water.)

In Yiddish, they said that they understood my predicament, and they led the way. We arrived at the gondola in seven minutes.

The next time, I thought, I may not be so lucky; I started taking Italian lessons.

On New Year's Day, the station went on the air at 7:00 a.m. I had let all of the other announcers take the day off, so it was just me. The glass broadcast booth was warmed by the generator, and I was smashed from drinking *Spumonte,* (Italian champagne) the night before, so I kept drinking lots of water. After the equipment warmed up, the light went on over my mike.

I played the national anthem and then, uncontrollably, blurted a slurred, "Goood Muurrring!" I heard the slurring, cut myself off the air, and just played records all day, finally putting on some recordings that lasted for hours while I took a nap.

One day, an officer appeared outside my glass booth while I was on the air. First I saw the eagles pinned on his shoulders, then the medals down both sides of his chest: a colonel. Nervously, I did my broadcast, while he sat there watching me. Since I was in my pajamas and bathrobe, I figured that they were on to me – that they knew all the strange things we did. This is it – I'm off to the brig! I put a record on and went out to talk with him. Shaking, I was about to apologize for being out of uniform, when he confided, "I've always wanted to meet you. I've admired your shows and the great innovative changes you've made with the station; I'm a big fan."

I was floored. I thanked him and asked about the medals and crests he was wearing. He said he had been assigned to the Allied Generals as a pilot and had even flown Churchill, when Churchill was in the American zone. Now he was stationed at the major airport in Udine.

"What are you going to do when you get out of the Army?" he asked.

"Go to college." I replied. He seemed surprised.

"Take my card. Perhaps I may be able to help you, if you want to get into radio in New York. I live in Washington, D.C., and I have influential friends."

He invited me for dinner, but I wasn't able to make it.

Somehow, I was leery of his attention. I took the card anyway, but I never called. I was determined to go to college and get an education. I thought to myself, "If I've accomplished this much at age 19 *without* a college degree, imagine what I could accomplish with a college education."

One of my duties was to administer the radio operation's payroll, a duty I never suspected would pose a problem . . . until an officer from headquarters showed up.

He said, "We want to give you a commission."

"Me? A commission, why?" I asked.

He explained that the Army couldn't have a corporal in charge of payroll, distributing monies, and buying things in town. "We'll make you a lieutenant," he said.

By now, I'm not even halfway through my required 14-month enlistment requirement and, to my dismay, I knew that a field commission would require me to give the Army another 12-14 months of my life. I tell him that I can't do it; I'm honored, but I can't do it. Then I explain why. He's annoyed but comes up with a solution.

*Doing "The Night Watch" -
December 1946.*

"See this name?" he asks, pointing to a piece of paper in his hand.

"I see it: Christopher Donald."

"Get a piece of paper and a pen, and let me see you write his name."

I got the paper and pen and I wrote the name.

"No, you idiot, write his name exactly as it appears."

"Sir, you mean as if I was forging his signature?"

"No, soldier, I would never order you to forge a signature; that would be a crime. Just write it exactly as Donald would."

So I sit there practicing exactly how Christopher Donald would write his name. When I get the payroll and disburse it, I'm Christopher Donald. By then, I have a little over six months to go as Corporal Goldsmith until I'm discharged. To get even, the Army wouldn't even make me a sergeant.

Another visitor came to see me, this one from the BBC. He was interested in the boxing matches between American and British soldiers that we'd been broadcasting.

"We'd like to use your facilities."

I say sure.

"And *you*."

"Me? Why?"

"By the time a British announcer says, 'The bloke took one on the chin,' the round could be over or the fight finished. We need a more articulate announcer broadcasting the blow-by-blows on the air."

Who's going to know?

So I broadcast the intramural boxing matches between the U.S.A. and Great Britain on the Armed Forces Network, transmitted by BBC to London, which relayed my voice over the BBC network live. I wondered if anybody in the U.S. heard me.

Somewhere during this time in *Gorizia*, Italy, I discovered the local synagogue, which was situated along a cobbled street not far from the radio station. Although I rarely went to synagogue in Brooklyn (usually on the High Holy Days), a sense of home – of not forgetting where I came from – drew me and two of my Army buddies to the Friday night services. Most of the members of the congregation were merchants. They generally sold souvenirs: Swiss watches, cigarette lighters, Italian ceramics, and all styles of silk scarves and ties. We went every Friday evening; it gave us a feeling of comfort.

One early afternoon, a group of MPs came to the radio station. We were all lounging around in our slippers and robes, probably looking like inmates of an insane asylum.

The lead MP said, "Close down the station. Announce that you're shutting down for maintenance on the antenna. All of you get dressed, you're coming with us."

I thought, "it's over, they're closing down the station; they're taking us in. I went on the air and quickly signed us off.

"Where are we going?"

"To headquarters in Udine."

He would tell me no more. I dressed, got in the truck with the others, and was driven to Udine, which was a city with parks, churches, hotels, and the Army HQ building.

"What's going on?"

"You'll see."

There was a line of soldiers in front of HQ, spanning more than three city blocks. We got to the end of the line and still didn't know why we were there. At least we weren't brought to headquarters because of our activities at the radio station. I told my men that I was going to the front of the line to find an officer who could tell us what was happening.

At the very front of the line, two officers sat at a table with piles of paper currency in front of them. During the occupation, the U.S. Army had issued currency called "scrip." Our salaries were paid in scrip, and it was only to be used for purchases at the Army's P.X., a virtual supermarket where food, tobacco, sodas, personal items, and off-duty apparel were sold. In addition, it was used for food, snacks, and meals at the Army clubs.

I explained to one of the officers that I was in charge of Armed Forces Radio in Gorizia. He smiled, told me that he was a fan, and explained that the color of the currency was being changed. It seems that scrip was being used illegally as money in the city and in various towns. The Italian stores and shops accepted it and used it to purchase what they needed from one another, as well. The Italian currency, the *lira*, had no recognizable value; local citizens had more confidence in the U.S. scrip. The lira was supposed to be used by the military for all purchases in local establishments. There were money exchange desks at each military outfit that changed scrip for lira. It got confusing because of the constant fluctuation in the value of the lira. Changing the color of the scrip made all scrip then in circulation *worthless*. From then on, only *new* scrip or dollars were to be used within the confines of the military and only lira were to be used in civilian establishments. I thought that these changes also had something to do with the black market that was flourishing throughout Italy, affecting the value of the lira.

I told the officer that not one of the MPs had told us to bring our money. He said, "Confidentially, you have a few more days. Many G.I.s are on vacation and will need to exchange later. Actually, today was the day to stop using scrip, in any color, immediately. No exchanges will be made with civilians, only Army personnel."

He told me to call him as soon as my outfit was ready to exchange. We should collect the scrip and pick a representative to make the proper exchange. He made arrangements for a truck to take us back to the station.

As we were being driven back, I was thinking that we had a few days of breathing space. I knew that I'd go back, but maybe not the next day. I had an idea.

I went to the synagogue and told the Rabbi the whole story. I knew that a lot of the men in the congregation were going to get hurt, because most of them were selling souvenirs to the G.I.s and would most likely get stuck with the old scrip. I had to warn them.

The Rabbi was dumfounded; he started to shake. "Do you realize what a disaster this is? They've struggled to make a living, and all of their hard work will go up in smoke. Their money will be worthless! I can't believe that this is going to happen."

He asked me to come back that evening. When I returned, six men from the congregation showed up, with two huge strapped valises full of Army scrip.

"You have to cash this in for us," one of them said. "This is our life savings. We implore you, as a fellow Jew, to do this for us."

"I'm a private; how many crap games can I tell the Army I've won to get this amount of cash? I'll try to get other soldiers to help with the exchange, but I'm sure they'll want a fee or a percentage."

The men in the synagogue reminded me, "You're one of us. You've got to help us; do whatever it takes."

So, I left with the two valises and headed back to the station. My four buddies agreed that for a fee of 20% we'd go back to Udine the following day to exchange not only our scrip, but also whatever we could of the scrip in the two valises. We opened the valises. There must have been over $20,000 worth of old scrip in each! It would be impossible to account to the exchange office for such a large amount. My buddies said that they would each try to get away with cashing in around $1500 worth; that would amount to a total of only $6000, less our 20% fee, leaving $1200 for us and $4800 for them.

When we got back to Udine, we saw the officer and made the exchange with no problem. None of us knew how much we were actually allowed to cash in. I went back to the synagogue, toting the valises. "Out of about ten thousand dollars in scrip," I told them, "I cashed in maybe six thousand; the net to you after commission is $4800. That's the best we could do. Here's your money. One suit case we didn't even try to change. From the other, here's the remainder of the unchanged scrip, less $1200."

"This is terrible – you've ruined us! We want our money back."

"My buddies and I have actually taken only $1200 for our efforts; we couldn't exchange any more."

"You're not leaving here alive."

Straight out of a scene in some B-movie, the men stepped in front of the synagogue door and blocked me from leaving. I looked at the Rabbi, who said there was nothing he could do. So, giving in, I took $200 out of my pocket – all I had on me – and handed it over.

I was told, "We never want to see you here again."

"You mean, I can't come to services anymore?"

"No!"

About a week later, the Rabbi came to the radio station to tell me that I could come back. They'd found an officer who would help them out.

So many rackets, I thought.

I had gotten very friendly with another army pilot who was leaving messages on my call-in show. This one would fly me to Zurich – it was wintertime, too cold for Venice. Eventually, I had a girlfriend there, Toni, who looked like the skating star Sonja Henie, but prettier – a very outgoing girl who lived alone, worked in a shop, and was happy to be dating a GI with money in his pocket. Although I was in love with her and would often stay overnight, we never had sex. I was respectful – or maybe I was just afraid that somehow my mother would find out. I guess it was my upbringing: you don't fool around with a girl you're serious about.

My enlistment was coming to an end. On our last night together, I told Toni that I would be heading back home to the States and that I couldn't make a commitment to her. I'd be in another country, going to college and trying to make a career for myself. We promised to write to each other regularly. She cried in my arms as we passionately said our goodbyes.

As I walked out the door into the snowfall, heading toward the taxi stand nearby, I heard her calling, "Herbert, Herbert." I turned to see her following me out into the snow, still in her nightgown; I had to drag her back inside crying hysterically.

When I eventually got on the ship to go home, the guys and I were comparing notes on our adventures with girls – discussing who got laid in Europe and who didn't. Of course, I said I did. Then one of the guys took out a picture of his girlfriend.

It was the same picture of Toni that I carried in my wallet.

I went back to my quarters and cried.

Toni wrote many letters to me, just as she promised. But I never opened a single one.

Radio Who's Who

Pfc. Herbert M. Goldsmith, called 'Herby', for short, is our scintillating Chief Announcer at AES, Gorizia. Added to his important duties as chief of the announcers, he writes and does "The 1 O'clock Jump," "Jive At Noon" and up until a short while ago, "The Night watch." In his offical capacity, Herby sweats over the schedule, supplies the right man in the right position at the right time and, supervises the training of student announcers.

Herb Goldsmith said goodbye to the stork and hello to the Bronx a short nineteen years ago. However, by this time he has branched out and maintains residences in both New York and Miami, Fla. Educated in the east, he graduated from Abraham Lincoln High School where he had participated in the varsity swimming team. Herby acted as emcee in school shows and wrote and directed the Senior Show. In June of '45, he graduated and joined the Maritime Service. He attended Radio School for the Maritime until it was closed and then shipped out on a Liberty Ship for LeHavre, France. Aboard ship, Herby was non-com in charge of army mess (no doubt a slightly disliked fellow).

After nine months in the Maritime Service, he entered the army in March of 1946. Herb started his world-wide tour by going to Camp Joseph T. Robinson, Ark., for infantry basic. In June he boarded a Victory Ship, the Wilson Victory, and set sail this time for Italy. Once overseas, Herby was assigned to Co. "A" of the 752 Tank Bn. By September his application for AES on TDY was accepted. He started out as an announcer and worked his way up to Chief Announcer in two months!

Radio Highlights

Well, fellows it looks as if we're going to have to say 'so long pal to our old Night Watchman, Herb Goldsmith. It seems that under the strain of training new-men and other added duties he must retire from the show. No doubt you will be happy to hear that your substitute Night Watchman, Arnold Fine, is taking over. Army has been doing a swell job and will continue to do his best to fill that mellow groove dug by Herb.

On Sunday at 2000 hours, "MAIL CALL" features it's usual array of personalities. Your lovely skipper will introduce such notables as sweet and lovely, Jean Peters; "I Wanna Get Married" gal, Gertrude Nieson; that amazing latin vocalist and expert of the pantomine, Miguelito Valdez; a woman who is above everything a great American, Kate Smith, singer supreme, Frank Parker; the old Fire Chief himself, Ed Wynn and, a small musical organization that makes a great deal of nice noise, the Les Paul Trio.

COMMAND PERFORMANCE, aired at 2030 on Sunday, presents a swell show as usual. On hand will be enchanting and capable, Constance Moore; a fellow who knows what's what, Jack Douglas; a fast rising and brightly shining star, Rickey Jordan; the rotund and rascally casanova, Harold Peary alias the Great Gildersleeve; smooth tap and vocal man, George Murphy and silver-voiced Glen Niles.

HOLLYWOOD STAR TIME, heard on Sunday at 1730, continues in the O.S.S. series of stories starring a well known actor every week. This week "Operation Monsoon O.S.S. stars that popular and excellent actor, Brian Donlevy. The story concerns the trials and tribulations that the O.S.S. men contend with the Jungles, the natives and Japs. Oddly enough a good part of their worries are caused by an American Missionary in the wilds of Burma.

At 1900 hours on Sunday, The Frank Morgan Show hits the air waves with a bang once again (This serial type program has become quite popular with the Blue Devils). Dr. Tweedy's students hire a night club in which they intend to hold a surprise party for him on his birthday. The glib doctor doesn't know of this and decide that this very club is indecent and should be raided. On the very night the raid is scheduled, he is forced to attend the birthday party. The result is, as always, uproarious.

"Stars and Stripes - Radio Who's Who" article... talking about the Herby Goldsmith - Chief Announcer!

Army of the United States

SEPARATION QUALIFICATION RECORD

SAVE THIS FORM. IT WILL NOT BE REPLACED IF LOST

This record of job assignments and special training received in the Army is furnished to the soldier when he leaves the service. In its preparation, information is taken from available Army records and supplemented by personal interview. The information about civilian education and work experience is based on the individual's own statements. The veteran may present this document to former employers, prospective employers, representatives of schools or colleges, or use it in any other way that may prove beneficial to him.

1. LAST NAME—FIRST NAME—MIDDLE INITIAL			MILITARY OCCUPATIONAL ASSIGNMENTS		
GOLDSMITH HERBERT M			10. MONTHS	11. GRADE	12. MILITARY OCCUPATIONAL SPECIALTY
2. ARMY SERIAL No.	3. GRADE	4. SOCIAL SECURITY No.	2	PVT	BASIC 521
42 275 173	T/5		7	T/5	CHIEF ANNOUNCER 442
5. PERMANENT MAILING ADDRESS (Street, City, County, State)					
12 WEST 72D ST NYC N					
6. DATE OF ENTRY INTO ACTIVE SERVICE	7. DATE OF SEPARATION	8. DATE OF BIRTH			
4 MAR 46	12 JUN 47	3 SEP 27			
9. PLACE OF SEPARATION					
SEP BR CP KILMER, NJ					

SUMMARY OF MILITARY OCCUPATIONS

13. TITLE—DESCRIPTION—RELATED CIVILIAN OCCUPATION

CHIEF ANNOUNCER AND CONTINUITY WRITER 442

WAS ASSIGNED WITH THE 88TH DIV AT A RADIO STATION WRITING SCRIPTS
AND ANNOUNCING OVER AES GORIZIA ITALY WROTE HIS OWN SCRIPTS ON "DISC
JOCKEY" SHOWS SPORTS AND SPECIAL PROPAGANDA PROGRAMS WROTE SCRIPTS
FOR OTHER SHOWS THAT WERE BROADCASTING TO ALL EUROPE OF SEVERAL LARGE
BOXING EVENTS WAS ON THIS DUTY SEVEN MONTHS AT GORIZIA ITALY

WD AGO FORM 100
1 JUL 1945

This form supersedes WD AGO Form 100, 15 July 1944, which will not be used.

*My separation papers
from the Army.*

Chapter Four

TWO OR THREE DAYS BEFORE we docked in New York, I took my knapsack and duffel bag and threw them overboard. Goodbye, Army. All I had left, as the Statue of Liberty came into view, was my little cap and a cane I'd bought in Switzerland – a beautiful piece with a carved knob on top, and metal medallions from all the cities I visited attached to the staff.

My father was waiting on the pier. By then, he was living in the Oliver Cromwell Hotel on 72nd Street and Central Park West in Manhattan.

"You'll stay with me," he said.

He took me directly to his one-bedroom apartment, with its twin beds, and we became roommates. My mother had let me know that she was starting to date and that she didn't want men to know that she had a 20-year-old son.

It was June of 1947, and I was ready for college. Because of my low grades at Lincoln High School, I was concerned that I wouldn't be accepted; luckily, Long Island University had a policy of accepting all ex-servicemen who were high school graduates, regardless of their grades. You needed only a passing grade in your first semester at LIU to continue; it was truly a blessing. Thanks to the G.I. Bill, my tuition and books were paid for by the

U.S. Government, and I received a check for $50.00 every week from the 52/50 Club. Before long, I was enrolled in college.

The LIU campus consisted of six floors in the former Con Edison building on Fulton Street in upper Brooklyn. The building stood alongside several dilapidated shops with signs in the windows that read, "These Buildings are Condemned." In my art class, we weren't given *canvases* to paint on; we were told to paint directly on the *walls*, since the building was going to be demolished at the end of the semester. Jigg's luncheonette, which was across the street, became my hangout. I made friends quickly and found many people with the same ideas and drive that I had; quite a few, like me, were going to school on the G.I. Bill. Our tuition was paid directly by the government, but we were only receiving $50 a week to support ourselves, and who could live on $50 a week? I tried to manage by having dinner at my mother's place twice a week and meeting my father for a meal on Sundays.

> DURING MY COLLEGE YEARS: I BECAME AN ACTOR AND MET THE WOMAN I WOULD MARRY.

Two momentous things happened during my college years: I became an actor and I met the woman I would eventually marry.

LIU's speech department was setting up a theatre and looking for people to audition for various roles. I told Professor Brown (the Speech Department chair and director) what a big *macher* I was. It didn't help; I still had to audition. Acting was an entirely different experience from being chief of Armed Forces radio, because now I didn't have a crew to work with. It was just me, face-to-face with my own desires for notoriety and fame, trying to satisfy my need to stand out from the masses. Fortunately, I had enough talent to win a role in Moliere's *Imaginary Invalid*.

My parents' relationship was still tempestuous. Although my mother was dating someone, she also saw my father from time to time. It was as though they were "cheating on each other, with each other." It became clear after a while that my father really didn't have enough room for me to continue living with him.

*On a boat ride up the Hudson
with my friends from LIU.*

Brooklyn must have been calling me back, because I found a room for rent in an elderly woman's home off of New Lots Avenue. Actually, the room she rented me was her dining room, with sliding doors for privacy. She also had another boarder, a taxi driver who worked nights, but I never saw him. The room cost $10 a week, and since I was only getting $50 a week, I needed a part time job.

Macy's on Flatbush Avenue hired me to work in the men's sock department on Thursday evenings and all day Saturday. Right away, I started getting marketing ideas. The socks were displayed on tables and were all mixed together – black socks, brown socks, navy socks. It was a mess. When I got to work, I'd not only fold all of the socks and straighten the piles by color, I'd also check them over and make pronouncements like, "We're running out of socks," or, "We need more brown socks." I shanghaied other people working there to do inventory, which they'd never done before.

Despite my management skills, the socks remained a mess and I got fed up. Because of the movie *The Man in the Gray Flannel Suit*, something new arrived on the men's fashion scene – gray socks – and I thought we should order some of those. I found out where the store bought their socks and called them up as though I were the buyer for the department. I ordered more socks in all colors, but especially in brown, and I threw in an order for some grays also.

My school life was going really well; I was in the theatre group, and I was always with my friends, meeting people in the hallways. It was a close-knit community, where teachers and students were friends. The Speech Department held a weekly tea in a lounge, where students were welcome to read poems or excerpts from other interesting writings. At one of these teas, I came with the theatre group to make a speech encouraging students to join the theatre. I told them how important it was to support the school and how intimate the experience would be. We were mingling with the students when my good friend Marvin walked over to me.

"My friend Dolores would like to meet you," he said.

Guess my response.

"I'm too busy, Marvin. I can't even handle everything on my plate now."

It was true. Besides school work, I was working at Macy's on Thursday nights and all day on Saturdays, plus trying to make our first play production a big hit for the school. My schedule was already full, and that left no time for dating. Seeing all that I had already accomplished without a college education, I was determined to get my degree. After that, the sky was the limit!

In those days, dating meant going to a movie or going dancing. It was the Swing Era and everybody was going out to dance halls to hear the big bands. But my mother – a terrific dancer – had assured me that I had "two left feet," that I could never dance, and that I shouldn't even think about it. Still, she had tried teaching me to dance. My mother had a Victrola and dance records (many times, I'd find her dancing by herself in the apartment), and although she gave me countless lessons, I wasn't a very promising student.

Besides, like I said, I didn't have time.

I found out later that Dolores had performed that same day. My group had gotten there after her performance because we didn't want to interrupt what was going on. Dolores had asked who I was, and Marvin had answered, "Oh, that's Herb Goldsmith. Everybody knows him." Unbeknownst to me, Marvin already had his eye on her, but she'd told him, "You're a good friend, Marvin, but beyond that, it ain't gonna happen."

A few days later, I bumped into Marvin and he said, "Do me a favor please. At least look at her. She's a beautiful girl, and maybe you'll change your mind."

In his pocket, he had Dolores's class schedule, including her row and seat number in each class. I went to one of the classrooms, opened the door, and said to the teacher, "Excuse me, professor, but it's important that I make an announcement about our upcoming theater production of *The Imaginary Invalid*. We need the support of the class."

I made my spiel. And I looked. Marvin was right – Dolores was really pretty. She had short dark hair, very large eyes, a perky nose, thick lips, skin like alabaster. More than pretty, she was beautiful – a knockout – and that was from a distance.

Marvin was waiting outside the classroom.

"Well, whaddya think?"

"She's very pretty, but she was sitting down; I'd like to see her standing up."

"Well, she's having lunch at 1:30 at Jigg's luncheonette."

Before long, Marvin and I were at Jigg's. I saw Dolores sitting with her girlfriends in a booth way in the back. We sat on a stool at the counter looking unconcerned. After a while, Marvin looked up and said, "Here she comes."

Dolores walked right past us, her eyes on the door. Her walk was dynamite. I could see that underneath her felt skirt she had hips! And so, of course, I called to ask her out, hoping we wouldn't end up dancing.

It was a Friday. "I'd like to see you tomorrow night," I said.

Her answer floored me: "You can't call me on a Friday night for a Saturday night date." Years later, Dolores admitted that she'd been waiting and yearning for my call but wouldn't give me the satisfaction of knowing it then.

Her response bothered me all weekend, but it taught me what was expected of a gentleman, and on the following Monday I dutifully called. We made a date for Saturday night. There were, however, a few logistical problems. Dolores lived near the next-to-last subway stop in the Bronx and I lived near the last stop in Brooklyn. The trip would mean a long train ride and a transfer from the elevated line to the underground. What kind of first impression could I make showing up on the train? And besides, what kind of action could I expect on a crowded subway car? Clearly, I had to get a car.

My father's work life had changed. Instead of traveling all the time, he had gone into his own business, joining another salesman to establish a company in downtown Manhattan that sold the same kind of men's outerwear he'd represented on the road. So he didn't always need his car. Grudgingly, he allowed me to borrow the gray Cadillac for my big date.

I gave myself two hours to get there and got lost twice. But there I was, in my tie and sports jacket, on the second floor of a four-story walkup . . . with Dolores standing partly in the hallway, holding the door nearly closed behind her.

"We're having the apartment painted," she explained, "and all the furniture is pushed together; I didn't want you to see a mess."

I didn't care. All I saw was how beautiful she looked in a pretty print dress that shimmered like silk and clung to her body. Just my luck, the place she had chosen for our first date was a dance hall.

Marni's Casino reminded me of Madison Square Garden. It was a long room the size of a basketball court, with a dance band at one end and places to sit at the other. We headed for a corner banquette far from where the band was playing. Dolores took off her beaver coat and put it on the ledge, behind our seats. As we headed toward the dance floor, I could feel the ice in my veins.

Surprisingly, my dancing turned out to be adequate, and Dolores never once complained about my stepping on her feet. After several turns around the dance floor, we returned to the banquette, where an awful animal odor assaulted us. As it turned out, the heat vents were located in the tops of the banquette, exactly where Dolores had thrown her coat. We survived that too.

We got into the Cadillac.

"Where do we go now?" I asked, having no idea where we were.

She offered to show me and proceeded to give me directions: "Go to the second light. Make a left and then a sharp right. You'll come to a very bright streetlight, but don't park under it, just let it shine on the hood of the car."

Oh boy, I was thinking, "This girl knows where it's at." I did exactly what she said, and we parked. I loosened my tie, pushed the car seat back a little, and put my arm around her. We both said what a special night it had been. I was thinking, "Goldsmith, don't screw this up."

Dolores looked up, moved her mouth toward mine, and gave me the most unbelievable French kiss. Then she pushed the door handle and hopped out of the car. We were right across the street from her house.

"Thanks for a great evening," she said, skipping into the building.

I just sat there cooling off, playing that kiss over and over in my mind before driving back to the far end of Brooklyn. The next day I returned the car to my father. A week later, I went to dinner at my mother's.

"I met a girl. I've never had this experience before – we went dancing and I was actually okay. The funny thing was, ma, while we were dancing she just seemed to . . . fit."

> THE FUNNY THING WAS, MA, WHILE WE WERE DANCING SHE JUST SEEMED TO . . . FIT.

My mom chuckled. "God bless you son, don't screw it up. This must be the girl for you."

And she was. After their apartment painting was done, I was allowed to come in and meet her parents. Her mother was very European and worked at Lerner's Department Store on 14th Street in Manhattan; her father sold kitchen supplies to restaurants. Claire, her older sister, had married and moved to Chicago. The atmosphere in that family was so different from mine. Her father was a gentle, charming man; her mother was a homebody. Their home was their castle and their children were their jewels.

They wanted to know about my "lifestyle." After all, I had been in the Merchant Marine and the U.S. Army, cooked on a rolling ocean, and run a radio station. I was a man of the world, whose parents were separated. Strangely, Dolores parents didn't seem to mind any of it.

One of her father's customers owned a delicatessen-restaurant, where the owner's wife was the cook, and we started eating there a lot. He must have given me a break on the price, because the bill was never as high as the price on the menu. This was much better than my customary "liverwurst on rye with lots of free coleslaw" at Jiggs. After a while, Dolores's mother invited me to eat at home with them instead of eating at the restaurant. Later I was allowed to sleep over, which meant that sometimes I had three meals there: breakfast, a light lunch, and dinner. Benefits like those were important because I was still trying to live on $50 a week after paying $10 rent.

*Dolores, the cheerleader at
Long Island University.*

Looking good at LIU.

One weekend, I got a call asking me to come in early Monday morning to see the manager at Macy's. Boy, was I excited – I'd done such a good job that I was probably in for a raise, maybe even a promotion.

"What would you call yourself here at Macy's?" the manager asked.

"A clerk," I responded.

"So why are you acting like the buyer?"

I told him that I thought certain things needed improvement, and that I was just trying to help.

"It's not *your* responsibility," he said coldly. "And you won't be doing it anymore because you're fired!"

I felt humiliated. This was my first firing and it really hurt.

On my way out, the executive called after me, "You're too smart for this job."

It didn't help.

Money was always a concern for me because without it I couldn't date Dolores "properly." Nevertheless, we still had great rapport and so much to talk about. Like me, she was interested in theater and the arts and had real ambition – she was studying to be a speech therapist.

We dated all throughout college, mostly with our friends – in groups. For two and a half years, I couldn't get her past the kissing stage (not for lack of trying). Although I was stuck on first base, we had good times in so many other ways. A friend of Dolores's family worked as a chauffeur on an estate in Westchester, where he lived in the gate house. Whenever the owner was away in Newport, we'd picnic on the estate. We spent Saturdays and Sundays together, but there was one aspect of my life that I wasn't so eager to share with Dolores for fear she'd be turned off: my bohemian friends.

Back in Brooklyn, I had a group of friends, including girls, who all hung out on a section of Brighton beach called Bay One. A lot of artistic people from the city congregated there: drama students, actors, dancers. They were a strange group. I vividly remember that one of the girls had a two piece bathing suit, which nobody had ever seen before; my friend Lee knew her.

A weekend at the Catskills.

Lee had set his sights on an acting career, and after his stint in the Navy actually became an actor. His first show on Broadway was *Twelve Angry Men*. He then went to Hollywood, where his first film role was opposite Lana Turner in *Peyton Place*. Lee was a handsome, dark-haired guy, who looked a little like Dana Andrews (or, for today's audience, George Clooney). The trouble was, he had a high squeaky voice – which didn't bode well for an acting career – and he eventually left acting to become a successful television director.

Norman, a good pal of mine from high school, was primarily interested in music and wanted to write jingles. At one point, Lee, Norman, and I decided to write a musical. After school, we would meet at my aunt Dottie's house because she had a piano (and because we knew we'd always get a good meal). We actually thought that we knew what we were doing. It was never completed.

Norman apparently *did* know what he was doing because he went on after his Army service to become one of the top songwriters of all time. One day, Norman suggested that I come to his office; he was working in the Brill Building in Manhattan, where all the songwriters were. "You gotta come up here, meet my bosses, they're testing some of my songs," he said. There were twenty agencies on the floor, each door with a frosted glass window, all were selling sheet music. In the hallways, there always were guys looking to make a few bucks by playing the piano. Norman would grab anyone in the hallways who would play the piano, sing a little, or interpret a tune; demonstrating the songs. Once, Norman grabbed this little guy who was always hanging around and asked him to come in and play. The guy smiled and introduced himself: "Hi, I'm Sammy Davis, Jr."

In my sophomore year, I had the lead in the school's production, Moliere's *The Farce of Pierre Patelin*, a zany over-the-top French farce originally performed by strolling groups of players in the Middle Ages. Professor Brown did a theater-in-the-round adaptation, which included showcasing the entire cast in wonderful period costumes marching in to medieval music. Reviewing my performance as Pierre Patelin, a shrewd shyster, a local reviewer called me:

"A great comic" and technique, "A combination of Bob Hope, Groucho Marx and Menasha Skulnik."

It was a big hit. In fact, it was such a big hit that my father took me to the Copacabana, where radio personality Jack Eigen broadcast a show that mixed music with celebrity interviews, and Jack Eigen actually interviewed *me!*

The following year, we did an even more ambitious production: Henrik Ibsen's *Ghosts*. The reviews called the show brilliant and described my portrayal of Oswald, Mrs. Alving's slowly dissipating son, this way:

"A powerful and tragic performance, displaying his versatility to great advantage. In that transition from sanity to an abrupt, violent derangement, he offers a turbulent, terrifying characterization."

I didn't know what was ahead of me, but everything was looking up, and I wanted to grab the ring. The world was changing and the feeling that anything is possible made everyone optimistic. We all knew we were talented, but we had no idea how far that alone would take us. I didn't have aspirations for any profession I knew of, but I was determined not to do what my father had done. I saw his life as hard and lonely. I, on the other hand, had already been exposed to a multitude of opportunities and was eager to grab hold of them all. As for acting, it was something I thought I should at least consider.

My college grades were excellent and I graduated in three and a half years. My roles in the various theatrical productions made impressive additions to my resume, although I had no idea what kind of future business I was aiming for. LIU was a very small university, and if not for the success and national fame of their basketball team, I doubt that they would have had the impressive growth they did in the 1950s. The publicity that the theatrical performances brought was important and helped to create the impression of a very well-rounded school.

Theatre Group Continues Use Of New Methods; 'Pierre Patelin' To Be Presented In-The-Round

By SAM BERKOWITZ

In "Pierre Patelin," the third in-the-round production of the LIU Workshop Theatre, we are presented with a robust carnival of jubilant minstrels who give us a succession of farcial scenes that make up a fanciful play. "Patelin" was written by a 15th century friar who, intrigued by the amorous ballads of the nomadic minstrels, preferred to remain anonymous. His play holds the satirical embodiment of that reckless age of fierce passions and unscrupulous shysters.

The play was translated from the French by Richard T. Holbrook, and adapted for the arena production by Prof. Dennis Brown, director of the group. His adaptation has given the comedy a topical, zany, whirl-wind atmosphere; his prologue and epilogue give the play added zest and color.

As the lights gradually illuminate the wide expanse of the arena stage, Wally Beinfeld, as the leader of the minstrels, comes pirouetting in like an elegant, swishing balletome followed by his entourage of mad jesters. The accompanying music is Dimitri Kabolivsky's highly spirited "Comedians;" the prologue is practically a ballet, one in which the choreography is both ingenious and colorful.

'Patelin' The Shyster

The title role, Pierre Patelin, is played by Herb Goldsmith. Patelin is a shrewd, welching shyster, unscrupulous in his shady deals, but nonetheless a likeable hero. Herb is a great comic, and his pantomime, in the prologue, of a gay, ne'er-do-well husband is hilarious. He goes through his antics with a combination Bob Hope-Groucho Marx-Menasha Skulnick technique.

Maxine Schacter plays Patelin's shrewish wife Jeannette, with plenty of gusto. Her delivery of the wise-cracking remarks, the luring pivot-sway of her seductive torso, is a fine caricature of the French traditional **femme fatale** (this one's domesticated.)

Draper, the cheated cloth merchant, who is the victim of Patelin's shennanigans, is played by Jerry Koenig. His portrayal comes off in a striking manner, and the contorted facial expressions together with his leering smile make him an excellent buffoon.

'Patelin' Most Attractive

The **pas de quatre** is completed with Enzio Napoli as the supposedly half-witted shepherd, who has eaten his flock, and is brought to account for his misdemeanors.

As an experimental project "Patelin" proves to be the most attractive and unique of the three productions presented by the Workshop. Prof. Brown has prepared a wonderful script, and his arena presentation, introduced and completed with his carnival of players, is a happy and valuable innovation in the University Theatre today.

Herb Goldsmith

"Pierre Patelin"

"The Imaginary Invalid" -
my role, Cleante.

The Reviewing Stand

By Toni Barbieri

"The Farce of Pierre Patelin;" Adapted and directed by Prof Dennis Brown; University Workshop Theatre; Starring Herbert Goldsmith, Maxine Schachter, Jerome Koenig and Enzio Napoli.

"The Farce of Pierre Patelin" presented last week by Prof. Brown's Workshop Theatre is an engaging, frolicsome and, at times, maniacal in-the-round presentation of one of the earliest French farces penned. Wringing every drop of humor from spent, yellowed stock situations which, at the time of composition were far from the hackneyed interpretations of today, the drama group creates a delightful and entertaining genre.

Headed by Herbert Goldsmith in the title role, Maxine Schachter as his shrewish wife, Guillemette, and Jerome Koenig as Joceaulme, a draper, the play encompasses the roguery of one Pierre Patelin, erstwhile lawyer, and his unscrupulous antics. These antics are executed in a laughable triple-play fashion from walking off with a full 6-yards of woolen material, to feigning sickness and insanity to escape paying the debt and making a mockery of French "justice" by instructing a sheep-stealing client, Lambkin, to respond to all judicial questions with a "baa."

The essence and backbone of "The Farce of Pierre Patelin" emerge from Patelin's crazy capers.

Prof. Brown made a wise choice in casting the lead role. Herbert Goldsmith is a likeable Pierre Patelin. Patelin's conniving bargaining with the draper, his earthy "waking up scene" replete with scratching, devouring breakfast and crude mannerisms, are familiar gimmicks reflected in various forms in the contemporary drama. But, the red-bearded Goldsmith has added a freshness to this role which strengthens one's ability to endure the farce. Goldsmith's outstanding ability to get lost in the role is shown in his spontaneous ranting and raving when pretending sickness to ward off paying the draper. This scene is amusingly crazy!! Never have we thought such ludicrous facial contortions could be so well done by a comparatively unseasoned actor.

As Guillemette, Maxine Schachter is called upon to interpret one of the comedy's most difficult roles. Not only is an alert switch of emotions from feigned "weeping" to realistic wifely nagging called for, but Guillemette must convey her disgust with her husband via face-making and pantomime. Miss Schachter's nagging and shrewish take-off is utterly convincing. Unfortunately, her sterling portrayal is marred only by marked, and spotty forced acting during delivery of some straight lines and action. In spite of this one flaw, the pert co-ed carries a complex role in fine form.

Enzio Napoli's Lambkin, the shepherd, Wally Beinfield's manager of the players, and Leon Goldstein's performance as the judge, give a gay tone in supporting the leads. Not to be missed is Morton Press' sad clown which is straight from Murray Hill 5-1133!

Prof. Brown's adaptation of the farce and his knowing direction, merge to make the presentation untiring, since farces can get out of hand and, for the most part, border on the boring. By way of comment, it was the professor's major intention in directing "Pierre Patelin," to make his cast overact in true, farcical tradition. All the evidence of "hamming it up" were effectively injected in each key spot of the play,

'Pierre Patelin" review.

As Pierre, Mr. Goldsmith has the opportunity to run the gamut of characterizations; first as a rather carefree unsuccessful lawyer and husband — through a haggling shopper (on credit) and dying, demented, babbling pauper—and finally as a cleverly haranguing and ultimately created, devilish barrister. He is countered throughout by his very amusing wife, Guillemette, played wonderfully well by Miss Maxine Schachter. She has managed to capture the effect of the shrew, whining and discontented, not only in her shrill voice but in the desultory movements of her hands, body, and facial expressions. Her one scene where she satirizes the siren is undoubtedly the most hilarious one of the entire show. She played that one complete with the twisting torso and a rose between her teeth. Jerome Koenig was an effective straightman and buffoon in his role of the draper, Joceaulme. He was obviously the one to be fleeced by all the participants and the butt of all the pranks.

The most perplexing role of all was the shepherd, Lambkin, done quite well by Enzio Napoli. Mr. Napoli had the paradoxical job of portraying a simple, browbeaten shepherd in the beginning, and a shrewd welcher of a lawyer's fee at the end of the play. I must say that Mr. Napoli carried this off excellently despite the fact that the majority of his lines consisted of one word—"Baaa"—the bleating of a lamb.

Professor Brown surmounted the puzzling task of scene changes very effectively by reverting to the original strolling players type of performance. There were five scene changes in all, accomplished comically, but nevertheless deftly, by the big Happy Clown, Jack Gitelman, and his little friend, the Sad Clown, Morton Press. Their speed of movement and careful timing to the fast music lent a great deal to the speedy overall effect of the farce.

STAFF

Stage Manager
  Don Zeitz

Costumes
  Eleanor Winston

Student Producer
  Al Phillips

Student Director
  Gene Pressel

PLAYERS

  Herb Goldsmith
  Wally Reinfeld
  Maxine Schacter
  Jerry Koenig
  Enzio Napoli
  Jack Gitelman
    (See cover)
  Morton Press
  Leon Goldstein

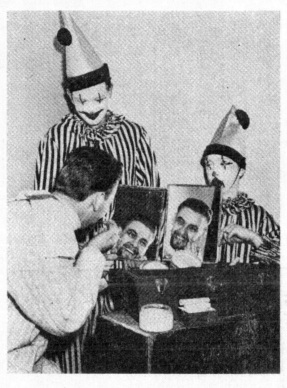

Applying makeup for,
"Pierre Patelin"

"Pierre Patelin"

The Reviewing Stand

By Samuel Berkowitz

A PROMISING START

GHOSTS THAT REMAIN WITH US

LIU Workshop Theatre production of Henrik Ibsen's "Ghosts," directed and adapted for Arena staging by Prof. Dennis Brown.

A whole nation of thought-provoking ideas are presented in this noteworthy LIU Workshop Theatre production of "Ghosts." Ibsen's demented hero, Captain Alving, lives and

 stays with us long after the lights have dimmed. This Alving—this pestilence—this horror drives us strongly within ourselves so that we might find the courage to look at life, the way it was prescribed in Ibsen's time, still dominant, still possessive, in all its' contempt for humanity. It is a brilliant production, a harrowing experience that enables us to reflect and evaluate the dilema that has taken hold of western cultures, subjecting its' peoples to false ideals and traditions.

Mrs. Alving: I think we are all Ghosts, Pastor Manders. It is not only what we have inherited from our fathers and mothers that exist again in us but all sorts of old dead ideas and all kinds of old dead beliefs.

Pastor Manders: There is the result of your reading this abominable subversive free-thinking literature.

Mrs. Alving: You're wrong there my friend—it was you that first made me think.

The student-actors contribute expert and precise performances, that intensify the tragic events that occur. Lore Alfredson (a Junior, who has never performed before) brings forth a superb portrayal of the embittered Mrs. Alving. This young woman is a wonderful actress, possessing the fire and imagination that gives the role that rare quality of meaningfullness. As Mrs. Alving's slowly dissapating son, (Oswald, Herb Goldsmith delivers a powerful and tragic performance, displaying his versatility to great advantage. In that transition from sanity to an abrupt, violent derangement, he offers a turbulent, terrifying characterization. ..

Martin Zagon,, as the hypocritical Pastor Manders, offords the audience with one of the most contemptable of peoples ever written into a play. Eleanor Winston as the not-too naive, ambitious Regina Engstrand, once again proves her talents a competent actress. The surprise of the evening was the excellent performance of Al Landa as Engstrand, the caretaker.

"Ghosts" -
my role was Oswald.

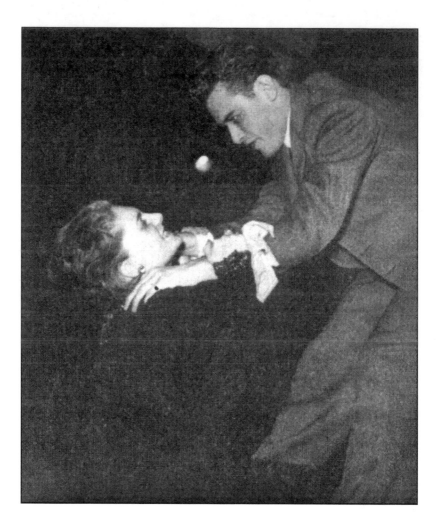

In Ibsen's "Ghosts"

"Ghosts"

Through my dramatics professor, I'd been introduced to New York theatre people, including a professional actress who'd volunteered to be in one of our productions and who offered to help me if I decided to pursue acting. As soon as I graduated, I got a small part in a play called *Dame Nature* at the Cherry Lane Theater in the Village. It wasn't long before I missed my friends. They had normal day-jobs, while I worked in the evening and had the entire day free. I was also uncomfortable in a world that was so different from the one I was accustomed to. My new friends seemed to enjoy all-night parties, booze, and superficial chatter. I wasn't much of a drinker, and I hated beer. And then there was the dog-eat-dog mentality among some of the actors: I had mentioned to a friend of mine that I had an audition at 2:00 p.m. on Tuesday (we were scheduled to have lunch together at 12 p.m. on Tuesday). On Tuesday morning, he canceled our lunch date, claiming to have a dental appointment. When I arrived at the audition (it was a "cattle call" with a long line of aspiring actors), I saw my so-called friend standing at the very front of the long line of actors. This kind of lifestyle, and the sudden interest I was drawing from gay men, unnerved me. The status and attention I'd enjoyed at school was great, but now I was concerned.

Luckily, I met some people who worked in television (which was just getting started), and I considered a new career path. WABD Dumont television, with offices in the John Wannamaker Building, created shows that aired a few hours a day: fashion shows, cooking shows, sewing shows – little drama and nothing creative. I worked for a producer/director as a gofer, learning the business, doing everything from assembling the sets to writing, even doing some voice-overs. I was happier there; it reminded me of Armed Forces radio.

And then I started getting ideas again. When I told my boss that I had developed two concepts for TV programs that hadn't been done before, he told me to write them out. I did. Two weeks went by without my hearing anything.

"Whaddya think? I finally asked him.

"I'm too busy. See me in a week."

Another week went by.

He finally called me into his office.

"Sit down," he said. I sat.

"I'm gonna do you a favor. You have no talent. Even your writing is terrible. You're never gonna make it in this business."

I left dejected. Great, now I hated the theater and had been thrown out of television. I was devastated.

A few weeks later, the television shows I'd written appeared on the air. They were directed by, and credited to, the man who'd told me I had no talent. What a business.

But I still had ideas.

One of my ideas was about radio, where I'd already had a great deal of experience in the Army. Radio stations in the early 1950s had disc jockeys playing music continuously, and showcased personalities like Jack Benny or *Fibber McGee and Molly*. Why not do an interview show on the road, I thought – get outside the studio and have someone visit places most New Yorkers had heard about but hadn't seen, like Silvers Baths (Turkish baths in Coney Island). Why not do interviews with a barker at a freak show, or with women trying on clothes at a store like S. Klein in Union Square, or with people waiting to get into the store before it opened in the morning. Then I realized that those stores and businesses could become the shows' sponsors, paying for their own publicity.

I could call it *The Inquiring Reporter*. I loved the idea, but would anyone else?

Someone gave me the name of a contact at a local radio station. I wrote up my idea and immediately went to the station. A woman came out to talk to me. "Before I can look at *anything*, you have to sign a release giving us the right to use your idea."

Not knowing any better, I signed it.

Weeks went by. I hadn't heard a thing, so I went back up to the radio station. The same woman came out and handed me the pages I'd written up.

"Sorry," she said. "We went through it; there's no interest."

About a month later, on the radio:

> *"From Union Square presenting our new program The Inquiring Recorder, brought to you by S. Klein on the square."*

At least they changed the name from *The Inquiring Reporter*.

I was getting knifed in the back daily and getting more and more depressed. Who could I fall back on? Dolores. I started staying at her parent's apartment and became like a son to them, albeit a despondent son. I'd tried. I knew I was a good actor and a good writer, but I had no idea what to do next. After having experienced the dark side of show biz, I realized that I had better find meaningful employment, even temporary employment. I needed an income; the G.I. Bill was used up, my job at the TV station was over, and my acting career was sidelined.

Chapter Five

THEN A CALL CAME THAT CHANGED MY LIFE: it was Lou, my father's partner. "Would you entertain the idea of working for the new company that your father and I have started?" My father had gone into business with Lou and another salesman from his previous company. They'd named the new company *Chief Apparel*. Soon, Lou and my father had bought out the third partner. They hired the same contractor who had manufactured merchandise for their former employer. He was now designing *their* merchandise and putting *their* labels in the garments: SPORT CHIEF for outerwear and RAIN CHIEF for rainwear. Except for the labels, there was no difference between their goods and the outerwear styles that my father had sold previously.

Lou explained that it was common for a father to want his son to work in his company, and that my father wanted me to seriously consider the offer.

Here was a way to earn some much-needed dollars. I had no idea what my job would be; I only hoped that it wouldn't be in the stock and shipping department. In order to make some extra money while I was in college, after leaving Macy's, I had worked on Saturdays in Chief's warehouse and shipping department, packing orders and unpacking cartons from the manufacturers. They didn't hang the jackets on pipe racks. Instead they folded and stacked them, one on top of the other. In the warm weather months, I had to sprinkle camphor balls between each jacket in order to protect them from moths. Since there was no air conditioning, only open windows, it *really* stunk; I can still remember the smell and the tears those mothballs caused.

Until now, my experience was in radio and theatre. What did I know about the business world? *Bupkis*, that's what. But I went to their showrooms at 1199 Broadway, between 26th and 27th streets. At the rear of the showroom were the storage and shipping areas; a freight elevator brought up shipments from the manufacturers. After packing the orders that had been sold, the cartons were shipped to the customer. Everything was done just as I remembered from when I was a kid.

> WHAT DID I KNOW ABOUT THE BUSINESS WORLD?

"Dad, what do you want me to do?"

"What do you think you *can* do?" my father asked.

I told my father that I didn't have the slightest idea.

He said, "Why don't you go in the back and see Johnny; find out how the company works."

Johnny was an Italian guy who, in addition to being their only salesman, was in charge of receiving and shipping. He had two assistants and a lot of local customers on whom he would call for orders. He would go out in the morning, to Queens or Brooklyn, and come back with orders that were entered on a chart and then given to an assistant to pick, pack, and ship.

I started asking him questions. "Why are you the only sales person?"

He explained that a lot of my father's old customers called in orders or came to our showrooms to see the line. Because the building had 11 floors of apparel firms, there were always new customers wandering around and coming in to look and sometimes buy. He didn't seem to need more salesmen. His partner Lou had one very important customer – Montgomery Ward, one of the largest national chains. It was much like Sears is today, and they were actually major competitors at the time. Montgomery Ward bought nothing but raincoats from them. There wasn't a man in America who didn't own a raincoat with a zip-in wool lining for winter. Raincoats were an all-year-round item.

The men's apparel business was about to change. At the end of the war, the soldiers were returning to a different world; the suburbs were growing. The G.I.'s

were starting families of their own and didn't want to live with their parents in the city. Inexpensive housing was being created on the city outskirts, and G.I.'s were eligible for subsidized government loans to buy those houses. Interest rates were negligible. You could buy a house on a quarter acre lot for $10,000 and pay it off in – what – 20 years? So now everybody's got a plot of land – they landscape it, put in new trees, and suddenly they're experiencing a different kind of life. They're not living in apartment houses anymore. They've got all this room: a basement, big bedrooms – it's unbelievable, and there's a lot of leisure time to enjoy it. On Saturdays and Sundays, you didn't have to go to the office. During the week, you went to work wearing a suit and tie, but on weekends that didn't make sense anymore. Men started to wear flannel shirts, denim shirts, things that workmen would wear, instead of their regular white dress shirts – and without a tie.

Companies got smart and started making casual shirts for those men, and some made outerwear in lighter fabrics than before. Little by little, the Army Navy stores disappeared. The new apparel went into mom and pop stores, where you started to see not only shirts, ties, and shoes, but also a special section in the store for this new outerwear merchandise. Everything evolved – even socks and pajamas. Suddenly, men's underwear was being made in different colors. It was an exciting time. The apparel industry started to evolve, and more people went into the men's side of the business than ever before.

Working at Chief Apparel became a great learning experience. After I'd been there for a short time, I learned about apparel trade shows. The

Men's Apparel Club of New York, for example, would rent several floors in a hotel and have a show twice a year, spring and fall. If you joined, they gave you a room at the hotel to show your line; hopefully, buyers from out of town would stop in and buy your brand. Several hotels were interested in hosting this show because all it took was removing the beds from the room and bringing in a rolling pipe rack and a large table. There were usually three or four floors, each with 20-25 distributors. Since major highways and thruways were still being built and travel was difficult, these shows were an important part of the out-of-town customer's life. They also gave him an opportunity to come in to the big city with his family, see a show or a movie, and have a good time. Later, it became easier for salesmen to travel to the customer instead of waiting for the customer to come in to the city.

Chief's business was expanding so much that the company moved to 902 Broadway, which had a much larger combination of showrooms and warehouse space. They started to hire a few more salesmen, including another one from their old firm. My father decided that it was not in his future to keep traveling, but rather to stay in the city and do whatever he needed to do to make the company grow.

New fabrics were being developed. The fabric salesmen came around, claiming that our competitors were buying these new fabrics and that we should too. Sometimes we did, and along with new materials, we started to develop our own distinctive line of men's outerwear. Instead of six or seven styles, we had fifteen to twenty-five. To make a garment warmer, we used quilting in the lining and added a fake fur collar that looked like beaver. Then we made detachable collars, with pieces of fake beaver buttoned or zipped on. And we started using zippers on pockets; men's fashion was being born.

> MEN'S FASHION WAS BEING BORN.

Many times I was called in from the warehouse to work with a customer in the showroom. I educated myself by reading the men's trade paper, the *Daily News Record* – owned by Fairchild Publications, who also owned *Women's Wear Daily*. I got an idea: why were we restricting ourselves to the

East Coast market, which was New York, Eastern Pennsylvania, Westchester, New Jersey, Connecticut, and a little bit of Massachusetts? Why not the whole USA?

My father said, "Are you crazy? How are we going to see those customers? They already have their resources. Besides, traveling by car is too difficult."

I said, "Well, I did my research and this Men's Apparel Club (MAC) has a show not only in New York, but all over the country. We should sign up for those, go to whatever hotels they're in, and start to expose our line." This, I hoped, would give me the opportunity to get out of shipping and into sales. I told my father that I wanted to start with a state where we had not yet sold our products; by doing that, we could market Chief's product line to a new group of stores and investigate who those stores were currently buying from, which outerwear styles were selling, and at what prices. It would give us important information about our competitors in that state so that we could decide if we were in a position to do business there as well, and alert us as to what was missing in our line.

I convinced my father and Lou that it was important to know what opportunities were out there. I assured them that I would bring back orders.

"Where do you want go?"

"Ohio. Let's see if I can write some business and determine what the buying climate is out there. If Ohio manufacturers sold only to Ohio stores, and if fashions were changing and everyone was creating their own unique designs, there was an opportunity for a New York firm to sell there. Purchasing our line would give the stores an opportunity to have a label and styles that were different from competitors in the same town."

My dad and Lou agreed for me to go ahead. I got a car, packed up four garment bags, and set off, remembering that when my father called on customers, they knew him. But no one knew me, so I had to come up with a gimmick.

I HAD TO COME UP WITH A GIMMICK.

My first stop was Steubenville. I checked out two or three mom and pop stores and went into the nicest looking one, where I asked for the owner. Invariably, the owner was there in the store.

"I represent Chief Apparel from New York."

"Never heard of them."

"Perhaps you can help me," I said. "I'm a newly married man, and I have an opportunity to be the salesman in this territory for a distinguished New York outerwear company. I noticed that you have the nicest store in town, and I hope you can tell me if I have any chance of getting business with this line of products."

"Is this your first traveling salesman job?"

"Yeah, I've never done this before; I usually work in the shipping department and learned that they don't have a salesman for Ohio, so I asked for the chance. That's why I'm here. Before I take the job, I need to know if it's possible to make a living here. Please take a look at my samples and tell me what you think."

"Okay kid, bring them in."

I brought in all five garment bags on my collapsible rolling rack, unzipped the bags, and presented the line.

"Wow," he says, "they look very nice. How much is this garment?"

"I have to go into my envelope here and see if I can find my pricelist."

"Young man, that's not how you do it. You get a pin ticket – write the style number and the price on it and pin it to the cuff of the garment. When the customer asks the price, like I did, you have it right there. Let me show you one."

Eager to teach me my business, he gave me a bunch of pin tickets to put on all my samples. Then he went through the line and set aside three styles.

"How much are these?"

I gave him the prices. "Have you written any orders yet?"

"No, being the nicest in town, I wanted to stop at your store first."

"Do you have an order sheet? I'll be your first order."

My order sheet was numbered 0001. A relative who was a printer had made a hundred double sheets for me, all numbered 0001. I took only one sheet and carbon paper with me when I went into a store with my line.

I started writing, but he interrupted me. "No, you've got to put the carbon paper between the pages; the first page is for the store and the second page is yours."

He actually wrote the order, wished me good luck, and said that I could definitely make a living selling Chief's line. I went town to town using the same spiel and getting orders. It worked every time.

Boy, was New York surprised that I was sending in all these orders. But I didn't realize that you had to check the store's credit to find out whether they were a good risk or not. Chief subscribed to Dun & Bradstreet, a credit rating service that published a book listing stores by state, city, and town and rating their credit risks. All wholesalers referred to D&B for the payment record of the retail stores they sold to. These reports were analyzed, and the credit scores were reported to subscribers. In the days before computers, all this analysis (which resulted in a history of each store) was done by hand. Later there were credit backers called factors; if they gave the manufacturers the okay to ship and the stores didn't pay, the payment became the factor's risk. You paid a fee on every order, much higher than a bank loan – if you could get one – an almost usurious amount, but it was like getting a loan and insurance at the same time. If your firm needed the money in advance, the factor would advance it with an interest charge. Chief didn't choose to go this route.

Since 90% of our yearly business was delivered and paid for in the fall, our ability to get loans from a bank was important. We needed the loans to cover overhead costs as we were building up merchandise and storing inventory in the warehouse from June until the end of August. Fall business represented 75% of the year's volume. The money end of things was in the hands of Lou, who maintained good relations with the bank. In those days, your banker was like part of the family; you knew him by his first name, he took the chances, he knew who you were and knew everything about your business. Your banker trusted you. The financial side was something about which I would eventually learn.

> BUT THE CREATIVE SIDE ALREADY EXISTED IN ME.

But the creative side already existed in me. Because of my trips, I was constantly giving the company new styling concepts. Everything was so new that it was impossible to make a mistake. They accepted some of my ideas and made samples. At the start of each season all samples, not only mine, were reviewed by my dad, Lou, Manny, and Henry. The styles were reviewed and costs calculated by the contractor to determine what the cost to the company would be. When the line was completed, salesman samples were made. At the sales meetings, salesmen were shown the line and told which fabrics and colors were offered in each individual style. Prices were always a heated discussion; the salesmen always wanted lower prices.

Because I had been successful in Ohio and had created an opportunity for Chief to expand by showing at Men's Apparel Club's seasonal shows in Chicago, Detroit, St. Louis, Kansas City, or Dallas, I was allowed to join those shows. Chief Apparel was ready to expand their sales representation because the move to the suburbs brought new Main Streets, new types of apparel, and stores that catered to the new demands of the suburban lifestyle. There were no large stores like Macy's, Gimbels, Montgomery Ward, Sears, or Marshall Field in these communities, just mom and pop stores. The new stores needed new fashions and new resources. Local manufacturers were becoming fashion conscious just as their customers were becoming fashion conscious.

Until then, towns had three or four men's shops, all with identical merchandise. The stores were owned and run by families with no incentive to travel. Why travel? Salesmen would come to them. The salesmen would show the best stores two or three styles they hadn't shown the other stores. There was no understanding of price points – a garment might sell for $20 in one store and $18 in another.

My idea was to go into those cities and towns as a New York manufacturer with the mystique and panache of New York and offer the stores an exclusive. Because I was a new resource for them, they were cautious and wanted to buy just a limited number of styles, so I offered them an exclusive on those styles. Astute entrepreneurs understood that they'd be getting something the competition didn't have, which they then could sell at any price and produce higher profits.

All the men's outerwear companies were small. McGregor was the exception, the largest and the best – a trail blazer – and my role model. Their prices were higher than most of the competition's prices. They had put into motion the idea of stores carrying a coordinated line of outerwear – jackets, shirts, and sweaters – though the term 'coordinated' didn't yet apply to menswear. McGregor's designed sweaters and shirts that worked together: a sweater with a color co-coordinated shirt and outerwear jacket. They developed a brand that the stores couldn't afford *not* to have, and they did it consistently, season after season. McGregor had a policy of "confinement," which meant that they didn't sell to every store, only to a select few. That left an opening for me with my product.

I was also thinking about regional differences in styling needs. In Chicago, for example, a customer might need a jacket with a hood and a lining of either, fleece, quilted, wool plaid, or even a zip out lining. I thought we should design a few new styles that would be specifically for a new area that we wanted to sell to. But when I told Lou and my father about the idea, they said, "Wait a minute. It's expensive to make production on a small scale. We can't make 400 jackets; we'll have to make thousands. How do we know this will work?"

"You don't know," I said, "but if you don't take a chance on this, you'll remain a small company."

McGregor was also my role model when it came to advertising. Except for them, there wasn't any national advertising for men's sportswear. The leading brands – Hart Schaffner & Marx, Eagle, and GGG did some advertising for tailored clothing accessorized with Arrow and Van Heusen shirts and ties, but it wasn't fashion, it was just clothing not outerwear. McGregor was advertising in national magazines like *Life* and *Look* and in men's magazines like *Argosy* and *True*. McGregor was way ahead of the bunch. They made a beautifully styled line, merchandised it, and marketed it in a very unique way. The salesmen had books with fabric swatches attached to a page opposite a color photograph of how the garment looked on a professional model. It showed how it would look when worn, as opposed to showing the buyer the garment hanging limply on a hanger. They spent a lot of money doing this and used the same layout in their ads in major magazines. Most apparel manufacturers didn't understand anything about advertising; they thought that spending money on ads was ridiculous, especially since the ad was not meant to reach the retailer, but the consumer. Many other companies held the same opinion that my dad held. "Since we don't know who the consumer is, or where he lives, how can we hope to reach him through national advertising? Let the retailers spend their own money on advertising. For us, it would be a waste of money. How could we motivate our retail customers, and eventually their customers, to buy Sport Chief outerwear and Rain Chief rainwear?"

Since national advertising was too costly, I concluded that the only economical way to promote the firm was through trade publications and publicity. Why not show a celebrity in an ad wearing our clothes – somebody from the sports world or the movies? That would motivate our customers to identify our apparel with a well-known personality. If they saw a movie star or an athlete wearing our clothes, they would logically think that the celebrity wouldn't pose in an ad if they didn't like the product. He wouldn't wear it if it wasn't good.

> THE ONLY ECONOMICAL WAY TO PROMOTE THE FIRM WAS THROUGH TRADE PUBLICATIONS AND PUBLICITY.

The way I put the question to myself was, how can I hope to create excitement for our brand at little cost? This was all new. Each day now, I couldn't wait to get to work. How do I pay for consumer advertising? I'd have to get money from my father and his partner, neither of whom realized how important advertising was. I just had to wait for the right time.

Fashion is in the eye of the beholder, and the country was developing a competitive attitude: who has the bigger car, the bigger house, the fur coat? What you wore became your badge, your uniform, another marker for making the statement, "I'm better than you."

In the meantime, I chose some styles from magazines and from jackets that I bought in Chicago, Philly, and other cities. I brought them to Manny, our manufacturer's designer, and asked him to make our versions of those garments. It was difficult convincing them, but for the most part, it got done.

The company kept growing. Lou had an Army buddy who owned a few stores in Connecticut and Massachusetts called Case Clothing, selling a large selection of merchandise at lower prices. Today you would call it a discount operation; they were buying from us. Case expanded and opened new stores in the New York metropolitan area under the name of Robert Hall. Our business exploded. The need for fashion outerwear at the right price became very important and Robert Hall advanced Chief the money to pay for fabric and our manufacturing costs. Robert Hall's spectacular growth caused our volume to explode.

Eventually, Chief built its own factory in Shickshinny, Pennsylvania. This was helpful in producing goods quicker, as well as in getting the samples we wanted. Instead of hiring an outside patternmaker, we now had our own team of sample makers. As volume grew, we added more salesmen.

It was time to get serious with Dolores. Since she was the practical one, when I proposed she answered, "We can't live on your $55 a week. When you get $75, come back and we'll talk." She was now a speech therapist at the Roosevelt Island Hospital, making $100 a week, but she was also thinking that if she got pregnant and stopped working, we'd have to make do on my salary alone; it wasn't enough.

I had to find ways to increase Chief's business; then I would ask for a raise. Positive things were happening, but not yet enough for me to dare to ask for a raise. So I kept thinking of ways to promote the company.

A catalogue: something no other menswear company did. Not a catalogue that customers could order from, but one that would showcase the

1951-52 Fall Catalog for Sportswear, Outerwear, and Rainwear

CHIEF APPAREL, Inc.

The first catalog for
Chief Apparel.

company, particularly its diversity, and showed that we sold not only men's outerwear, but boys wear and rainwear. How do I convince Lou and my dad to spend the money? They didn't believe in putting dollars into marketing or advertising. I got Mallinson, one of our fabric suppliers, Conmar the zipper manufacturer, and DuPont, whose water-repellant chemicals were used on our rainwear, to all contribute to the cost of the catalogue in exchange for their logos being featured. What did we have to lose? My father wanted to show what a great operation we had, so I enlisted the help of my friend Harold, who was just starting his own advertising agency. Our showroom, with its showcases set up to look like store windows, our shipping department, and our executives (Dad, Lou and I) were on the back cover. On the inside front cover, we reproduced our custom-made shipping box. I bought the mailing list from the trade newspaper *Daily News Record* and we sent the catalogues all over the country.

Dad and Lou were ecstatic; this was my first major contribution to the company.

What could I do next?

Our products had unique names, Sport Chief and Rain Chief. Our labels and sleeve tags had a profile of an Indian Chief wearing a long headdress.

The New York Yankees had a pitcher, an American Indian, Allie Reynolds, who had recently pitched a no-hitter. He was known as the "Super Chief." I called the Yankee home office. In those days, there was no such thing as a publicity department in the Yankee organization, but the guy I talked to about getting publicity in our trade newspaper knew that publicity for the Yankees would help them sell more tickets.

"Have Allie Reynolds come up to our showroom and I'll get the trade press to come for an exclusive article on Allie and the Yankees," I told him.

"Great! Pick a date and time and we'll be there, and thanks."

The trade press was the *Daily News Record*, a daily that was mailed all over the country, and Menswear was a national monthly magazine. Mostly they wrote about cloth, needles, sewing equipment, thread, dye, hangars, cartons, and buttons . . . boring. Not much on fashion, and certainly not on

*New York Yankee, Allie
Reynolds, who pitched a
"no hitter," with Lou on the left
and my father on the right.*

celebrities. The people working at those publications were young guys like me, eager for something new to write about, so I called them up.

"Want to give yourself something new and great to write about? Come up to our showroom, take a picture of Allie Reynolds of the New York Yankees, and interview him for an exclusive story. This will be a first for your paper – a new kind of feature article."

They jumped at it. The next day, the *Daily News Record* ran a front page story on Chief Apparel, with a photo of my father and Lou, together with Allie Reynolds signing a baseball while wearing our jacket.

I hadn't spent ten cents on Allie Reynolds for the article and yet we had received national exposure. All it cost was a free jacket for Allie Reynolds and one for the Yankee press representative. Now Chief Apparel was "nationally advertised." We reproduced the photos and the press articles and included them in a brochure that was mailed to all of our customers. Our salesmen were given copies to distribute.

We were a HIT! I had become a true asset to Chief.

> WE WERE A HIT! I HAD BECOME A TRUE ASSET TO CHIEF.

I had a few friends trying to get started in advertising and a few guys in show business who worked in the New York marketing departments of several Hollywood film studios, 20th Century Fox, Paramount Pictures and Universal. They were responsible for promoting films and getting as much exposure as they could. One day, one of them called me and said, "I've got this new actor; maybe you can do something to help me promote him and the movie he's starring in. It's about auto racing."

"What's his name?"

"Tony Curtis. I'd like you to meet him"

"Okay, I'm sure I can come up with something. Before we meet, send to my office all of the promotional material regarding Tony and the movie."

We set a date for two weeks later, when Tony would also be in town.

Closing the MG deal with
Tony Curtis.

I immediately called my friend Harold at the advertising agency. I asked him to do me a favor: make up a dummy ad featuring Tony Curtis in one of Chief's jackets. I was sure that Universal would allow Tony to pose in the jacket. All I had to do was mention the movie at the bottom of the ad. The movie would not be released for several months, so I had plenty of time to develop the campaign. It would be perfect in helping to increase the spring outerwear business. Since this was a movie about cars, I thought that if Chief could create a national contest with a new car as the prize, we would build our reputation and brand awareness, increase our business, and create a stir in our industry. I knew Lou and my dad wouldn't spend any money buying a car, but staging the contest was essential.

I personally loved the English convertible sports car, the MG; no American company had anything like it. The American representative of MG Motors had their office in the Empire State building. They treated me cordially when I called to make an appointment. I told Harold to make up some more dummy ads, this time showing Tony Curtis seated in an MG with the movie credits at the bottom of the ad.

The MG office was one room. The representative was an elderly British gentleman who acknowledged that MG wasn't doing satisfactory business in America and was ripe for a novel promotion.

The name of the promotion was WIN AN MG. Every store that purchases the MG jackets receives a counter card with application forms that read, I WANT TO OWN AN MG, BECAUSE . . . An independent contest-judging company would make the final drawing. Every store receives posters featuring Tony Curtis in the MG jacket, with the Headline "WIN A MG." Stores would have the jacket and poster cards in their windows, attracting the consumer, who had to come inside to find out how to win the car. The Englishman was truly excited and agreed to donate a car. Now we had to change the ad that we would present to Universal.

I was elated, but I thought that if there was something about the jacket that really defined it as an MG jacket, it would be more saleable and dramatic. I contacted Harry Ball and Sons, the company from which we purchased linings, and had them make up sample linings printed with the

Backed by Power Packed ½ page ads this April in

HUNDREDS OF VALUABLE PRIZES

and the grand prize of an MG

to the winning contestant

and an MG -- to YOU

if the winning contestant picks up his contest blank in your store*

NATIONAL CONTEST ENDS MAY 31, 1954

GRAND PRIZE

MG

TF Sports car

SECOND PRIZE

the sensational

SCOTT-ATWATER

3 h.p. outboard motor
with **POWER BAILING**

NEXT TWO PRIZES	"Wilson" Golf Equipment including Five Irons, Two Woods and Golf Bag
NEXT FOUR PRIZES	"Nufco" Caddy Master
NEXT TEN PRIZES	"Plymetl" Swim Ends
NEXT TEN PRIZES	"Plymetl Six Rng" Balls
NEXT TEN PRIZES	"Regent" Vac Racket Reversible Sets
NEXT TEN PRIZES	Wilson Match Play Tennis Racket
NEXT TEN PRIZES	Fiberglas Salt Water Fishing Rod
NEXT TEN PRIZES	One Dozen "Pro Stor" Golf Balls
NEXT TEN PRIZES	Fiberglas Fresh Water Fishing Rod
NEXT TEN PRIZES	Wilson Major League Fielder Baseball Gloves
NEXT TEN PRIZES	"Seal Professional Basketballs
NEXT 36 PRIZES	Louisville Slugger Baseball Bats

*MG CAR to be awarded to store owner or men's outerwear buyer if winning contestant picks up his contest blank in dept. store

to help you sell the contest to your customer, we have...

MG insignia. I took one of our new spring jacket samples and had the MG lining sewn into it. This was all done in less than a week. Now I was ready for my presentation to Universal.

No one at Chief knew about any of this. I thought it best to tie up all loose ends before making my pitch to them. My concern was making sure Lou and my father would be available to take photos with Tony Curtis. This meant that I would have to make my presentation to them, since I would be inviting the trade press to announce the promotion. I really wasn't sure they would agree to the cost. If I could get a major store to commit to this promotion, it would make it easier to get their okay. Chief had never been able to sell to any of the New York department stores. If I could get an order, I'd be in.

I called Macy's and asked to see the store's promotion director, not the outerwear buyer. I knew that he would be receptive. He thought it was a great idea, a plus for the entire men's department.

"How about getting us a loan of an MG that we would put right on the floor of the men's department next to the outerwear?" he asked.

If I could do that, I was assured of an order. In those days, promotions like this didn't exist. I thanked him. From there, I went straight to the MG office and sold the representative on the idea. Macy's had a way to get the car up in a freight elevator. DONE! But one more thing: I needed a *second* free car. The retailer would stamp the store's name, address, and phone number on the back of the entry form, and I thought it would be fantastic, if the winning entry came from either a mom and pop store or department store, either the owner of the store, or the buyer of the department store would also get a free MG. How could any store in America not feature this? MG agreed immediately.

It would be up to our salesman to insist on a decent sized order – one that would include other styles as well – if a store wanted to participate in the contest. Now I had to sell this to my bosses before inviting the trade press. Harold made up the dummy ads and window posters featuring Tony Curtis wearing a Sport Chief jacket and the name of the movie. The layout was outstanding. The cost, in my opinion, was do-able.

On a Hollywood set with
Tony Curtis - "Two Traveling
Salesmen"

On Monday, I told my Father and Lou that I had important information and items to show them. I knew that they thought I was going to show them more of the garments that our competitors were selling. If I told them that it was about spending money on advertising, they would turn me down. They agreed to see me any time that week. I made an appointment for Friday, thinking that they would have the weekend to think about it. I was positive that they would go for it. The trade press would eat this up – it was revolutionary. I didn't sleep for two nights. Friday came and I made my pitch.

> THE TRADE PRESS WOULD EAT THIS UP - IT WAS REVOLUTIONARY.

Not only did I get a positive reaction from both of them, but more important, congratulations and a slap on the back. They happily agreed to have the trade press come up, and of course, interview both of them. They'd loved their previous interview with the Yankees. Now I would be brave enough to ask for a raise from $75 a week to $100. This would be harder to get, but I didn't have to ask because at the end of the day, Lou called me into his office and handed me my weekly pay check . . . $100!

The following week, the trade press reporters and photographers were in our showroom, along with the English gentleman from the MG Company, and Tony Curtis and my friend from Universal Studios. Tony put on some of our jackets for the photographs. The press was thrilled – this was big news! The next day, the trade paper had us on the front page and three inside pages, with plenty of photos and interviews.

Our brand was now known to all competing salesmen and the stores they sold to. It was time to capitalize on this exposure and open new accounts with new orders. I had previously joined many of the out-of-state Men's Apparel Clubs scattered around the country, so I planned a trip to coincide with the dates of their shows. The reception for our company and our line was outstanding, and I wrote a lot of business. I knew that to maintain relationships with these new accounts, in these new areas, we should have local salesmen. Naturally, quite a few salesmen from local competing companies knew that a lot of their customers were buying from us in large quantities. Many of these fellows were eager to join us. Now we had new salesmen in new territories. For a while there, I even neutralized the competition.

In November, I was appointed Chief's Sales Manager and was finally in a position to propose to Dolores.

But first I needed an engagement ring. My mother had some time ago found a diamond ring in the street, which she gave to me. If you were ten feet away, you could see the imperfection in the diamond. I took it to a jeweler and paid $35 for a new setting. To Dolores, the ring was equal to the finest offering by Tiffany's. She quickly picked the wedding date; she couldn't wait.

Four months later, on March 30, 1952, we were married in the Savoy Plaza Hotel on Fifth Avenue, between 58th and 59th Streets. Dolores had found the suite through a girlfriend who worked for Adolph Zucker, the head of Paramount Pictures. He had just given up his custom-built duplex apartment there, and we were able to rent it for our wedding.

It had a library, a living room, a dining room on the ground floor, and up a winding staircase, several bedrooms. On entering, guests waited in the library while a maid in a French maid's uniform took and served drink orders. Our photographer was busy taking pictures. Among the forty guests were my father and his lady friend, wearing a white gown that looked almost like a wedding dress; my mother and her boyfriend, an accountant she'd met dancing at Roseland and our very closest friends from school and from Bay One.

Although it was only March, New Yorkers were sweltering in a heat wave. There was no air conditioning. After waiting an hour and a half for my father's sister to arrive from upstate New York, the ceremony finally began in the living room. All the furniture had been removed and rows of straight chairs were set up, with an aisle for walking to the *chuppa*. A trio of musicians played as Dolores came down the winding staircase in her bridal gown. My advertising friend Harold, who was also a rabbi, conducted the service. Immediately afterward, Dolores's uncle grabs me by the arm, pulls me through the sliding doors into the dining room and slaps me.

Our wedding photo, 1952.

"Why'd you do that?"

"For good luck; it's an old custom," he tells me.

I was learning about old customs and certainly needed all the luck I could get.

We all returned to the library where a butler served hors d'oeuvres and champagne until the furniture in the dining room was returned to the living room and the dining room was set up for the luncheon.

It was a great wedding.

We were officially man and wife by early evening, but our departure for our honeymoon, to a place Dolores had picked but nobody had heard of (including me) – the Virgin Islands – wasn't until 11:00 p.m. that night. I had a friend who worked on a game show at NBC, so we went over there to kill some time.

> OUR HONEYMOON, TO A PLACE DOLORES HAD PICKED BUT NOBODY HAD HEARD OF – THE VIRGIN ISLANDS.

"Anybody celebrating an anniversary?" the host asked.

I raised my hand.

"How long?"

"One hour."

The master of ceremonies called us up to the stage along with thirty sailors who were in the audience. Patriotism prevailed, because they chose the sailors as final contestants instead of us. We did, however, get enough money from the studio to take a limo to the airport, instead of a taxi. But it still wasn't anywhere near 11 p.m., so we went back to the Savoy Plaza hotel, back into the apartment, and up the stairs to the bedroom, where we became a truly married couple.

In bed, I looked up. My head was facing a mirrored closet door, slightly ajar. In the reflection, I saw the French maid standing just outside the bedroom door, clasping her hands and mouthing, "God bless you."

Dolores hadn't seen her, and I tactfully waited ten years to tell her about it.

Our honeymoon.

Finally arriving at Idlewild Field (now JFK) for the first leg of our trip to the Virgin Islands, we told the Pan American crew taking us to Puerto Rico that we were just married; they served us caviar and champagne, helping to make this a very special flight. When our plane arrived an hour late, we missed our flight to the Virgin Islands and were told that the next one would be an hour later. We waited about 45 minutes. Then a pilot came out and said it was time to leave, motioning toward a two-engine prop plane revving on the tarmac. The airport in Puerto Rico was a very casual affair with just a chain fence separating passengers from the planes, and we hadn't seen any other passengers either in the waiting area or boarding that particular plane. The gate attendant told us that the flight was full. Something was fishy, so I gathered our luggage and insisted that he allow us to board; he didn't budge.

"We're on our honeymoon; if you try to take off without us, I'm going to lie down under the wheels."

He budged. "Okay, get on." The plane was empty.

Thirty minutes later we landed in St. Thomas, B.V.I. and made our way to the brand new Virgin Isle Hotel, built on the top of a mountain with a beautiful view of the Caribbean. Although it was 9:00 a.m., we were greeted by a Cary Grant look-alike in a white dinner jacket and ascot. He introduced himself as the owner and manager. We were given a tropical rum drink while we checked in. Two barefoot bellhops put our valises on their heads and took them away to our room, two stories above the entrance. It was a spacious room with a balcony that had two chaises, but there weren't any screens on the windows. At this height, we were told, we wouldn't be bothered by flies or bugs.

We quickly unpacked and went to the pool area to relax before lunch.

Where the hell were we? Even though I had no idea, it was a beautiful spot.

After lunch, we spent some time on the pool deck, but when I started to get red, we went back to our room, relaxed, and changed for dinner.

We enjoyed a delightful meal while being entertained by a calypso band. We introduced ourselves to other honeymooners at dinner and wound up spending some time with them.

It had been a long day when we finally went to sleep. From the depths of sleep, I heard Dolores.

"Herbie, they're taking our things; they're in the room."

In the pitch black, I slid off the bed and onto the floor. I started doing the Army crawl toward the front door. This is 1952 and I'm picturing fierce natives with bones in their noses and spears in their hands slinking into the room from the open balcony. Slowly, I slid my arm up the wall until I found the light switch. Ready for anything, I switched on the light; there was no one in the room.

Dolores sat up in the bed, looked down at me, and said, "Herbert, what are you waking me up for?"

So much for the first night of our honeymoon.

Leaving behind the Virgin Islands and the tranquility of the tropics, Dolores and I returned to Puerto Rico and settled at the new Hilton Hotel. This island was active with a Latin pulse of its own: lots of restaurants, night clubs, and gambling. We became night people, sleeping late, lounging at the pool or beach, saving our energy for the evenings. It was a great, active time. Then on to Miami Beach's Sea Gull Hotel, where we got back to a routine of three meals a day, lots of rest and naps, dinner at a regular hour, and an occasional night club.

It was a great honeymoon. Dolores had really picked out all the right places.

Soon after we got back, we rented a one-bedroom apartment in Jackson Heights, Queens, a great family neighborhood with lots of newlyweds and new mothers pushing baby carriages. Within two blocks, there were shops galore, a hospital, and the subway – no need for a car. The only problem was that Dolores hated the old noisy refrigerator. The super of the building said he could get us a new one but only on the condition that we pay additional rent.

*Our honeymoon at Eden Rock
in Miami Beach, FL.*

We argued back and forth until the super said, "Take it or leave it, you can have it with a rent increase from $69.69 a month to $73.00." Dolores winked at me; I shook hands with the super and Dolores got a quiet refrigerator.

Somehow, despite working long, crazy hours I managed to have a happy home life. Dolores and I made many friends among the couples in the apartment building and my married friends from the New York offices of the Hollywood studios. When I wasn't travelling, our weekends were especially exciting – theatres, night clubs, dancing, and most important, great restaurants; we loved good food. George was the only one of our new friends with a car, and we had the best time seeing all parts of the city. Some weekends we even drove to the Catskill Mountains, staying at Laurel-In-The-Pines or Brown's or Kutcher's; Grossinger's and the Concord were still out of our league.

On weekdays, Dolores and I went to work. Dolores had her own pressure-filled days as a speech therapist at the hospital on Randall's Island. That is, until she became pregnant. It seemed that all the wives in our group got pregnant at around the same time. Socially, things slowed down. Dolores worked at the hospital until her seventh month.

She was making $100 a week. At Chief, I was taking in all of $100 a week. I couldn't believe I was going to be a father. Because I wasn't prepared for the additional responsibilities, I wondered how we would manage with only one salary. I was frightened. How could I go to my father and ask for another raise? I certainly deserved one, but I wondered why they hadn't given me one without my asking? Look at what I had accomplished for the company!

My dad, surprisingly, was truly happy for us. My out-of-town business trips continued, and Chief Apparel continued to grow as a result of my success in motivating the sales force and marketing our products. Dolores was very understanding.

The summer months were the least busy months for me, and luckily, our daughter Gail was born in July. All the designs and marketing plans at

Chief were pretty much finalized. I could spend more quality time with my new family.

Dolores decided that we needed a pet. She bought a parakeet, which she named "Beauty," and we both trained it to speak. Some of the windows on our third floor apartment faced the front entrance of our building. We developed a routine: upon returning home, just before walking through the front entrance, I would signal with a whistle. When the screened window was open, Beauty would respond, "Hello Herb, what's the word." Entering our apartment, I would hear, "My name is Beauty, I'm a good boy." He was a very special part of our family, a quick learner with an incredible vocabulary. Whenever Dolores cooked scrambled eggs or mashed potatoes, he would voice his approval by beating me to the dinner table. After all, I couldn't fly. Surprisingly, he reacted positively to our new baby daughter, Gail. Once, when Dolores and I went away for a long weekend, my mother-in-law checked on Beauty for us. Upon returning, we came through our front door and were greeted with, "My name is Beauty - Boy - a - la." It took weeks to correct him.

The Tony Curtis promotion was a major success. The existing accounts had banner sales; new customers were buying, and Chief opened hundreds of new accounts. The MG contest had been the real draw. Hey, why *not* try to win an MG? One didn't have to buy anything, just fill out the contest form. When the stores ran out of the forms they requested more; and when they called us, naturally we asked about reorders on the jackets they were selling.

The formula was there, always the same. Each season, our customers expected another star promotion. Now I began to contact other Hollywood studios and show them what I had done for Universal and Tony Curtis. "I'll promote your movie; you'll supply the male star." It was a natural. The trade publications ate it up, writing about us and printing photos of all the promotions, and of course including the jackets that were tied to them.

> EACH SEASON, OUR CUSTOMERS EXPECTED ANOTHER STAR PROMOTION.

My friend Jerry at Paramount Studios called and asked if I could help promote his new movie. "Herb," he said, "if you can do for me what you did for Universal, I'll be forever grateful. It's a really lousy movie and we don't have a decent budget to promote it. I don't know what to do with it; it's the worst." The movie was "White Christmas," starring Bing Crosby and Danny Kaye. It was scheduled to be released after Thanksgiving.

I saw a way to merchandise this around the theme of Christmas. Since manufacturers started showing the Fall line starting in June, for delivery from September through December. We could also promote the movie in June during our fall and winter selling season. I went to our lining supplier, who had done the lining with the MG logo print, and told him that this time I wanted snowflakes printed in various shapes and sizes. Based on the sales success of the MG promotion and the orders he got, he agreed. For the first time, I went to one of our outer fabric suppliers and had him make up sample yardage of printed snowflakes on a gabardine cloth. We offered four "White Christmas" jackets that season.

In June, I converted all three of our showrooms into Christmas scenes. The floors and garment displays were sprinkled with fake snowflakes. Each showroom had a trimmed Christmas tree with Christmas music playing softly. When the elevator doors opened, buyers were greeted with the sound of "Jingle Bells." The receptionist wore a red flannel hat trimmed with holly and berries. We put the buyers in a holiday mood from June right up to December. As usual, the trade press just ate it up and again printed our story with lots of photos.

> WE'LL GIVE YOU TWO WEEKS TO PROVE YOU'RE RIGHT.

My dad and Lou thought I was out of my mind. They said, "We'll give you two weeks to prove you're right."

The buyers were all smiles as they sat down to see the line. They couldn't afford not to buy, lest their competitors buy it. The garments were shipped. Sales were great at the stores. White Christmas ended up being one of the most successful and profitable movies of all time (but not because of us, I must admit).

*Our "White Christmas"
promotion with Danny Kaye
and Bing Crosby.*

*Display in Chief's
showroom and Herb's guest
appearance on TV for the
"White Christmas" promotion.*

ROCK HUDSON chooses *Sport Chief* as his star jacket

ROCK HUDSON
co-starring in
Universal-International's
ALL THAT HEAVEN ALLOWS
Print by Technicolor

ADVERTISED IN
LOOK

Be as fashion smart as the stars, pick this 100% WOOL TALSUEDE band bottom jacket. It features a contrasting color gridiron motif knit trim with multi-purpose lining. Zipper by CONMAR. **$16.95**

*Showroom at Chief, "Rock
Hudson" promotion,
discussing details
with a buyer.*

As new promotional opportunities opened for us, I expanded our sales force. We now had representatives coast-to-coast. The new salespeople were proud of the company they represented and were the envy of their competitors. They also earned more money than most.

Over the following years, other promotions were developed that featured movies starring Rock Hudson, Jeff Chandler, and many others. It was easy. The more we did, the more was expected of us. Not only did we have to develop a strong and contemporary jacket line, we had to have famous celebrities endorsing and promoting the brand SPORT CHIEF.

By now our second daughter, Michelle, had been born. Since we only had a one-bedroom apartment, we needed to move. Many of our friends were moving to Long Island, but we imagined that a house would be too expensive for us. I learned that as an Army veteran I was entitled to a government mortgage at an extremely low interest rate. My uncle Leo, who was a real estate agent in Queens, knew of builders on Long Island who were building new small communities out there. On a Saturday, I borrowed my father-in-law's car and we drove to Long Island. We were impressed with a development in East Meadow. After having lived in a cramped apartment, the model houses in that development looked like mansions to us. Because I really wanted my dad to see it first, I told the realtor I would come back the next day with my father. He promised to hold it.

My dad wasn't too thrilled about our owning a house – with all of the problems that he imagined a new home would bring – but after he spoke to his brother Leo, he agreed to see it. The next day, he picked us up and drove us to East Meadow. There was a different agent this time. I told him that I had been there the day before, and that they were holding the lot I had selected.

"Sorry," he said, "but I wasn't given the message. Unfortunately, that lot was sold early this morning, and it was the last one for sale."

I was disappointed and my dad was annoyed with me because we had wasted a trip. As we were about to leave the sales office, the phone rang.

"You're in luck. That was a cancellation, and it's on the largest lot in the development. Why don't you go see it?" Even my father thought it was an exceptional opportunity. The cost of the model was $10,500, and the G.I. mortgage made it affordable. The agent wanted a ten-dollar binder to hold the property, which my dad gave him.

The down payment at closing would be $1,500; I only had $800.00 in the bank. I waited until we got into the car and asked my dad to lend me the $700 balance. After several moments of silence, he said, "If you can't afford the down payment, then you shouldn't own a house." On Monday morning, I called Leo and asked him for a loan. He loaned me the money but insisted that I never tell my father. My father never asked where I got the $700.

I was finally a HOMEOWNER! It would take at least five months for the house to be completed. Now the anxiety starts. How do we furnish it? What colors, inside and out? Trees, plants, flowers, furniture – everything a new house needed; where was I going to get the money? We had some furniture from the apartment and a few knickknacks, but we didn't even have a car. I always borrowed my father's or my father-in-law's car; I couldn't afford to buy one. To visit my mother or father on weekends, we would have to take the subway, carrying the babies, their diapers, food, a change of clothes, and baby formula.

Surprisingly, it was my dad who paid for my first car, a brand new green Plymouth. I could never figure him out. I think that my mother, after hearing our stories, yelled and shamed him into that car.

Moving into a new community was a bit frightening. All the houses were about the same price, so we and our new neighbors were all in the same boat – newlyweds and new parents. It was like building a new family. Little by little, some fell out of favor while others joined in strong friendships. Wives became friendly with wives, and even the husbands found friendships developing. We formed car pools and bowling teams, had card game nights, and helped each other with whatever problems we might have with our homes. Slowly but surely, we were all becoming typical suburbanites. As a family, we didn't feel the need to go to "the city." It reminded me of my early years in Brooklyn, when we also had no need or desire to leave our self-contained neighborhood and go to New York City.

Our home was about a 20-minute ride to either Rockaway Beach or Lido Beach. They weren't crowded like Bay 1 in Brighton Beach or Coney Island, and the sand was cleaner and whiter. We schlepped towels, beach toys, beach chairs, food, and a change of clothes; each family had so much to carry that it was impossible to car pool. Then a phenomenon that was new to this area arrived: private beach clubs. They were built right on the beach with lockers, cabanas, adult pools, and kiddie pools. For those who didn't bring lunch, there were snack bars. Entertainment on Friday and Saturday evenings was at the club house, which had a great bar and its own bartender, a large dining room and dance floor, dinner, music, and dancing. On Saturday nights, there was professional entertainment. Friday nights were strictly formal attire. It gave us a feeling of being "upper class." No need to spend money on summer vacations; we simply joined the beach club and shared a cabana with another family.

We were participants in the changing fabric of American life. Suburbs were forming everywhere, with new houses, new communities, new schools, and entirely new towns. These new suburbs were small towns in themselves, consisting of a Main Street and a few side streets for shopping, restaurants, beauty parlors, and other privately-owned shops catering to the needs of families. There might be an A&P or a Bohacks supermarket, but there were no department stores.

These changes created new business opportunities. As middle class Americans across the country spent more leisure time participating in hometown sports and enjoying casual weekends, they needed new kinds of clothing. There were bowling alleys, roller skating rinks, and indoor ice skating rinks, and people played baseball, football, and basketball in schoolyards and park playgrounds. Families took weekend trips to zoos, country farms, carnivals, or outdoor concerts. All of these activities required the more "active" jackets that would become the new fashions worn by mom, pop, and the children. Our objective was to convince storeowners that Sport Chief was the favorite brand of this ever-growing consumer population.

As Chief Apparel grew, so did our competition. Each year, more and more companies came into the business, selling their products on the merits of their styling and price. Invariably, price was the most important factor. Chief couldn't compete with the low- priced firms, but our competitors couldn't compete with our successful promotion and marketing skills. We stayed. They came and went.

> MY CONSTANT DILEMMA WAS, WHAT DO WE DO NEXT?

My constant dilemma was, what do we do next?

Chapter Six

IN THOSE DAYS, EVERYONE IN BUSINESS – from the executive to the salesperson – wore a suit, shirt, and tie along with a hat. Ninety percent of the clothing in New York was bought in small stores like Phil Kronfeld, Eagle Clothing, Leighton's, and Witty Brothers, and small chain stores like Wallach's and Broadstreet's. The first four sold the higher-priced suits. Each store had a section for dress shirts and ties. It was usually a concession – somebody rented the space and paid rent or a percentage of sales. When you went into a store to buy a suit, you also bought shirts and ties. The suits could be altered and tailored to fit, in-house. The consumer had a lot of confidence shopping in those stores.

One day, as I was buying a suit for myself, I looked around the store and realized that no outerwear was being offered for sale in the store. I became friendly with the manager and eventually asked him why he didn't carry outerwear.

"We're a clothing operation," he said, looking down his nose at me. "We don't carry sportswear."

"What if you had outerwear designed especially for your customers?"

"Sounds interesting; if you come up with something like that, come see me."

I went away thinking about a highly styled line with a new label: a line made of exceptional fabrics, not sold by Chief's regular salesmen, and available only in men's tailored clothing stores and upscale department stores known for better tailored clothes. This might be a solution to the "competing-on-price problem" that Chief was beginning to encounter.

At that time, Chief's largest and most important customer was Robert Hall. Even though we didn't sew Sports Chief labels into the styles we sold to them, the styles were exactly the same as those we sold to other customers. Robert Hall was selling them at lower prices. We needed to enhance the image of Chief Apparel with a brag piece – a new "image" label – to give our company more credibility.

Because of the way American life was changing, fewer and fewer suits were being sold in clothing stores. Casual wear, which the market was demanding, was nowhere to be found in traditional clothing stores. I started thinking about a fall line of a few styles featuring advanced styling and fabrics. I designed four waist-length zipper jackets whose styling and fabric were not customarily associated with outerwear. The first had a body of patterned wool with wool-ribbed knit sleeves and collar. The second was the same style jacket but with a leather body. The third had an imported genuine Persian leather suede body with glen plaid wool sleeves and collar. The last design was a jacket of silk and wool tweed that reversed to become a solid color silk shantung.

My advertising friend Harold first proposed that we name this new line THE AMERICAN MALE. That wasn't good enough for Harold, though; he then suggested that we add a "year" to the label, the coming year (not '56, but '57). We could call this first foray, THE AMERICAN MALE '57, and for each new season rename it a year ahead.

> WE COULD CALL THIS FIRST FORAY, THE AMERICAN MALE '57

Before I presented my concept to Lou and my dad, I had to have patterns and samples made. Having purchased the fabric yardage, I first went to our sample department, but everybody said they were too busy. The styles were

especial
sport wear
for

the american male '57

FASHION A

Self jacquard patterned wool front and
back. Wool shaker knit sleeves and collar.
Entire garment including sleeves completely Bemberg rayon lined. White, Tan.
36-46. $14.50

American Male '57 brochure.

very labor intensive and it would take too long. Even though I was the boss's son, they told me to get lost, so I had to go to an outside sample maker. The samples were great. Harold hired a model and had them photographed. He designed a dummy ad appropriate for a men's fashion magazine like *Esquire.*

Now I was ready. Knowing it would be limited production, I was afraid that Lou would throw me out of the office. He didn't, but both he and my father asked, "What do we need it for?" I did the whole pitch – why we needed this new label and where we should confine our selling. AMERICAN MALE would give the company the prestige it deserved. I laid it on thick. Although impressed, they still insisted that selling this line was not to interfere with our regular business. I agreed to test my concept by personally taking the samples to stores in New York City to see what would happen.

I had the confidence but didn't know the problems yet to come. With my great samples in hand, I hit the street. Much to my surprise, I immediately got orders. Usually, to get a size scale, the stores would take a minimum of a dozen pieces. While each store ordered small quantities, I nevertheless sold between two and three hundred pieces of each style. That provided enough for a "test" – for us and for the stores. They took their chances and so did I.

When I told Lou and my father about my reception, they warned me that I might have a problem getting the pieces made because my designs were very detailed.

I went to our factory in Schickshinny, Pennsylvania, planning to have 500 pieces of each style made. I offered more money than they were use to. The floor manager immediately shot me down. These pieces were, she said, slow production numbers; they would take a lot of hand stitching and it would be very labor intensive. The factory workers, mostly women who lived in the local community, didn't want to do this kind of work because, "We like to talk to each other while we're working, and these styles need too much attention to details." At the end of the day, it was presented to the factory workers and they threatened to strike if they were forced to make my garments.

I called Lou and he recommended that I find an outside contractor. I had boxed myself into a corner, knowing nothing about contractors or where to find them. I needed help. I was also the Sales Manager of Chief's sales force and needed to devote productive time to that, in addition to overseeing advertising and marketing. I had a full plate. Maybe this time I had bitten off more than I could chew. I left the factory depressed and went to the local hotel where I always stayed, in Allentown, Pennsylvania. I had dinner alone, as usual.

I tried thinking about anything but my current dilemma. Nearby, also eating dinner alone, was a guy I'd seen every time I'd stayed in that hotel. I went over and introduced myself. Andrew, it turned out, sold exclusive outerwear styles to stores like J. Press and Brooks Brothers, very upscale type stores, and at prices higher than what we were thinking of for AMERICAN MALE. I said I was from Chief Apparel and we started talking about business.

"Where do you make the garments?" I asked.

He didn't have a factory. "I deal with the Mennonites," he said.

"What's that?"

"They're a local religious group; they make money by manufacturing candles and by sewing. My problem is that I can't give them enough work."

"I've only seen their quilts," I said.

"What are you doing tomorrow?" he asked.

"I'm going back to New York," I answered glumly.

Andrew persuaded me to stay another day. He drove me to a building that was essentially a long room that looked like a meeting hall. Women were sitting near the windows, sewing on machines with old-fashioned foot pedals. No electric motors. No production line. Each worker made an entire garment from start to finish.

I took Andrew aside and told him about AMERICAN MALE and the problem I was having getting the jackets made. He told me that because he couldn't give the Mennonites enough work he was afraid someone would come along and poach his labor force. I offered to solve both his problem and mine by sharing the production capacity. He agreed; the few machines allotted to me would be sufficient for the amount that I had sold. I negotiated the price with the Mennonites and gave them the production order. I now had plenty of time to deliver for the fall season.

To quick-start the new American Male collection, as usual, I called the *Daily News Record*. Again, a tremendous article appeared. I convinced Lou and my father to let me take a full-page advertisement for AMERICAN MALE '57 in the huge Olympic preview Issue of *Sports Illustrated* magazine. (The Olympics were held in Melbourne, Australia that year.) The ad emphasized that the new line was an integral part of Chief Apparel's new prestige branding and that I was breaking new ground by advertising directly to consumers instead of simply showing goods to retailers.

> I WAS BREAKING NEW GROUND BY ADVERTISING DIRECTLY TO CONSUMERS INSTEAD OF SIMPLY SHOWING GOODS TO RETAILERS.

The test was successful. The stores sold out their original orders and placed reorders. Now I began thinking about the next season. How could I continue the line on a volume basis? AMERICAN MALE styles were flying out of the stores and I was running out of Mennonites. My next line would be much broader and more balanced. I could continue to use the Mennonites for the styles that required hand detailing, but I could also simplify production and create designs that emphasized fabrics and styling and that could be made in our factory.

One day, the receptionist called my office and said that there was a gentleman there who spoke in a heavy accent and had four garments over his arm. He wanted to see the man in charge. Thinking he must be a customer from the East Side, possibly returning some damaged jackets, I went out to see him; he wasn't a customer. He represented a fabric mill in Germany, and the jackets he was carrying were actually samples made of the fabrics that the mill produced – brushed velveteen-like cotton, and cotton ribbed velvet corduroy; I'd never seen fabrics like those in the United States. The garments had leather buttons and button holes, silk stitching . . . and some of the styles had leather piping – amazing workmanship.

*American Male '57 ad ran in
"Sports Illustrated"
December 1956.*

I asked, "What is the minimum I must buy?"

"One hundred yards."

He was trying to sell fabric, but I was interested in purchasing complete garments. The mill, he told me, had a small sample department, making samples just to show how their fabrics could be used in garments. Their objective was selling yard goods to potential outerwear manufacturers, not making or selling garments themselves.

"How many people do you have in your sample department? I asked. They had 20 people and I only had 15 Mennonites.

I told him that I was only interested in purchasing a ready-made garment – like the four styles he had shown me. "Please call your factory," I said, "and find out if they would consider making small production amounts of each style. If they are interested, ask what the price would be."

He returned the next day, all excited. The price was so low that I applied for an emergency passport that day. Three days later we were on a flight to Germany.

I met with the owner, who told me that his was the largest mill in Germany producing fabric from raw cotton balls all the way through to a finished product. Actually, his business was selling to upholstery and drape manufacturers. Upholstered velvet-like couches and chairs, as well as drapes, were then in fashion, but he considered apparel another outlet to consider. I convinced him to start his own small sales force and sell those same four styles to men's retailers in Europe. That way he could control his own destiny and have the exclusivity of producing styles in fabric that only his plant made.

"Start small; make only a thousand of a style. I'll take 500 pieces and all you have to sell is the other 500. Whatever you don't sell, I'll take," I told him. I would help design the next collection so he didn't need to hire a designer. He agreed and quickly added more sewing machines and hired salesmen.

The cost of European labor in the late 1950s was significantly lower than it was in the United States. While shopping for fashion ideas in the European

the American Male *is an especial grouping of domestic and imported sport outerwear that has been created for a specific market and anticipate its ENTIRE need.*

st. louis

norfolk

portland

venezia

imported from italy

cortina

gorizia

temple

stores, I noticed the influence of leather trimming in button holes, as piping on the edge of a collar and as leather elbow patches. These touches would have been costly to make in America but were no problem for the Germans to price competitively. I brought back samples and asked our production manager to price the styles in our Pennsylvania factory. He said that it could not come close to the price I got in Germany and the designs were too detailed to sew in volume. Too labor intensive again!

Originally, the concept was innovative styling that enabled us to sell to the better men's stores. After the first season, I wanted to balance out the line with some traditional styles. I added basic contemporary styles – a jacket with an all wool raglan sleeve and a shawl collar, another made of black and white leather square, similar to a pattern I'd seen in a sweater. Our Pennsylvania factory was able to produce these.

To promote AMERICAN MALE '58, I got in touch with Anita Colby, the executive assistant to the president of Paramount Pictures and former editor of *Harper's Bazaar* – the Anna Wintour of her day. I persuaded her to sponsor our launch. Ms. Colby sent out invitations on her elegant personal stationery to the trade press and the prestigious New York stores. On June 19, 1957, we had a private reception and fashion show at the Waldorf Astoria Hotel. We hired models and were off to the races. Everything about the show was a class act. As I stepped to the podium to introduce the first fashion line of Especial Sportswear (Especial was another of Harold's inventions), I thought about how I'd always believed that selling was show business. I would tell my salesmen, "You're the director. Those garments are the actors. Your showroom is your set, and the buyers are the audience."

There in the Waldorf, I felt, "This is Broadway!"

In my opening address, I told an audience of local accounts, buying offices, and the national press that AMERICAN MALE, the country's first high-fashion line of outerwear and sportswear, was best described as the "ten percent line." The ten percent line was purchased by consumers who are fashion conscious, adhere to the sporting casual way of life, and have the dollars to spend; those consumers make up ten percent of the male population of the United States.

I quoted a study by *Fortune* magazine that detailed how, "The American market of 168 million people is not one homogenous market. Rather, it is made up of clusters of families, bound together by friendship, location, business, or social interests, who influence each other's purchases profoundly. Whereas the average family was timid about being the first to try a new idea, such as wearing Bermuda shorts, buying a color television set, putting colored tires on its car, or sporting a new Corvette. In every cluster there is always one family that responds first to innovations – 'The Ten Percenter!'"

I continued, "That one family, the first-to-act family, the self-starters – that is our target. They are the ones who installed separate phones for their teenagers, did their kitchen over in pastel appliances, discovered new vacation spots, served new drinks, bought hi-fidelity and color televisions, and drove a second or even a third car. They would do our selling by word-of-mouth."

"These people," I concluded, "are not only your best customers, they're your best salesmen. The designing and merchandising of the AMERICAN MALE '58 line is designed for the Ten Percenter."

How did I know all that? I knew it not only from studies in Fortune magazine, but from what was happening in my own life.

Our mortgage with the government on the new home, had been approved at the end of 1954, and from then until March 1955 we were always there on weekends, making sure that the house would be ready. We were so proud – look how many rooms we have, how large our back yard is. With the grass, trees, and shrubbery, it seemed like a small park. The first thing I thought about was buying swings for my little daughters, who were only 18-months-old and five-months-old. Dolores said it was probably a little early for swings.

Since all of the homes had been completed at about the same time, we all moved into our new neighborhood together. Friendships were quickly established, especially with our immediate neighbors. One way or another we helped one another. When spring arrived, we all took advantage of our back yards. Grilling, especially on the weekends, was common. The smell of the various aromas from the grills filled the air. After dinner, some of us would stay outdoors. Because our rear property bordered three homes on our left side, three at the rear, and one on the right, we could all see what the others were doing. The hedges were not large enough to actually separate our back yards, and over-the-hedge conversations eventually led to friendships.

Socially, not much was happening; we needed a get-together. Since our section of homes was in a cul-de-sac, we had a block party at the end of the street with everyone chipping in six dollars a home; it was a great evening. Then, since getting a sitter to watch our kids on a Saturday night was a big problem – there weren't enough older kids in our neighborhood – I said to Dolores, "Let's have a Saturday night party in our back yard."

My idea was to ask my friend Jerry at the Paramount Films office in New York if I could borrow one of their films so that we could have an outdoor movie party in our back yard. (Drive-in-movies were very popular at the time.) I'd also ask him to find us a projector and a guy to operate it.

Dolores said I was crazy. "Why go to all this trouble?"

"Why not? It won't cost a lot, and we could really make an impression on our friends and maybe motivate them to come up with other entertainment ideas."

If we did it, she wanted to have a long table set up with packaged candies and popcorn, just as they have in the theatres. We sent out invitations on Paramount stationery and rented the candy table, folding chairs, and a popcorn machine. Then we prayed that it wouldn't rain. It was standing room only. The film was *The Man in a White Suit*, starring Alec Guinness. We were a hit, and so was the film. We had set a precedent, and our friends continued with lots of fun outdoor parties.

How would we top that one? We would have a year to prepare.

The presentation of THE AMERICAN MALE '58 at the Waldorf was a success. The publicity in all the trade publications was specific, complimentary, and featured photos of the models wearing the AMERICAN MALE jackets. Harold and I had found a photographer named Maurey Hammond who created beautiful, original images in a style that didn't exist in fashion advertising. Using an intense black background, he created the impression that the models were floating in space. My father and Lou were thrilled. We sold to small clothing stores all over the country. By displaying the new line, the stores themselves became, in effect, my magazine and newspaper ads. Another feather (or is it headdress) in the cap of Chief Apparel.

Initially, the new line had not been sold by Chief Apparel's salesmen, only by me. Starting with the second collection, however, the sales were made by a separate sales force that also represented high-price fashion tie and shirt companies. They were selling to the same customers that Chief wanted to break into with its line. Eventually, the better department stores woke up and realized they needed more casual sportswear and outwear, not only tailored clothing. Because we already had our foot in the door, they came to us. The neighborhood mom and pop tailored clothing stores also began adding sweaters, shoes, and casual slacks.

The styles were an immediate seller and literally blew out of the stores. They were also a hit in Germany. The Germans increased the number of sewing machines. AMERICAN MALE had found their needed production facility. We were on a roll and I could do no wrong.

We moved our main office and showrooms to Fifth Avenue and 33rd Street, across the street from the Empire State Building. The industry's newest sportswear companies occupied space in our building or across the street. We had three Sports Chief showrooms that were open to the general trade, and a private showroom for THE AMERICAN MALE line. It had two glass doors and a heavy brass chain locking the brass handles on the door. When a customer came to see the line, the lock could only be opened by a special key that hung on a brass chain around the salesperson's neck. The whole thing looked like it was out of King Arthur's Court – all hype to set an atmosphere of exclusivity.

Not only was I busy being creative at Chief, I had the same urge to do the unusual at home. As summer approached, I saw an advertisement in the *New York Times*: "Have a Clambake in Your Own Back Yard." They shipped, overnight by air, lobsters, clams, and mussels from Maine, packed in dry ice in a wooden barrel; they were guaranteed not to melt on arrival. "Dolores, I've got the next great party idea."

She thought I was crazy. "What are you trying to prove? Where and how can they be cooked? I'll tell you one thing, there's no way they'll be cooked in my kitchen."

She was right. We didn't have the right sized pots. Our stove couldn't handle it. But restaurant supply houses had huge restaurant-sized seafood pots. They suggested that I get heavy canvas from a ship's sail maker, spread a square section on my lawn, and sprinkle lots of grilling charcoal on it – at least three inches high. I should get several cinder blocks and put the pots on them, making sure that the burning charcoal was right under the pots.

I ordered forty lobsters, steamer clams, and corn on the cob – enough to feed forty people. Just as the ad promised, barrels of lobsters and steamers arrived on Wednesday, fresh and packed in ice. The clambake was scheduled for Saturday. Even though the barrels were sealed, I couldn't take a chance on the ice melting. The restaurant supply house had delivered the pots, tables, and chairs; I had already received the cinder blocks, canvas, and plenty of charcoal briquettes. Now, Dolores insisted that the lobsters and clams had to be cooked by the next evening, or they would spoil.

I came home from work a few hours early and opened the barrels in the back yard; they still had plenty of ice. I set up the canvas, charcoal, and cinder blocks and then filled the pots with water. I lit the charcoal. When the water boiled, I emptied the barrels into the boiling water, separating the clams from the lobsters. As they were cooking I suddenly panicked.

Where do I put the lobsters and clams to cool off and store till Saturday?

Dolores never stopped laughing. "You better get to the store before they close and get plenty of ice. After they are cooked you'll have to put them back in the barrels."

I got plenty of ice.

Another problem: if I put the hot lobsters and clams in the barrels and cover them with ice, the ice wouldn't last the night and everything would spoil.

Problem solved: When all was ready, I lined up the lobsters in rows on my front driveway and spread out the clams to cool. The scene was like a bad monster movie, "Attack of the Killer Lobsters."

A half hour later the police were at my door.

"Sir, what do you think you're doing? The neighbors are complaining about an odor coming from your home. And why in hell are all those steaming things lined up on your driveway?"

I explained politely about the clambake on Saturday and my dilemma of having the lobsters and clams spoiled.

"Officer, in another half hour it all will be cool enough for me to repack."

"Okay, I'll give you thirty minutes to get all of this stowed away." It cost me one lobster, but he never did come back.

The next two days, I loaded the barrels with fresh ice. On Saturday night, I again filled the pots with water and lit the charcoal, so that all would be hot for dinner. Our friends couldn't get over it. One problem though: the cop had cost me one lobster, so I made myself a sandwich.

What else could we do? Eventually, the outdoor parties inspired our neighbors and friends to form a Mystery Group. (More on that later.)

Starting in November 1957, the men's apparel shows took me on a two-week trip every year, showing Sport Chief's spring line – first in New York, then in Chicago, and next in Dallas. It was evening during that first year, after the selling hours at the Chicago show in the Palmer House hotel. I was fixing up the showroom, making sure the garments were presentable for the next morning, when I got a tearful phone call from Dolores.

"I have bad news. Your father passed away."

"He had an attack in his office and was taken to the hospital, where he died."

I wrote a note for the Sport Chief Illinois salesman, telling him to ship the displays and advertising materials, blow ups, etc., back to New York at the end of the show. I automatically made sure that all the company business was taken care of before I left; then I packed and left for the airport. By now it was after midnight and the last plane to New York had left hours before. The next one out was at eight in the morning, so I stayed in the terminal.

> HAVING THE WHOLE NIGHT GAVE ME TIME TO THINK ABOUT HIM.

Having the whole night gave me time to think about him . . . about what he meant to me, what he meant to the business.

What am I to do? How could anyone replace my father? He was the image of the company.

My father was only 54 years old, with a new wife. A dozen doctors had told him that he needed surgery, but he was deathly afraid of surgery. Outwardly he appeared to be a healthy man, in good physical shape but a heavy smoker (Chesterfields). His lunch usually came from Gertner's Restaurant. A chef with a rolling cart came to our showrooms each day, lunch was "open house" to all buyers. His lunch that day had been a tongue sandwich, literally fat on rye. He'd already had one small heart attack, and he had lots of gall stones. When his buddies would come in from out of town, he'd say, "You wanna see my x-rays?" He had finally found a 13th doctor who told him it was okay not to have surgery. "Wait until you have an attack," that doctor said, "then you'll have the operation."

Shifting on that hard uncomfortable airport bench, I recalled how my dad would berate me about money. "Why are you always worried about money? Why are you always asking for a raise?"

"Well," I'd stammer, "I know I'm contributing to the company . . ."

No one had ever told me what my job was. All along, as the country and the industry changed, I was seeing opportunities for Chief Apparel to do something creative, like the various promotions I had set up with Hollywood studios and sports stars. First, I had become the sales manager; then, I took on the duties of advertising and promotion director. Now I'd started a new line, AMERICAN MALE. Although nobody had hung the title of designer around my neck, I was a designer.

I'd already understood that fashion was in the eye of the beholder. I'd learned to shop fabric mills and think about how changing a fabric changes a style. I knew that you could find fashion innovation anywhere – even in the closure on a ladies pocketbook – and that I had to ask myself, "is it feasible to make it at a price point that will be acceptable to retail stores?" You didn't want to frighten the stores with prices way out of line. I used my eyes and my imagination – reading foreign fashion magazines, imagining how the simple act of taking a pocket from one garment and a collar from another might make it look more interesting.

"Look," my father would say in those often repeated conversations, "we're not holding you back. As you grow into the company, you should remember that one day this will be your business. If I'm gone, you'll replace me."

> YOU SHOULD REMEMBER THAT ONE DAY THIS WILL BE YOUR BUSINESS.

*My father Irv getting ready
to be crowned "Sport Chief"
in Madison Square Garden
during a rodeo.*

Chapter Seven

LOU, MY FATHER'S PARTNER, was only in his 40s, with very young children. I thought my father always felt guilty that as their company was just getting started, his own son was getting a salary, taking money out of the business. He wanted Lou to be the one to determine whether I was an asset to the firm, so he pushed me onto him. For decisions concerning the company, he would say, "Go to Lou." That night in Chicago, waiting for the plane back to New York, seemed as though it would never end. Finally, at 8:00 a.m., I was on my way home.

I returned home from Chicago, grieving. Dad's funeral was held in New York's Riverside Chapel, it was filled to capacity, with a loudspeaker set up outside for the overflow: a well-deserved tribute to a leader of his industry. After sitting *Shiva,* I went to the office, unsure of my situation. Lou explained that he and dad had a buy-sell partnership agreement, funded by insurance on each of their lives. When one partner dies, all of the company stock goes to the survivor, paid for by the insurance proceeds. So I had no ownership interest in the company whatsoever; I was still just an employee. My father's brother Ben was the executor of the will; Ben said that he would talk to my brother and me as soon as he could put two and two together.

> I HAD NO OWNERSHIP INTEREST IN THE COMPANY WHATSOEVER.

Lou said that I could go ahead with AMERICAN MALE as long as it didn't conflict with anything I had to do for Chief. At this point, the salesmen had Chief's spring line and the shows were being covered, so I could devote some time to AMERICAN MALE, which was good for me. The public loved the clothes and our customers' inventories sold out rapidly. The fact that we couldn't take reorders helped us to obtain larger orders for the next season. As usual, styles that sold well at retail were repeated in the next season's line, sometimes only with new colors added to show change. The stores in Germany also had great success. The positive reaction brought increased demand for the mill's fabrics from industries other than apparel.

AMERICAN MALE was now a major outerwear source to the better men's stores, with almost no competition. Our sales were terrific. We started knocking off our own products, creating styles for Sport Chief based on discontinued AMERICAN MALE styles. For AMERICAN MALE, we started a sweater line made in Pennsylvania, as well as a cross-over vest in suede. In outerwear, we developed an assortment of new products: a walking coat of imported cotton poplin with contrasting silk thread, a reversible town coat, and a jacket made of a cashmere blend fabric with fleece lining – all to be made by the Mennonites.

THE PRESS CONSTANTLY WROTE ABOUT THE AMERICAN MALE.

The press constantly wrote about THE AMERICAN MALE. All of the men's fashion magazines featured our styles. As a result, Chief Apparel was still the talk of the industry.

Sadly, my father had not lived to see this new success. He had agreed on the concept but didn't get to see how well it sold. Nor did he see me become a designer – the creator of a new line – with all of the prestige that flowed from that. I was still trying to prove myself to him, but I was disappointed again because he was no longer there to recognize my achievements.

The industry was growing so fast that the Men's Apparel Club's hotel shows weren't sufficient to keep up with it, so a new organization was formed, the National Association of Men's Sportswear Buyers (NAMSB). It

The American Male
best-selling style.

organized trade shows twice a year where menswear manufacturers could show their fall and spring lines. In New York, it was initially held at the trade show building on Eighth Avenue, and later at the NY Coliseum on Columbus Circle. In Los Angeles, another organization was formed to cover the West Coast: MAGIC – The Men's Apparel Group In California. Now the men's industry had two major exhibitions each season. The spaces were huge, booth's with plenty of room for displays, providing a pleasant working atmosphere while working the lines with customers.

Constantly trying to think up ways to entice new customers to our booth, I took inspiration from an article about a young golfer in his 20s who seemed phenomenal. One of his friends was acting as his manager, and for $300 I hired the young golfer to promote our line for the first two days of the show. In addition to our racks of garments, we set up a putting green 30 feet long by four feet wide, covered with synthetic grass, on a platform two feet above the ground with a hole at the end. A sign at the door proclaimed, "Beat the Pro and Win a Prize." Every other company just had racks full of clothes, though some also displayed trimmed mannequins. I was looking to attract customers and at the same time garner free publicity in the trade papers.

Lines of buyers quickly formed in the hallway, waiting to get in and putt. When Lou came in he turned pale, which was not like him. He had never been involved in the sales side of the business; his part was to maintain the company's relationship with the bank and with two clients, Robert Hall and Montgomery Ward. Since my father was gone, it was important that Lou make an appearance at our booth on opening day; after all, he was now the boss. This was a first for him.

He said, "Why are you taking up all this space? You could have a lot more racks showing our lines. Take down that golf setup and bring in more product!" I explained about marketing and how using a celebrity was a method of attracting new customers. Since most of our line was heavy fall stuff, we could expand into something lighter, appropriate for golf, especially for our southern stores.

I introduced Lou to the young golfer, who had just signed an agreement with a company that made men's slacks. I told Lou that we could bind this young up-and-comer for a full three years, for only $1500, and use his name on the label along with Sport Chief's. We could make a golf jacket that he could promote by wearing it at televised golf tournaments. I'd given a lot of thought to putting an embroidered emblem on the chest, and I came with up with the idea of a golf umbrella. Lou, unfortunately, did not understand the concept of brand identification and thought the whole thing would take too much time and energy. My confidence was shaken; this was the first marketing decision I'd made that had been rejected. But my instincts were on target – that kid subsequently became one of the greatest golf legends of all time, and that umbrella logo is still associated with him.

Remember the Mystery Club? Our social lives in the suburbs had expanded as much as my life in the industry had. Dolores and I, together with a few of our neighbors, came up with the idea of

> OUR SOCIAL LIVES IN THE SUBURBS HAD EXPANDED.

a "Mystery Club," where one couple would organize an event for the first Saturday night of the month. Each couple contributed $20 and the hosts supplied a full evening's entertainment, including transportation and dinner, all for $10 a head. We were told only where to meet on the assigned night, not what would happen. Six couples joined.

For the first event, the hosts had us drive to a strip mall in Glen Cove, Long Island. It was evening and all the stores were closed except an art and sculpture studio. Inside, the artist (a man in his mid-fifties, with a goatee) had us sit at tall tables, facing him. He described the process by which he made sculptures, starting with molding the clay by hand. Then, giving us each an apron and pointing to the bowls of clay and glasses of water on our tables, he urged us to begin by softening the clay. We squeezed, pounded, pinched, and sprayed. When the clay was soft enough to mold, we sculpted. The women made dishes, necklaces, or bracelets. The men? You guessed it: they all sculpted penises.

Dolores and I enjoying our
new social life.

We were hysterical, but of course the artist was annoyed. This was the first time he had agreed to meet with a group that wasn't taking his class, and he expected us to be as serious as he was about the class. Our hosts apologized and begged us to restrain ourselves, saying, "Cool it, you're all acting like a gang of teenagers."

Next, the sculptor surprised us with a female model. Disrobing, she sat demurely on the center chair. The room suddenly became quiet. We were instructed to each sculpt a specific part of her body. The truth is, if we had put all of our individual pieces together, they would have formed the ugliest women imaginable. After the hour was up, platters of food were brought in for dinner.

We drew lots to determine who went next.

One time we met in a beauty salon. Each man was assigned a woman, not his wife, for whom he had to create a hair style that was completely different from the one she wore. With much reluctance, the women agreed. The men washed, dried, shaped, and sprayed. In most cases, we had to re-do, but the women were good sports. The friend to whom I was assigned had always worn her hair combed straight back. I styled her with a part and a bouffant. She and her husband liked it so much she never wore it combed back again. Dinner was chow mein in a local Chinese restaurant.

Then it was our turn. I had read that the Metropolitan Opera needed male extras for their next production, a month away. I went backstage and found out that they could use us and that we would be paid $10 apiece. I also read that Mama Leone's Italian restaurant was introducing strolling singers during the dinner hour. At the restaurant, I told the publicity manager that our six men would be appearing at the Met for that scheduled night's performance. We could stroll in the restaurant with our makeup on and sing a bit of O *Sole Mio*, along with their musicians. One stipulation though: I only had $20 per couple to spend. I needed the $10 that the Met was giving us to buy balcony tickets for our wives." Could we get a bowl of spaghetti and a simple dessert, including tip, for that amount? She said that it would be no problem. The publicity would be worth it.

LIFE Magazine had a regular feature called LIFE GOES TO A…! It was the last feature in each issue. Someone in their advertising department did me a favor and arranged for the editor of that segment to interview me about our mystery. She thought it was a great idea. I was all set.

My friends and I arrived at the original Metropolitan Opera House on Broadway for our roles as lance carriers two hours before curtain, for costumes and makeup. We were instructed on how to march across the stage, take our positions at the back of the stage, and hold the lances still and vertical (the bottom of the staff must rest on the floor). The music started. We dutifully marched to our positions, standing at attention. During the second aria, one of our guys started rocking his lance back and forth to the rhythm of the music; he had really gotten into the beat. The stage manager was livid. Under the music, we could hear him pleading from the stage wing, "Stop!" When the male lead finished singing, we turned to our right and marched off, out of step. Luckily, we got paid despite our improvisation.

We got into our regular clothes, kept the makeup on, met the girls, and started toward the restaurant. It was only five blocks away, but Broadway was closed. Cops, mounted police, and crowds of people as far as the eye could see, were behind wooden barriers. We couldn't get through. A police lieutenant explained that the astronauts were riding down from upper Broadway. When I told him that we had just performed at the opera and were now going to perform for opening night at Mama Leone's, he ordered an officer to escort us as we paraded down the middle of the street to the cheers of onlookers not realizing who we were.

At the packed restaurant, I instructed my friends that they were to sing *O Sole Mio*. The publicity manager with whom I had originally made the arrangements wasn't in, but the maître d' escorted our group to a table. Stroll we did. Sing, if you could call it that, we did – in our loud if not operatic voices. We managed to have the entire restaurant sing along.

A waiter handed out menus and then asked, "What would you like to drink?" I panicked. Dolores kicked me under the table and whispered, "You'd better straighten this out."

I appealed to one of the managers, reminding him that we were only supposed to be paying $10 a person which included the tip and that all we expected was spaghetti, desert, and coffee. "No problem, sir, I know all about the arrangement. Thank you for that tremendous entrance. There is a lot of very enthusiastic press here, so order anything from our menu and drink to your hearts' content because we are picking up your check; *grazie mile* from the management. Naturally, including the tip, I left our planned $60 and we all got home at one the next morning. Unfortunately, *LIFE* Magazine discontinued the LIFE GOES TO A...! section, that week.

THE AMERICAN MALE was selling all over the country and taking up too much of my time. I decided to hire a separate sales force. Because I wanted to maintain exclusivity around that label, Chief salesmen would not be allowed to show the line; they weren't happy about that. Next, I hired an assistant to help me with production and coordinating.

In 1959, we decided to drop the year from the AMERICAN MALE name. Now it was just AMERICAN MALE. The third collection included a lot of repeats (our classics) and variations on what had been successful before. Unlike other manufacturers, we were using imported fabrics: a golf sweater in Alpaca wool, imported from Austria; jackets in wide wale corduroy fabric imported from West Germany and the finest leather and suede. We continued to be fashion-forward: side vents in a jacket, which most outerwear didn't have, and front pockets that could be closed by a zipper – equally innovative.

Chief Apparel also brought to the market one of my proudest innovations. I happened upon it one day while I was staying at an inn near the factory in

> CHIEF APPAREL ALSO BROUGHT TO THE MARKET ONE OF MY PROUDEST INNOVATIONS.

Germany. The housecleaner came in and asked if I would mind her cleaning the parlor while I was still in the room. As she went to roll up the throw rug, I heard a ripping sound. Wondering what had made that sound; I went to the rug, bent down, lifted an edge, and heard the same ripping noise.

Something was glued to the floor as well as to the corresponding corner area of the carpet; they looked like Band-Aids.

So I asked, "What is this?" She held the rug in place and showed me that the corners of the rug had the same kind of tape. She was amused that I had never seen this before.

"Look at the way the drapes in your room are tied back," she said. The same kind of tape was holding the edge of the drapery ties to the wall.

I immediately thought that using the tape instead of a zipper would be great in children's jackets because kids always had trouble with zippers. Their jackets were almost always open. Using this tape, all they had to do was overlap and press. Mothers would love it.

Where could I get this magic tape? The maid and the innkeeper knew that the product came on rolls and was purchased in their local hardware store. I asked for a short strip and showed it to the factory manager in Germany. He laughed and said that they recommend it to their furniture clients for holding down pillows on couches and chairs, but that they had no other practical applications.

> MY MIND WAS GOING A MILE A MINUTE WITH NEW CONCEPTS FOR THIS REVOLUTIONARY PRODUCT.

"Where can I buy this and what do they call it? Who is the distributor? What does it cost?" My mind was going a mile a minute with new concepts for this revolutionary product.

All he knew was that it was called "Velcro." Because I was leaving for New York the next day, he said that he would try to find where the company was located. In the meantime, I was able to get about two feet of this tape from the innkeeper.

As soon as I got to my office, I looked in the Manhattan telephone book for the company. Nothing was listed for Velcro. I guessed that they didn't operate in the U.S. and that I'd have to wait for Germany to fill me in. In the meantime, I'd use the tape I brought with me. I went to the sample department and had one of our production people remove the zipper from an old sample and replace it with this tape. She had no idea what she was sewing. She thought that instead of leather it was some kind of cloth trimming.

I put it in a bag and took the jacket home to show to Dolores. I put it on and demonstrated how it worked by simply touching the two sides together, creating a tight fit, and pulling them apart to open. She started laughing, thinking that I had finally flipped out. When I told her to blindfold me and showed her that it worked easily by touch, she tried it and was impressed.

I had to show it to Lou, but not until I found out where I could purchase it, what the minimum quantities were, what colors they came in, and what the costs were.

My desk was loaded with messages from fabric mills whose new lines were available to be seen. In my dealings with them, I'd insist on an exclusive first look, before our competition. Many of the mills had showrooms in the Empire State Building across the street from our offices; I made my appointments. In the lobby, I realized that I'd forgotten the floor and the room that my first appointment was in. I looked at the directory on the wall, under companies affiliated with the fabric industry. As I jotted down the information for all my appointments, I looked up a mill whose name started with a "W."

My eye caught a glimpse of a name under the letter "V." There it was: *Velcro International.*

I couldn't believe it. All this time, they were right across the street. Not even listed in the phone book. Why had they never called on our firm? After all, we were so well known. And why haven't any of our competitors, used it? I went to a phone in the lobby, called my secretary, and told her to cancel my first appointment, not even knowing if the Velcro Company could see me.

I went into the elevator, excited. The office door was like the one the MG Company had, frosted glass, with only a room number painted on it. I knocked and entered. The office was very small. Seated behind a small table was their sole representative. I told him that I had seen Velcro in Germany but wasn't able to find out where to buy large quantities. I made a point to stress the word "large."

"Mr. Goldsmith, does your firm make carpets or drapes, or is it perhaps furniture?"

He had never heard of Sport Chief or AMERICAN MALE. He and the company were Swiss and after almost a year in America, they'd had little success selling large quantities of their product. Most American homes had wall-to-wall carpeting and not many had area rugs or light curtain fabrics suitable for draping.

"My office is just across the street. I'll return in 15 minutes with a sample of how we want to use your Velcro and I'll show you some of our advertising and marketing successes."

"No problem, I'll be here."

I couldn't believe what was happening. My first thought was that I had to get him to agree to an exclusive agreement. I brought back the sample with the Velcro closure, even having him put it on and close and open it several times. He smiled. I showed him how the MG Jacket and White Christmas products were promoted and advertised by us. I had copies of the advertising that our retailers did on their own. He admitted that the Velcro Company had never thought of using their product on apparel.

I pointed out that on a jacket, a large amount of Velcro would be used. "Since we have to manufacture a minimum of a thousand pieces of a style, our purchases could end up being very substantial. With our national distribution, Velcro would quickly become known throughout America. It would cost the Velcro Company a lot of money and time to get that much exposure."

I had him. I asked him to agree to an exclusive in the apparel industry for at least a year. He said he would have to contact his boss in Switzerland. By the following day, he had confirmed everything I needed.

I immediately called Harold at the ad agency and told him what was happening. He designed the string tag to hang on the sleeve. Now we had to come up with an advertising and marketing campaign appropriate for this new concept. Up until now, no one in our company knew what I was doing with Velcro. I had the sample jacket locked in my office closet. When Harold and I finished creating the Velcro promotional material, we presented it all to Lou. He surprised me.

"Herb, this is really fantastic. Even if we don't sell a lot, the exposure that we'll get from the press will be worth the cost."

Lou was becoming my star pupil. In a few weeks, when I was ready to show the styles and marketing concept to the Velcro representative, I brought Lou along. I needed their commitment to pay some of our advertising cost; after all, we only had a one-year exclusive. This would open an entire new market for Velcro. Lou convinced them to give us the exclusive, as well as to contribute money to our advertising campaign. My star pupil!

For the fall line of 1958, Sport Chief made men's and children's lines of jackets with Velcro closings. Our salesmen were thrilled. This would be a door opener for them, allowing them to sell to more of the major stores in their territories. Again the trade press featured our story with photos and our sketches. We had no problem selling to major department stores and top independent stores. We offered them a marketing kit with a basket of promotional items and advertising materials: sketches of the jackets on models, as well as a reproduction of our hang tag that pictured a flat hand, palm down, with vertical printing that stated:

"THE JACKET THAT CLOSES BY TOUCH."

Sport Chief's Velcro jackets were an immediate success. The men's stores ran ads with headlines like:

BIGGEST NEWS SINCE THE ZIPPER JACKET;
THE REVOLUTIONARY NEW CLOSURE FOR JACKETS;
BEST NEWS SINCE THE ZIPPER;
THE AMAZING TOUCHDOWN JACKET.

From the Steve Allen Show,
Louis Nye.

They sold out.

While this was happening, I had to come up with a spring line of Velcro jackets and a national advertising campaign. Velcro closures made sense for winter jackets, but would they work in lightweight jackets? I had more success thinking up a promotion.

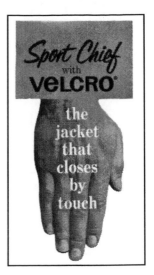

The Steve Allen Show was one of the most popular TV programs on the air. Each show had a segment called *The Man In The Street*, where Steve would interview three guys, asking the same questions. One of the guys, Louis Nye, would always respond with, *"Hi-Ho Steve-a-reno; your playboy, Gordon Hathaway here."*

We decided that he would be a great spokesman in our ads. He agreed to be photographed with a beautiful, partially nude model for an ad that we hoped to create for *Playboy* magazine and *Sport* magazine. In addition to our zipper and Velcro line of Sport Chief Spring jackets, we added three jackets for the "playboy" types: one for golf, another for tennis, and one for boating. We brought with us to Chicago several layouts that we were planning to photograph, along with a photo of the model, for our meeting with Hugh Hefner. I had to suffer getting my knuckles rapped. Our ad made liberal use of the nearly-naked girl, the kind of photo the magazine was famous for. Hefner nixed it. "Nude beautiful women are my business," he said. "Don't mix in *my* business; put her in a *bikini*, and I'll run your ad." So be it.

The fall and winter Velcro jackets had very good sales, so the stores were eager to purchase our spring Velcro line. Unfortunately, the spring retail sales were not as good. The *Playboy* ads in March, April, and May and the inside cover ad in *Sport Magazine* did help sell the non-Velcro line. Stores ran their own ads:

Sport Chief's
Indian
and
Playboy's
Rabbit
are getting together this spring

in a fashion promotion featuring
VELCRO CLOSURE JACKETS

Sport Chief

TENNIS JACKET FOR PLAYBOYS *featuring the* VELCRO
CLOSURE THAT CLOSES THE JACKET BY TOUCH

And, another ad:

WANNA BE A SPORT CHIEF PLAYBOY?

At home, as our social, family, and vacation obligations expanded, we found it harder to have a Mystery Club every month. One of the most memorable ones Dolores and I organized before the idea petered out came to me when I saw an ad in the *Journal American* for a bartender school on 49th Street and Broadway. I went to see the owner and explained my limited budget: $10 a head. He said that his classes didn't start until 8:00 p.m. (most of his students came after working full-time jobs elsewhere), so if we could get there by six, he could give us an hour-long class for $60 on how to mix about 20 different drinks. For teaching purposes, he normally used water instead of alcohol in the mixes, but I convinced him to let me provide a bottle of vodka instead.

What could I find for the rest of the evening? From my acting days, I remembered a small theater in Greenwich Village, owned by a drama coach who asked only for a small voluntary donation after the show. If I gave a dollar a head, I'd have $48 left to spend for food. I went down to the theater and reserved 12 seats. Nearby, I smelled the terrific and pleasing aroma of sautéing peppers and onions. Sure enough, there was an Italian pizzeria and take out store, with a guy busy at work on a flat steel grill that faced the street. Above the window was an exhaust fan; no wonder I caught the smell. Inside were two small tables and, mid-afternoon, just a few customers. I explained the idea to the owner, but not wanting to take a chance on ordering "heroes" for everybody – since some might not like it – I asked if he could make spaghetti with tomato sauce for $4 apiece, including coffee. We would be out of the theater by 9:00 p.m. He agreed and asked for a $25 deposit, which I gave him.

A week later, I told our group where to meet. The temperature was at least 85 degrees and very humid. The bartender school didn't have air conditioning. We were shown how to make various cocktails, and the owner pretended to be using water instead of alcohol. We all had to taste the various drink concoctions. Between the heat and the sipping, a lot of people were getting tipsy. When it was time to go, some of my neighbors needed help navigating the stairs.

I'd been worrying about how we would get down to Greenwich Village and stay within our budget, but on the corner was a bus stop with an empty bus. The driver said he was at the end of his run and was headed back to his terminal. Meanwhile, my friends were starting to board. I told him about our club and that we were headed for the Village.

"Get on, no charge," he told us.

He put a NO PASSENGERS sign in the front window, and off we went, laughing and singing. He dropped us off a block from the theatre. I pleaded with my friends to control themselves. They took their seats in what was really a loft, with folding chairs. It was a two character play. When the lights came up, a young guy and girl were in bed, nude. She kept moaning, crying, and kissing the actor while we sat there with our mouths open. They were no further than ten feet from us. After about two minutes, one of our guys, half-potted, walks to the bed, sits, strokes the girl's head, and slurs, "You want me to get rid of this jerk?"

We pulled him off the so-called stage.

His wife grabbed him by the arm and sat him down in the lobby. He came back later, quiet as a mouse. After an hour, we strolled to the pizza joint. It was not quite nine when we arrived. No aroma of onions and peppers, and a CLOSED sign on the door.

Looking inside, the two tables were empty and there was no one in sight, only a dim light at the rear of the store. What am I going to do? He has my $25 deposit.

"How could you even think of eating here, let alone give him a deposit?" "Listen, Dolores, he looked and sounded like an honorable man. It doesn't make sense that he would screw me out of the $25."

Our friends were getting loud and impatient. I tried the door; it opened. The owner, hearing us enter, came from somewhere in the back, smiling, and greeted me: "We're ready for you and your friends. Follow me." He locked the front door. We walked past the sales counters and those two tables. At the back of the shop he opened a door.

I couldn't believe it. A table was set for 16 with silverware, china, and cut glassware, a vase of tea roses in the center. His wife and two teenage children told us that they had come from Italy exactly a year before, and since they had no other family in New York, we would be their guests for a four-course dinner to help celebrate. Hot and cold antipasto; two different pastas; two main courses, chicken and veal – both with different combinations of peppers, onions, eggplant, and cheese – all in two kinds of tomato sauces. Chianti, Spumonte, and a bevy of delicious desserts with our coffee rounded out a perfect meal.

It was midnight when we said our goodbyes. The owner not only declined to take the balance of the money owed him, he returned the deposit. We had enough money to take cabs uptown to the garage where we had parked at the start of the evening. We agreed to chip in and send the very gracious family a gift from Tiffany & Co.

That was the last Mystery Club evening that was assigned to us. After two years, we all decided that it was enough.

Macy's ad on the Velcro jacket.

Chapter Eight

THE ANNUAL MAGIC TRADE SHOW for the fashion industry, held every January on the west coast, had started in Palm Springs, California but by now had moved to the Los Angeles Convention Center. Later, the show would move to Las Vegas, where it became known as *The Big Show*. In Los Angeles, the show got so big that it spilled over into the park land around the hotels. The booths had to be set up in tents.

As usual, I'd gone out to Los Angeles five days earlier to get our booths set up. I'd paid for my window treatment guy to come out and build display sections like the ones you would see in department store windows. Having dramatic booths was becoming an integral part of doing business, giving retailers a sense of pride: "Look at this great company I'm buying from!" We also needed to attract stores that were not currently buying from us. The whole thing was about hype. With THE AMERICAN MALE and Sport Chief, movie stars and sports stars, we knew we were going to write orders, but perhaps we could also attract new customers.

The show started Saturday and ended seven days later. As sales manager of the company, I had to be in attendance at all times. On the seventh day, Sunday, we were dismantling our displays. I'm dead, knocked out. I really needed a break, so I called Lou and told him I wasn't coming back on

Monday – that I had asked Dolores to come out to California and would be returning to the office by the end of next week.

"No," Lou said, "you're coming home tomorrow."

I said I was exhausted after having worked two full weekends, ten hours a day!

"That's part of your job," Lou said.

I told him that Dolores was already flying out and that we were going to Palm Springs for a few days. I needed to relax, to catch my breath.

"You're no better than everyone else," he snapped.

"Listen, Lou, I need to do this."

"Well, you had better think about this; if you decide to stay in California, I'll have to make arrangements to replace you.

After all I'd done for the company, I couldn't believe Lou was treating me this way. It almost seemed that he had become my father, not the guy who always praised me and had confidence in my abilities. I stayed in California.

When Dolores arrived, we rented a car and drove to Palm Springs. I told her what Lou was threatening to do. Dolores urged me to do what I felt I needed and wanted to do. We had a great time, relaxing and talking about our future. Together, we reached a decision.

At the end of the week, I walked into Lou's office and resigned. I gave him 11-months' notice and offered to help him find someone to replace me.

I'll never forget what Lou said: "You can't leave. I have an investment in you, and I'm still waiting for it to pay off."

That was the final nail in the coffin.

It was the end of January, 1960 – a new decade and a new beginning for me. In addition to the responsibilities I still faced at Chief, it was my future that presented the greatest dilemma.

IT WAS MY FUTURE THAT PRESENTED THE GREATEST DILEMMA.

In the eleven months I had remaining at Chief Apparel, I tried to figure out what to do next. How would I support my family? One of the first things I did was visit our competition, one firm in New York and a very strong company in Philadelphia. I knew that people thought I'd inherited a fortune from my father (which I hadn't), so I was confident that I would be seen as someone with serious assets to bring to the table. Also, although the word *marketing* didn't yet exist, I'd become an expert at marketing men's apparel. During my interviews with each company, I said I was not only interested in a job, but also an opportunity to earn a percentage of the company. Sitting at those meetings, I had the uncomfortable feeling that they were just trying to get information out of me. They hemmed and hawed . . . there was no way I could have a piece of their business.

This tactic wasn't going to work; the money I had wouldn't last long, so I looked elsewhere. My friend Bernie was the publisher of the men's trade magazine *Esquire Apparel Arts*, where I had advertised for years and made publishing news by having a number of 22-page inserts in several of its issues.

"You're the kind of innovative guy I'd like to have on my team," he said.

Bernie was leaving to start his own national consumer men's magazine. Although men's fashion had evolved considerably, the existing national fashion magazines were still almost entirely devoted to ladies wear. *Esquire* had only a few pages dealing with men's fashion. Bernie wanted to fill that gap. He showed me a layout that I thought was pretty exciting. He was thinking of calling the magazine *GQ, Gentlemen's Quarterly*.

"But I don't know anything about the magazine business," I told him.

"It'll be easy," he said. "You'll be the editor in chief and I'll be the publisher."

I wasn't convinced. Then my friend Harold said, "Why don't you join up with me?" His advertising agency created ads for publication in newspapers and magazines, but mostly they did catalogues, the kind salespeople left with retailers. It was called a "leave piece." But that didn't seem to fit either.

Perhaps, I thought, I should go back to the theatre. Television was growing by leaps and bounds, and I'd never been the least bit intimidated about performing. My ace in the hole was that I could always stay at Chief; I knew that one person alone couldn't possibly do the three different jobs I was doing there.

In June, I got a call from the general merchandise manager at Ohrbach's department store. He'd been told that I was unhappy at Chief. He said, "I've got something you should consider. Skiing is becoming very popular and we're starting to buy apparel items designed for skiers." To me, talking about skiing was like talking about astronauts. But I listened. "We're buying wool ski pants, heavy sweaters, loden-style coats and hats – mostly from a company called "Europe Craft," which imports them from Europe. They sell primarily to stores in ski areas in the Northeast. Do you know them?" I didn't.

"Well," he continued, "the company's owner, a man in his eighties, just died and his widow doesn't want to continue running the business. It's up for sale. Are you interested?"

Maybe this could prove interesting. I went to meet the widow, Mrs. Feigenheimer, a woman in her late 70s, at the York Hotel on Seventh Avenue, where she had her showroom and office. I saw numerous items for men and women, including sweaters, pants, and toggle- and loden-style coats. It was a seasonal business. I sensed opportunity here, especially in the coats – which were made in Germany, where I'd already done business.

Conducting some research, I discovered she was financed by a factoring company that I was familiar with through my father. I went to see the president and asked if he could tell me about Europe Craft's financial condition. He sent me to their back room, where John, who was sitting at a desk and wearing an old green visor, reached for a tray full of vertical cards – sales records for each of Europe Craft's accounts. He left me alone to review the data; within a few hours, I was able to see how much each account purchased and how they paid their bills. I knew exactly how much business they were doing. Their volume for the previous year was around six hundred thousand dollars, a tremendous amount to me.

I met with Mrs. Feigenheimer again. Her husband, I learned, had been very generous. In Germany, right after the war, he loaned money to local factories, many of which still felt obligated to him. They allowed him to pick and peck through their production in order to select the precise garments he needed. Over the years, Europe Craft had accumulated over 100 suppliers. Would those obligations cease now that Mr. Feigenheimer was gone?

I took a week's vacation from Chief and during that time Mrs. Feigenheimer accompanied me to Germany. Our objective was to visit her suppliers and see if they were interested in working with me. I also considered hiring the German buying agent for Ohrbach's, whose office was in Frankfurt. Fritz turned out to be not only credible, but also helpful with translations. Of all the places we visited, only one factory in Germany and one in Belgium were perfect fits; their prices were right, the mentality of the owners was perfect, their merchandise was versatile, and both operated on a handshake, requiring no letters of credit, just trust. There was great potential here.

When I was doing AMERICAN MALE business in Germany, I traveled around Europe looking at garments in stores, where I quickly learned that quality was of the utmost importance. Any garment with damage was sold in the little factory stores, not in department and retail stores. I called the owner of the factory in Germany with whom I was doing business and told him that I was leaving Chief. Would he agree to back me if I decided to go into business? He offered his full support. As a matter of fact, he was surprised that I hadn't gone into business earlier.

I was more and more certain that buying Europe Craft would be a good opportunity for me, different from what I'd done before. My head was into more than just *selling*. I wanted to create a line and then merchandise it properly; but how could I do everything by myself: run the business, develop a line, travel back and forth to Europe . . . I couldn't – I needed a partner. And the widow needed an answer by the week after Labor Day.

I had become friendly with a man who worked in another office in the Chief Apparel building. He ran the New York office for a boys' outerwear company in the Midwest, selling their finely manufactured jackets exclusively to top department stores. He was always complaining about his job. He and I talked for days.

Mrs. Feigenheimer wanted $15,000 for the company. For that amount, I only wanted the name – no inventory, no showroom – and I'd keep the two people she had working for her: a secretary-bookkeeper who spoke German, and a showroom salesman.

My friend couldn't come up with that kind of money, but he knew somebody who could. He introduced me to Sol. Sol was 5 feet 3 inches tall, weighed two hundred pounds, and smoked cigars. He offered to put up half of the money, in exchange for a 60% share of the business. In addition, he wanted interest on the $9,000, plus a salary and $200 a week in cash. He'd be an investor, not someone who worked in the business. When I heard his offer, I almost threw up; I wanted nothing to do with that kind of arrangement.

By then, it was three weeks before Labor Day. The widow said that she had another interested buyer and needed a decision after the holiday weekend, so I went back to her office. I was speaking with the salesman and the bookkeeper when Sol walked into the office! *He* was the other interested buyer! Sol didn't say a word.

I called my old friend Ed Wachtel, whom I'd first met in Texas when I traveled to the seasonal MAC shows for Chief Apparel. Ed was a buyer for Weiner Stores, a chain of low-end specialty stores in both the Midwest and the Southwest. I had never been able to convince Ed to buy my Chief line, even at closeout prices. At one trade show in Houston, I recall, a bunch of salesmen, buyers and I went to out to dinner at a private club. Texas strictly prohibited the sale of alcohol in public restaurants but private clubs were the exception. I had a few too many, and I asked Ed to call it a night and go back to his apartment, where I was staying. Hardly able to get undressed, I fell asleep immediately. At around four o'clock in the morning, I heard loud music and yelled, "Turn off the damn radio, Ed!" The music never stopped. Barely able to open my eyes, I tried to find that damn radio and shut it off.

The next thing I knew, Ed was soaking my forehead with a cold towel. Three other guys stood over my bed, laughing. "Hey Herb, the party's just beginning." At the foot of the bed was a live mariachi band. The laugh was on me. After my pleading, they all left – no more private clubs for me.

So here I was in New York, thinking about Ed, who had been brought up in Panama and spoke perfect Spanish. He had left Texas for an important position with the Campus Sweater and Sportswear firm and was now living in New York.

"I have a problem," I confided to him on the phone.

After we'd talked about Europe Craft for a while, Ed asked me, "Do you believe this is a home run?"

> Do you believe this is a home run?

I did. But I didn't know what to do about it.

"Okay," Ed said. "You and I are going to buy this company. Put up the money and I'll pay you back my half." A telephone handshake and we were in business.

Standing next to Dolores's side of the bed at six o'clock the following morning, I called Dr. Shulten, my contact in Germany, and told him I was leaving Chief to buy my own company. I had found two factories that I wanted to do business with in addition to his. We agreed, without any paperwork, to continue working together. He would give me full credit. I wouldn't have to pay for shipments until 120 days after receipt of delivery (stores typically made payment within 90 days of receipt of delivery).

"Dolores," I said, "how do you feel about all of this? We have two little girls and a future together that is so uncertain. Should I take a chance?"

"Honey, you believe in it; you have confidence. I know you'll be successful. If it doesn't work out, you'll always be able to get a job – maybe as a waiter. And even then, you'll be the *best* waiter."

Ed and I drew up the papers. By the end of December, Chief found a sales manager to replace me and decided that THE AMERICAN MALE line was no longer of interest. I had no regrets about leaving Chief. In January, Ed Wachtel and I announced our partnership in the trade press. I wanted Ed to be the company's president in order to create the impression that, coming from Texas, he must be a millionaire, even wealthier than people believed I was.

I hired Fritz as our agent in Germany and instructed him to look around for resources for our new company. Europe Craft's limited business had been a cushion for its owners, but for how long? That was not what I wanted; I had bigger ideas. The quality of European-made goods was extraordinary. At a time when people in Europe needed work, sewing was a big part of the post-war economy; it was one of the biggest industries. I was confident that I could continue to produce a line of unique and fashionable items at competitive prices not achievable in America.

The Goldsmiths and Wachtels had a celebration dinner at The Forum of the Twelve Caesars restaurant.

We moved our company out of the York Hotel, which was in the heart of the ladies garment business, and into a building on 23rd Street. In February, Ed and I took our first trip to Europe together. We'd done a minimal fall collection using new versions of styles made at our original German factory, plus some of the Europe Craft styles. In Belgium we went to the Salik factory, whose specialty was brushed cotton suede jackets with intricate linings. I didn't have time to do detailed sketches of new styles; I needed help. They introduced me to Teo, a Dutchman who made wonderful sketches of men's jackets. Teo and I came up with 20 sketches of new styles to be made into samples.

Ed turned out to be brilliant with figures. He calculated just how much we could afford to pay the factories, taking into consideration the duty, freight, clearing costs, and internal packing costs. His negotiating style was pure charm: would they be so kind as to lower the price? I wouldn't have had his patience.

During our first few years, Ed and I made many trips together because we couldn't afford a designer or a quality control manager. We shopped the stores for fashion trends and innovation. At the factories, we made final decisions as to measurements, styling, fabrics, colors, everything necessary before starting production. Most of our time was spent in Frankfort and Munich, where we had our most reliable factories. On one trip to Munich in January, we learned of a festival called *Fasching*, which consisted of dances, banquets, parades, and costumes every night for almost three months. It seemed like Mardi Gras in New Orleans.

American movies were the rage there, with German dialogue dubbed in. It was a little disconcerting to watch Jimmy Cagney and Edward G. Robinson speaking German. What did they wear in the movies? Just what all American executives wore – a suit and tie, a wool winter overcoat, and a hat, usually in black. Since that was how Ed and I were dressed, during *Fasching*, some revelers in the street thought we were locals in costume, dressed like Chicago gangsters. We were pushed into many parties and came in second in one of the costume contests.

We knew what to expect when we got there a year later, again without costumes. This time we were very innovative. We turned our suit jackets inside out so that, instead of seeing a solid flannel suit, they saw fancy linings as our outer material. It was the year that American clothing companies began to use linings with not only solid colors, but also fancy prints, colorful stripes and plaids, and even small polka dots. We were a hit again, and we loved Munich and its people.

While Ed mainly oversaw our sales relationships with retailers, most of the details relating to style and quality were my responsibilities. We alternated taking trips to Europe and kept a book with written notes regarding what needed follow-up and what needed finalizing.

Like a sprinter grabbing the baton in a relay race, whichever partner went to Europe took the book with him. Fritz was fantastic in locating quality oriented factories that met our price and production demands. He constantly visited the factories to make sure that what had been agreed to was actually done.

It was 1961, the first year that I started Europe Craft Imports, I had to do a personal favor. My very close friend Al had a brother Bob who was attending medical school in Amsterdam, Holland. He asked if I wouldn't mind bringing Bob some of the foods he loved from N.Y. I gladly brought salami, bagels, rye bread, Milky Way's and a bottle of Fox-U-Bet chocolate syrup.

When I arrived, I called and told Bob that I would take him to diner. This was the first time that I was in Amsterdam, so I asked him to pick a top restaurant. We met at the restaurant and I told him that I had all the "Goodies" at the Hotel, and after dinner I would give them to him.

It was one of the top of the line restaurants in Amsterdam, right on one of the canals. The food was exceptional. Bob looked like he hadn't eaten for weeks, so very thin. As we were having our coffee, the waiter asked me if everything was satisfactory and would I like to have a "Little Fucking" after dinner.

I looked at Bob and he smiled and he said, "of course." This was the custom at the conclusion of dinner in a fine establishment. The waiter left and a few minutes later he returned with a tray containing two cordial glasses and a bottle of "FOCKINK," the most popular brand of liqueur in Holland. It took about five minutes for both of us to stop laughing

I knew Bob liked to smoke cigars as much as I did especially after dinner. Before we lit up, Bob asked if I wanted to have a "FART." As a matter of fact I did. "Bob, here in the restaurant while smoking?"

"Of course not, we have to go outside." That seemed like a good idea. We lit up the cigars and Bob said, "The "FART" area is about two blocks from here. We walked a few minutes, and there on the canal was a river boat. The sign above it said "FAHT," English translation, "RIDE."

Twice he got me. We smoked and laughed all the way to my hotel. It was the best time I ever had in Amsterdam, Holland.

Some of our factories were located in small villages in the German mountains. One day in the fall of 1962, Fritz and I left Munich very early in the morning in Fritz's Mercedes. He had hired a driver to take us to the factory, which gave us the opportunity to go over the notes in the book. After an hour on the Autobahn, we exited to a two-lane country road and

FOCKINK

started to climb higher into the mountains. On both sides of the road were farm lands, no villages yet.

A ten-wheeler truck passed us, going slowly in the opposite direction. Fritz was asleep on the left side of the rear seat and I was making notes to his right. As the truck passed, we started to skid. It was not raining; the road was dry, with a covering of leaves.

The car spun into a ditch, flipped over on one side, then flipped again onto the other side. It landed upright, ten yards from the road. We were all shaken up. The driver and I got out of the car. Fritz, having awakened from his nap, remained inside. We walked completely around the car looking for damage: nothing, not even a dent. Fortunately, it was the time of the year when the farmers fertilized their fields, which had softened the ground.

When we got back into the Mercedes, Fritz said, "What's that horrible smell?" The driver and I looked at our shoes. We had manure all over them.

"You're dirtying up my car!"

"Fritz, we're lucky to be alive; count your blessings."

Our wheels were spinning and we couldn't move. Meanwhile, the driver of the truck had backed up and driven onto the field. He went down into that damp muddy ground, got his chain, hooked us up and pulled us out. Back on the road, the driver and I put our shoes into the trunk, and at the first village purchased new ones.

At home in Uniondale, I owned a Cadillac. In inclement weather, on turns, it occasionally skidded a bit. After that experience with the Mercedes, I decided to buy a Mercedes – after all, I had two small children to be concerned about. I have owned many Mercedes, and to this day not one has ever skidded.

Our first year in business, we did almost a million dollars. Not bad, but we needed more manufacturing capacity and more diversification of factories in order to create new styles in the fabrics that I wanted to use.

In the village of Gronenbach in the Bavarian Alps, Fritz found the factory: *Marte*. It was a two-hour car ride from Munich to this village. The town was straight out of *The Sound of Music*. I expected people to come out in their lederhosen and small felt hats and start to yodel. Everything in the town – clothing stores, grocery stores, furniture – was owned by the Marte family. I stayed in their ten-bedroom inn, which had a restaurant and bar on the main floor. When I checked in, I was given a bucket of coal to use in the potbelly stove in the middle of my room. It was cold, and the communal bathroom was at the end of the hall.

The Munich factory was becoming automated; as a consequence, its capacity increased and the minimum I needed to buy from them was increasing. Moreover, the number of styles they were able to make under these new circumstances was quite small and they would only make garments in wool. So Marte answered my needs very well. It was a small factory. We had sent sketches in advance and samples had been made and priced. The basic style we were developing was a wool Melton coat – a below-the-knee coat with wooden peg toggle closures and a detachable hood. Our model was inspired by the British Navy, which outfitted its crew in a garment called the Convoy Coat. Some of the variations we came up with included different linings, like a Tattersall plaid or quilted lining, to the waist only. We also designed shorter jackets with zipper closures.

Back in New York, I got a call from the Merchandise Manager of Wallach's men's store, which was roughly equivalent to today's Brooks Brothers or Paul Stuart. I had called on him when he was a buyer, but he never bought a thing from Chief Apparel or AMERICAN MALE because he felt they weren't right for his store. I wouldn't call him a close personal friend, but we were a friendly industry and he wanted to help us out. He was going to buy the Convoy Coat.

He proposed that Wallach's would create an ad to run in *The New York Times* featuring our Convoy Coat by Europe Craft, with a sketch of a battleship in the background and Wallach's as the place to buy it. Then, I should reproduce the ad in a mailing piece showing the Wallach's name. He said, "Once the stores see that Wallach's is selling it, you can bet that they'll be calling you for orders." He was right; it was a boon to us, and what a marketing lesson it was for me.

We didn't have a sales force. Out-of-town stores did business with us at trade shows, as well as on occasional client visits to New York, and through buying offices in the city. Our Convoy Coats were selling across the country and we opened many new prestige accounts thanks to the Wallach's mailing piece.

With an eye toward fashioning styles that couldn't be made in the U.S. (where both materials and labor were more expensive), we created a four-button above-the-knee car coat that had patch pockets, leather elbow patches, and shoulder patches. Pretty soon, Marte couldn't handle all of the orders because their plant was too small. Also, Siemen's Electronics had opened a plant down the road, siphoning off some of Marte's workers by paying higher salaries and even sending an air conditioned bus to pick them up in town and take them to their air conditioned plant. Marte was now sub-contracting our production to a newer source of available labor: Yugoslavia.

After a while, I said, "This doesn't make sense. Why don't we go to Yugoslavia directly?"

The people at Marte agreed. Electronics manufacturing was exploding all over their area and they didn't think that they could service us, since their labor pool was constantly being diminished. Even going to Yugoslavia was a burden for them – it was too far, too long, and required too much time. We continued utilizing Marte's expert manufacturing and attention to detail on our smaller-volume fashion items.

Munich became our major headquarters. The Germans were very loyal, plus I loved the food at the inn in Gronenbach. It was like eating at your grandparents' house; there was hardly ever a menu. It was all delicious home cooking, including a cheesecake that reminded me of Junior's in Brooklyn, only better. Fritz, our agent in Munich, would call the inn before my arrival to make sure that they had the *kaise-kuchen* ready for me.

The Europe Craft catalog.
"The Convoy Coat"

I also loved figs, raisins, and nuts – which were sold in specialty stores in Munich. One day I saw figs in the window of a sweet shop that sold items by either the kilo or half-kilo, and I went inside. Behind the counter stood two buxom women, wearing loden-jackets and Bavarian hats trimmed with peacock feathers. Thinking that my German was pretty good by then, I told them what I wanted: *"Figen, en die fenster."*

They laughed, so I repeated myself, slightly louder, pointing to the window.

"Figen, en die fenster." (Figs in the window!)

Still laughing, one replied, *"Vi pheell?"* (How many?) I replied, *"Tsvi Mahl."* (Twice.)

They laughed harder, doubling over. I left with my figs, perplexed.

Later, Fritz told me that figs in German is pronounced "FEYEGEN"; when I pronounced it as "FEEGEN" it meant fuck.

"You actually said, 'I want to fuck in the window' . . . twice!"

It was mid-December, two weeks before Christmas, and I was trying to finish up work in Munich after a trip to Belgrade. I called Dolores and asked her to come join me for the holidays instead of my coming home; my mother-in-law could watch the kids. She agreed. My German shipping-forwarder knew a small town in Austria that would be great for a ski-holiday vacation. Bad Gastein, he said, had easy slopes. Sounded good to me.

"Don't bring any clothes," I told Dolores. "We'll buy what you need in the stores." I was thinking of our manufacturer and their ski wear.

My hotel, *Der Bayerisher Hof*, had one of the best restaurants in Munich. At dinner, there was always a piano player who played soft dinner music. One early evening, I told him that my wife was coming to Europe for the first time and that I would like to surprise her by having him play our favorite song, "Our Love is Here to Stay."

"Do you know that song?"

"Nein" he said.

I had to sing it to him. We rehearsed for half an hour.

Dolores came off the plane carrying only a small, square cosmetic box. She had no luggage – no underwear, nothing – because, as she reminded me, I'd told her not to bring anything! It was Sunday. All of the stores were closed. We were leaving the next day for Austria, so I called our shipping friend and he arranged to have several of his customers open their stores for us. We got everything we needed. That night in the restaurant, I made sure there were flowers on our table. The piano player sang our song and we danced the night away.

In the morning, with no time to stop for breakfast, we caught our train. No dining car! We were so hungry that when the train stopped at a station, I jumped off. There was a snack-seller on the platform with a basket full of frankfurters, sandwiches, and beer. I was filling my arms with food when the train started to move. The doors were electronically sealed shut.

I chased it along the platform, arms flying, letting go of everything I was carrying.

I was keeping even with the engine and shouted, *"Halt, Halt! Meine frau! Halt."*

Eventually the train stopped and the doors opened. I climbed on and raced through the cars toward Dolores.

She let me have it: "What was I to do if you didn't get back on to the train? I don't have anything with me, no passport – nothing."

Dolores looked up at me angrily.

"And where's the lunch?"

" . . . Don't ask!" I replied meekly.

After all that, we had a wonderful time skiing. In the *Hotel Weismayr*, we made friends with a French couple (the man looked like Charlie Chaplin); with another guy whose face was scarred and who looked like the actor George Macready; and with the Mustards, an American family traveling with their two children. On New Year's Eve, there were ten tables of eight in the dining room. We were at a table for two, which we preferred. Dolores wore a shimmering evening dress we'd bought in town, and I wore a rented tuxedo.

The dance floor started to slowly empty around us.

"What's going on?"

"*Eine minutin*," came over the sound system. They were counting down the minutes to midnight.

We were alone on the dance floor. Suddenly, a bell rang. In their seats, people joined hands and started singing. A man came on the dance floor wearing a black suit and a black top hat, his face smeared with ashes: a chimney sweep. In his arms he carried a baby pig.

"*Shmeiss*," he said, wanting me to kiss the pig. (Later, I learned that I was actually being honored; according to the tradition, the first person to see a chimney sweep and kiss a pig on New Year's would be granted good luck all year.) No way. There was no way I was kissing a pig.

The Mustards were very friendly and over coffee asked where we were headed next. I said we'd be leaving from Paris to fly home to New York.

"Have you ever been to Paris?"

"Only to connect at the airport," I replied.

"You really must stay a few days in Paris. You'll love it."

Dolores believed that in our past life we had lived in the court of one of the kings of France. She felt that this would be the ideal opportunity to spend a few days in Paris. The Mustards had recommended a very old, small hotel – the *Hotel Duminy* – in the residential area near *Rue St Germaine*. It reminded me of an old-style bed and breakfast hotel of the 1800s. When we got there, it was early evening. We opened the hotel's front door, and it almost touched the reception desk. An elderly man showed us to our room, and I offered to carry my own luggage. The room was large with a slanted floor that required wooden blocks under the front legs of the bed to keep it level.

Dolores and I celebrating New Years in Bad Gastein, Austria.

We quickly unpacked, as we wanted to dine at one of the restaurants the Mustards had recommended. Dolores decided to have a quick bath. I heard her voice, "Herbert, come in here – fast."

I dropped my *Herald Tribune*. Anticipating a hot-water problem, I opened the bathroom door.

There stood Dolores against the wall wearing only a towel, pointing toward the glass transom at the top of the bathroom wall.

"I saw a man looking at me through the transom as I was about to get into the tub." I looked up and saw only that the frosted glass transom was slightly ajar. It opened into the hall in order to ventilate the bathroom.

"Go outside and see if he's still there, and do something about it."

I slowly opened the hall door and there on a tall ladder was the old gentleman who had shown us to our room. The hall was dark, he had a bulb in his hand, and obviously Dolores had seen his shadow as he was replacing the bulb. She laughed and got dressed.

Returning from dinner, Dolores remarked how dark the hall was, even with the new bulb. We looked up at the ceiling above the glass transom, and to our shock, there was no light socket. For the rest of our stay, we didn't see the old man again.

The next morning, we strolled the *Champs D' Elyse* and later lunched at the local restaurant, *Le Bonne Fourchette*, The Good Fork. No one spoke English. We were given a menu, which listed a four-course meal at a really inexpensive price. With a little high school French and pointing we ordered. We later found out that a specific wine was included with each course. Wow, what a lunch. The French know how to enjoy good food and wine. The wine was brought to the table on a cart that held four small barrels with spigots, no bottles. As we finished one glass, we were offered another.

We planned to go to the *Louvre* at around 3:00 p.m., but we were just starting desert and coffee. Yes, and brandy was offered as well. By then, nature called and the room was spinning. We both had trouble getting out of our chairs to go to the bathroom, which was only ten or so feet from us. Laughing hysterically, we held on to each other and finally made it. The check came at 3:30 p.m.

Although our hotel was only one block from the restaurant, we finally stumbled into our room 20 minutes later.

"Let's take a nap for an hour; the museum is open till 8:00 p.m. We'll get to the Louvre in plenty of time," I said.

Our nap lasted until midnight; no *Louvre* today. We knew from the Mustards that there was a restaurant in the meat district called *Les Halles*, famous for their onion soup and their large selection of oysters. Since they would be open until early in the morning, off we went, not returning to our hotel until 1:30 a.m. Again our timing was screwed up. We awoke at 11:00 a.m.

Next on our list was the summer palace at Versailles.

"Let's go there first, and since the Louvre is open late, we can catch it on the way back," I suggested.

We got on a tour bus that was equipped with earphones and translations in French, English, German, and Spanish. During the hour's ride to the palace, we were given highlights of Paris in English as we drove through the city.

I never studied or read about the history of France. Although I was always interested in history (the older, the better), all I knew about France was what I had seen in the movies. The only time I had visited France was when I was in the Merchant Marine and had been restricted to 50 square feet at the pier in Le Havre. I was excited.

Since it was January, we didn't get to see the magnificent gardens. We entered the palace and were quite overwhelmed at the beauty of the marble and wooden floors, the tapestries and paintings – all kinds of plush furniture and fine art. We read about the Hall of Mirrors in our brochure; it was breathtaking to see. We didn't join a tour group and guide, but by the time we passed the Hall of Mirrors it was too late to find one. The next

Hall was immense. There was a large group with an English-speaking guide. Dolores and I snuck up and listened to her explain that the wood-paneled hall with its magnificent parquet flooring was used for court dinners and dancing. The king would lurk on the other side of the wooden wall panels to hear what the guests were saying. At dinners, he would have those he suspected, those he didn't trust, seated at tables close to the panels to better hear them. Some of those panels covered hidden stairs and rooms. If King Louis grew bored at a dinner and decided to leave, instead of walking the entire length of the hall and then the length of the Hall of Mirrors, he would press a spot on a panel, which would then open. This was the shortest route to his private quarters.

I moved closer to the guide and said, "Why don't you press one of those secret spots on the panel to show how it opens?"

I don't know what made me say it, especially since we weren't in her group. She didn't know which of the panels opened and said that she had never seen one open in the 20 years she had been a guide.

I walked up to one of the panels. "Let me show you," I offered.

Dolores was pulling on my coat. "Are you crazy, shut up. You'll get us in trouble." At the top left corner of one panel there was a curved wooden molding that ended at a point. I walked to it.

"Here it is," I exclaimed pressing down on the molding. The panel started to creak and it partially opened. The entire group and the guide gasped. I broke out in a sweat. Dolores and I retreated as fast as we could, breathing hard, but laughing. Dolores was not upset. As a matter of fact, I remember her saying, "Now do you believe me? I told you that we were married and lived in France and participated at Court. I can see you with ruffled cuffs on your sleeves. You were even a good dancer."

The Louvre couldn't top that, even though we were impressed with the enormity and variety of all the art. This time we joined a group and guide, and I managed to hold off on making any more suggestions or comments.

All of the restaurants were great. Of course, it was Paris in 1961 and our first trip to Europe together. Of the many trips we made during the 57 years that we travelled to all parts of the world, this was the one that remained our most memorable; I can still remember it clearly today. Of all the places over the succeeding years that we visited in Europe, Paris would remain Dolores's favorite.

When it was time to leave, I paid our hotel bill and asked for our luggage to be brought down. They called for a taxi. As the taxi pulled up to the hotel entrance, the elderly gentleman who had supposedly been fixing the mystery light bulb in the hall appeared, carrying our luggage. We hadn't seen him since the transom incident.

He came over to Dolores, said "*Excusez moi,*" took her hand, and kissed it. "*Merci, Madame.*"

When we got into the taxi, Dolores turned to me and asked, "Was he thanking me for not reporting the incident or for the view through the transom?"

On another trip, I spent the weekend skiing by myself in Kitzbuhl, Austria. I stayed in a small lodge and rented boots and skis. So far, so good. I excitedly took the ski tow to the middle level of the mountain and then the funicular to the very top. Halfway down the slope, the trail was all ice. What the hell was I doing? What if I broke a leg? On the skis, I sat down on my "tush" and slid to the bottom of the mountain. That was the end; I wouldn't ski again. Travelling throughout Europe with a cast and crutches would be difficult. Far worse, it would affect my ability to continue fulfilling all of my business responsibilities.

Chapter Nine

BACK IN NEW YORK, on 23rd Street, we had an ideal setup. It was a whole floor, which we divided into one office for Ed, another for me, two showrooms, a receptionist area up front, and a large office for bookkeeping, clerical, and order analysis, as well as a telephone reorder section. Near my office, was our fabric and trimmings room (with zippers, buttons, labels, etc.). Since the fax machine hadn't been invented yet, we kept in touch with our foreign suppliers by Telex, a machine that converted typed messages into radio signals that were received overseas and converted back to type. Our warehouse and shipping department was on 22nd street, on the fourth floor. A large freight elevator was used for receiving shipments from Europe, as well as for cartons of shipments going out to our customers.

We were doing very well. Our first year we had shipped almost a million dollars of goods, and we managed to nearly double that by the second year. We were flying, but I had a lot to learn about the financial side of running a business.

Our factor was acting as our banker. We had paid $15,000 for the company and originally opened an account at Chemical Bank with $30,000.00, the amount our factor required us to have as capital. When we needed more money for operating expenses, we borrowed from the factor, who was advancing against receivables. We had to get a credit okay from them on orders we wrote, so they always knew how much our future shipments to customers would bring in. Months later, after our customers paid the factors, our debt to the factor would significantly be reduced.

By fall of 1962, our second year, we were doubling our bookings and our expenses went up accordingly. In February 1963, when our bookings doubled again, we had to hire more office, shipping, manufacturing, and quality control personnel. The factor was waiting for our final accounting statement for the previous year. This was the responsibility of Hal, our accountant, who had come to us upon the recommendation of the factor. We had found him to be very knowledgeable about the apparel business, but now suddenly, he had disappeared.

We didn't see or hear from Hal for over four months. He didn't answer his phone, and we looked everywhere but couldn't find him. We had no idea what the figures looked like, and submitting a financial statement in February was impossible. The factor knew this.

Meanwhile, we knew that borrowing from the factor was costing too much in interest, and that the interest was eating up our profits. Instead of selling only a fall line in February through May and getting paid in December, we needed to earn money in the first six months of the year so that our borrowing costs would be negligible. So we went to work on developing a spring business. We designed a line of spring-weight versions of our already popular winter styles, using cotton poplin and leather trim. On some garments, we eliminated the zipper and substituted genuine leather buttons and buttonholes. Our German company made the fabrics and manufactured the jackets on time. We shipped the spring line in February and were paid in April through July.

In July the factor called and told us that Hal had reappeared, not mentioning where he had been or what happened. Hal apologized to us and proceeded to work on our year-end statement. The first week in August, he came to our office and told us he had some bad news.

> AS OF DECEMBER OF LAST YEAR, YOU WERE TECHNICALLY BANKRUPT.

"As of December of last year," he said, "you were technically bankrupt."

But it was July, and we had already fixed the problem; our spring line had saved the day. Months later, we discovered that the reason Hal had disappeared was to find a cure for his alcoholism. Thank God he had; otherwise, the statement would not have been prepared on time and we would probably have been out of business.

We had to face reality. Although by our third year we were doing triple what we had done when we started, we hadn't put in any additional operating capital since the first $30,000. Because of our fast growth, the factor's risks were substantially higher. They insisted we deposit an additional $50,000 of new capital into our bank account or they would no longer finance us, and they were adamant.

There was no way; neither Ed nor I had any capital to speak of.

But somehow it all worked out. I mentioned the problem to Harold, my mother's new husband. He asked one of his clients to lend us the money at a lower rate than we were paying the factor. We kept growing, continuing to increase both our spring and fall business. Our leather business in particular was phenomenal. In addition to using our leather supplier in Belgium, we were now manufacturing leather jackets in Yugoslavia, where the cost was significantly less.

On the strength of our reputation for unique leather garments, the designer Oleg Cassini came to see us. Because of all the publicity he received as First Lady Jackie Kennedy's personal designer, he was starting to become very well known. He was young, dapper, short, and slight – a charming man whose heels were a little higher than normal. More important, he knew what he wanted: men's leather jackets.

"I need to augment my business," he said. "I don't make menswear, but if you could design for me some men's jackets, I could put my own label on them and probably sell them at a very good price.

"They have to be very special jackets, of course." I told him that every jacket was made almost one at a time; the skins were cut by hand by experts who understood the rigorous demands of working with a material that could not, for example, be folded. Our suppliers understood all there was to know about grains of skins, thickness, and color. He wanted us to design a line comprised of ten styles. We were now in business with Oleg Cassini. His main concern was the quality of the garment, but he also had a keen sense of knowing what would sell. Our association lasted only one season because as he broadened his ladies collection and became one of the leading fashion designers of that era, he didn't have time to concentrate on his men's business.

Soon we were outgrowing our warehouse space. The Loden King label was in great demand and the Convoy Coat had become a classic. Although our warehouse on 22nd Street had started out as a perfect setup, we had various kinds of trouble in the building. We had problems getting deliveries because transportation was squeezed too tight at the 22nd Street entrance, making it difficult for the trucks to park and unload. Some cartons shipped from Europe had been broken into, and there had been shortages. The truckers insisted that all cartons placed on the elevator were sealed and that only the elevator operator was allowed to bring the cartons to our floor. Eventually, we paid someone to keep watch – to spot what was going on. He discovered that a group of men were stopping the freight elevator on unoccupied floors – on the way to ours – breaking open a few cartons, removing a few garments, and tossing them off the elevator on to those unoccupied floors.

Because of our growth in sales, it was time to look for another warehouse. If we stayed in New York City, we would need at least two floors in a typical warehouse building. I heard about new, one-floor facilities being built in Secaucus, New Jersey. I contacted a commercial real estate agent and went to look, but everything was too big, too expensive, or too old. The agent was a bit annoyed when I said that the new buildings, although perfect for our needs, were too expensive.

A GOOD BUSINESSMAN LOOKS CLOSELY AT INVESTMENTS THAT NEED TO BE MADE IN THE EARLY STAGES, SO THAT HE WILL BE READY WHEN THE COMPANY GROWS IN THE FUTURE.

"You know, Mr. Goldsmith," he said, "a good businessman looks closely at investments that need to be made in the early stages, so that he will be ready when the company grows in the future. You're only looking at the space you need for today, not at what you'll eventually need.

Let me show you how a big company thinks and plans."

He took me to a relatively new building that was fully air conditioned and close to the Holland Tunnel. It was owned by the Bali Bra company. The building manager showed us around. Bali occupied two of the building's three floors; according to the manager, they left the top floor empty for expansion, expecting to use the space in about three years.

"You see, they've allotted space for growth. Their business plan calls for extensive growth in the next three years. When the time comes, they will have the space under the same roof."

I had an idea. "Why don't you ask them if they'd like to rent us the empty floor? Look at the extra income that they will have for the next three years."

We became Bali's tenant. The third floor, which became our shipping and warehouse operation, not only had its own freight elevator, but the entire space was air conditioned.

Since there was no way to meter our floor, Bali paid the electric bills!

The building had an interesting layout. Between the first and second floors was a huge opening that allowed conveyor belts to run through. Cartons of assembled bras from the Caribbean arrived on the first floor and were carried up the belt through the opening in the ceiling to the second floor, where they were packaged according to style, size, and color. Another conveyor belt took the cartons down to the loading dock, where the trucks were loaded and the cartons shipped to their customers – a very ingenious and cost efficient process.

Shortly after we moved in, Bali was sold to the Hanes Company, which decided to do all of the warehousing, packing, and shipping at their operation in the South. The ingenious hole between the first two floors made the building impossible to sell, so for two years it stood empty except for us.

It looked like we would need more space, so one night I was poking around the other floors with the building's superintendent. I said it was surprising, despite the huge opening in the ceiling, that after more than a year no company had expressed an interest in the space, even as a rental. He told me that he didn't understand why no one had asked to see the architectural plans because the opening could easily be closed up. The pillars surrounding the opening were covered with sheetrock, and underneath the sheetrock were extended horizontal flanges on all pillars. All that was needed for the opening to be closed and secured was to hoist a few concrete slabs, supported by the flanges. I borrowed the plans and showed them to my builder friend, Shelly.

We bought the building at a ridiculously low price because Hanes was happy to sell their "white elephant." We installed the concrete slabs and closed the opening. With so much space to spare, we had to find tenants for the first two floors, and we did. Among them were Krupp's and a local school board office, along with the Port Authority of New York and New Jersey, and a few others.

Because our company was growing so fast, we also needed more showroom space. At 390 Fifth Avenue we took an entire floor, which we used for showrooms, office space, advertising and marketing, the fabric department, the design department, and a pattern maker who created sketches that were sent overseas to have samples made.

By 1966, after five years in business, Europe Craft outgrew the Bali building and went to Secaucus, New Jersey. We also outgrew 390 Fifth Avenue and moved to 441 Fifth Avenue, where we needed two floors to accommodate departments for merchandising, design and fabrics, and an actual sample department, where the samples were made. By then, we needed a separate office for our women's line, so we took an office and showroom at 1407 Broadway. The daughter of our agent in Germany, who had years of experience in the buying office and contacts in every major department store, came over to work with us on the women's line. My daughter Gail was in charge, Michelle worked at the men's office with me. Eventually needing more warehouse space we moved to Secaucus, New Jersey.

Today, the entire three floors of the former Bali building are rented to our tenant, the Port Authority of New York and New Jersey.

Chapter Ten

OUR ITALIAN AGENT WAS a man called Marco, who had once owned a men's retail store on Manhattan's East Side. At a time when there were no apparel importers in the United States, Marco was bringing in his own men's knitwear, made in Italy. His styling and quality was superb. Adding Italian knitwear to our line would increase our volume. We made him an offer to be our agent and guaranteed him the income he wanted for the first year. He sold his store and opened an office in Florence, working for Europe Craft as our exclusive agent.

One day, during one of my trips, Marco said, "I have to take you someplace. I want you to meet two guys who are terrific talents."

At eight the next morning, we drove out of the city to a little town where two young Italians were just starting in business and needed a financial backer.

"Look at these samples that they're making," Marco said.

I was impressed with their talent. It was the kind of women's clothing you would see in Neiman Marcus or Bergdorf Goodman, a daytime line and a nighttime line in very advanced styling. Beautiful clothes but not right for Europe Craft.

"Marco, forget it."

I wished them good luck as we drove away from these two talented men, who went by the names of Dolce and Gabbana.

Marco also took me to see a small manufacturer in the silk area of Italy, a manufacturer that was producing silk scarves and using printed silk for men's shirts. Printing on silk was "it" at the time and this manufacturer was going wild with graphics; you could have the Mona Lisa on the back of your shirt. We turned that down, too. With our permission, Marco gave the contact to a company he knew in the men's suit business in New York. Nik Nik shirts became a huge international success not long afterwards.

Although Marco's inspired finds were not right for our business, he did set us off on a path that proved to be a very good one. He had personally taken over designing the Italian men's sweaters for us. The sweater samples arrived while I was in the warehouse looking over ladies outerwear samples for our new fall line. Karin, the merchandiser of our ladies division, was helping with the fitting corrections on over twenty new outerwear samples. I asked her to try on the first jacket, but the blouse and sweater she was wearing were too bulky to fit under it properly and we couldn't see what adjustments had to be made. I suggested that she look in the cartons of Marco's samples and put one on so that we could get a proper fitting. She changed into one of the lighter-weight men's sweater samples. It molded to her body.

Hours later, after we finished the corrections, I said, "Karin, how come that men's sweater fits you so well?" It was a skinny rib sweater, which I'd never seen in any stores in America. Karin, who just returned from Europe, laughed and said that this "one-size-fits-all" was the rage in Europe. On his factory visits in Italy, Marco had come across these tubular sweaters made with a circular knit. Because mixed yarns were used in production, no two sweaters were alike. I wasn't sure the body-hugging style would sell to men's stores, but I did know that this was a terrific style for women. Because of that happy accident, we went into the ladies knitwear business. THE SKINNY RIB became one of the leading new fashion items for both men and ladies.

The retail stores sold out. We couldn't get enough from our Italian suppliers to satisfy the demand for both men and women.

On a Sunday morning, in the summer of 1963, I got a call from my partner that a very close friend of ours Eddie White, was in a terrible automobile accident in East Hampton on Long Island. He said that the hospital wouldn't give out any information. My partner was getting ready for his trip to Europe, and asked that I check out what happened and most of all, find out how Eddie was and what we can do.

From my house in Uniondale it would take one and a half hours to get there. I arrived at the hospital, but they wouldn't let me see him. "No visitors" I found a supervisor and explained that Mr. White was an orphan and had no living kin. I was a very close friend. He said, okay, but only a few minutes.

Eddie was a song writer and had a great sense of humor. We always challenged each other with our latest jokes. He was loved by everyone in the Theatrical industry. I had to find out how bad he was and what he wanted me to do for him.

A nurse escorted me into his warm room. He was flat on his back in the bed, a cast on his right leg, from the ankle to his hip, it was raised and supported by a sling. His left arm and shoulder was also in a cast. Looking at me, his head bandaged, he whispered through his wired jaw and clenched teeth.

"Herby, whatever you do, don't make me laugh."

I fainted. I woke up on a gurney, in the emergency room. On my wrist I had a plastic bracelet with my name on it. My belongings were at my feet. I sat up and started to get off when the nurse who had escorted me to Eddie's room, said that she caught me under my arms, and I never hit the floor. They had brought the gurney to Eddie's door and lifted me on it. I needed to stay until a doctor could see me. About a half hour later, after checking me out, they said I was free to go. I got dressed and started to leave when I was told that the rules are that I had to be pushed in a wheelchair and at the front door, I could get up and be free to go.

I got all the information about Eddie's injuries and how long he was expected to stay. I asked to be wheeled into his room to say goodbye. Before I could say a word, through his gritted teeth, and in a whisper....

"Herby, I told you, DON'T MAKE ME LAUGH!"

Chapter Eleven

WHEN I FIRST STARTED GOING TO YUGOSLAVIA, there were no foreign newspapers or magazines in the country. People got their news exclusively from the artists or musicians who brought back stories from their travels abroad and shared them in one of Belgrade's many private clubs, where groups of lawyers or musicians would gather to associate with their peers. With stronger signals, American radio and television came to the country and Yugoslavians were able to see the world outside. The younger people started developing a taste for things like LEVI's jeans, music records, and a newer lifestyle. The popularity of The Beatles really changed things. One night, I went to a "discotheque" (which was just a basement and a record player) with some of the guys from work. The police came and shut them down, but two days later, another discotheque sprung up in a different location. Eventually, after many months of arrests and closings, the police decided it was useless. Thereafter, entrepreneurs started opening legitimate clubs. The country just *had* to open its doors.

Coming into town from the Belgrade airport, I passed lots of open fields covered with deep snow, and then apartment houses started popping up. In the midst of them ,stood one small straw-roofed house with mud walls. Why was it still there? My agent explained that the man who lived there refused to sell when the apartment houses were going up.

"Look at what's on the roof," he said.

I looked up at a TV antenna.

"In the last two years, he has gotten his own TV and an indoor toilet. As far as he's concerned, he's living like a millionaire."

One day in 1964, in the lobby of my Belgrade hotel I saw Omar Sharif, James Mason, Stephen Boyd, Robert Morley, and Telly Savalas, who were all there making the movie *Genghis Kahn*. I went over and introduced myself, telling them why I was there. We started spending time together. In Belgrade, there was nothing very exciting to do, and no interesting places to go. Mostly, we'd sit around after dinner in the lobby of the Hotel Metropole. To add some excitement, I said, "Let's have some fun; let's put on a men's fashion show for the guests. The next day, I brought samples from the factory. We had a semi-rehearsal. The actors tried on the jackets, and then we presented a fashion show for some of the guests and the hookers hanging around the lobby – the only people there. Although the hookers had no idea who the actors were (since foreign movies weren't allowed in), we got a standing ovation. We were all laughing and having a great time. It helped the guys to relax after a hard day on the set.

Another evening, after they had finished that day's shooting, Omar came racing over to where Telly and the rest of the cast were. He said, "I just got a cable from my agent. Wow! One of the film studios wants me to play the lead in their new film, *Dr. Zhivago*."

Everyone started laughing. Telly advised him not to take the part: "Not only are you wrong for the part, but you're also too short. You'll ruin your career. Read the book and you'll see. In fact, instead of acting, why don't you just focus on your expertise in contract bridge, where you really excel?"

Omar was nominated for an Academy Award for his part in Dr. Zhivago; so much for Telly's showbiz expertise and career advice.

Telly Savalas remained in my life for a long time after that. Wherever I went in my travels, I always seemed to run into him while he was making a movie. Once I was in London with Dolores, staying in a nice suite at the

Ed Wachtel, Eddie White,
Telly Savalus and me.

Hilton Hotel. After dinner, we went to bed, but loud music from next door was keeping us awake. I banged on the wall; the music didn't stop. I called the front desk to complain and waited another fifteen minutes. Nothing. In frustration, I put on my robe, went into the corridor, and knocked on the door of the noisy suite.

Who opens the door? Telly!

"Herbie baby," he says.

"Telly!"

"So, where we going tomorrow?" he asks.

"Well, I'm with Dolores."

"Oh," Telly says, "that's okay; she will make us look great."

Telly believed that every day was a super day; you never knew when it would all be over. He enjoyed his life, going out with lots of girls and hangers-on, convinced that his great life would only last a short time.

He once told me the strangest story about something that had happened years before, when he was with the *Voice of America*. He was driving along the Grand Central Parkway in Queens when suddenly, near the site of the old 1939 World's Fair, the car started jerking and sputtering; he realized that he had run out of gas. Telly wasn't the kind of guy to check the gas when he got in the car.

What to do? He starts walking in search of a gas station; suddenly, a white convertible slows to a stop. The driver, a handsome guy who looks like a movie star, asks if Telly needs a lift. They drive to a nearby gas station, where Telly gets a portable tank, says goodbye, and thanks his benefactor. But the guy says, "No problem, I'll drive you back." A grateful Telly says, "I'd like to thank you somehow," as the driver hands him his card.

Six months later, Telly is emptying his wallet and sees the card. He picks up the phone and dials the number on it. A woman answers. When she asks what he wants, he says, "I'm calling for Jim, the guy who helped me out."

The woman hangs up.

Telly calls back. The woman says, "Why are you doing this to me? My son Jim died a year ago."

Telly explains about the card in his hand; then he asks if her son owned a car.

"Yeah, a white convertible; he was in a horrible accident and the car was totaled."

He went to see the woman and they talked for four hours. That's all that Telly would say about it.

He told me that story in the context of explaining that he felt he was here on a pass; somebody was watching him, but his life had a clock on it. When he was diagnosed with prostate cancer, he refused to do anything about it. He was a tough human being, but also soft as a marshmallow.

In the mid-1970s, he had developed a cult following, after playing Kojak – the bald, lollipop-sucking New York City police lieutenant in the TV series. By then, he, my partner Eddie, and I had all formed a very close, personal relationship.

I can still see Telly at an October baseball game at Yankee Stadium in his big fur coat. Even though he was a rough guy, he was an immaculate dresser. Almost single-handedly, he was making the three-piece vested suit popular, at least among the people in the fashion industry, which gave him an Adam Award in 1976 for his influence on men's style.

When Ed said, "Let's make a Telly Savalas clothing line," my response was, "But we're in the sportswear business."

LET'S MAKE A TELLY SAVALAS CLOTHING LINE.

"So what?" Ed said. "We'll find a clothing contractor who only makes suits."

That was possible, I thought; not every clothing company made their own clothes. Some companies contracted out the manufacturing and just put their own label into the garments.

So we did it – we developed a Telly Savalas line that premiered in a fashion show at the Waldorf Astoria hotel in New York City early in 1977 to

Telly Savalas.

tons of newspaper publicity. But in spite of the appeal that Telly had (during every personal appearance, he was mobbed; thousands of people filled the streets), the line didn't sell as well as we had hoped it would. The clothing stores, as opposed to the sportswear stores with whom we did all of our business, thought that we didn't know enough about tailoring. We couldn't convince enough of them to carry the line. I think another reason may have been that the consumers, the people who actually watched *Kojak* on TV, simply did not wear suits.

In Yugoslavia, we were using six fabrics to manufacture 22 styles. The government assigned us to their garment and fabric control office, Centrotextil, which acted as our agent in every phase of the business. We placed our orders through the two agents assigned to us. When the garments arrived in the U.S., we paid the agents and they paid the factory. Hard currency was crucial to the Yugoslavian economy, so only 80% of the dollars we paid was converted to local currency and paid to the factory. The remaining 20% was placed in the bank, where it could be used as dollars or foreign currency to purchase critical items outside Yugoslavia – like machinery or the newest sewing equipment. Because of this, our business was very important to them.

In the early years of our association, it was like working in our own factory. They made every sample I designed and were able to secure the fabrics required. Their delivery was on time, and we never received a single damaged garment in their shipments. They became the most reliable, quality-conscious factory that we ever dealt with. They had a kitchen, with an excellent chef, and a separate dining room for customers and guests. Lunch was a real treat, equal to or better than the restaurants in downtown Belgrade. Ed and I were even assigned our own dishes and silverware, which were locked in a cabinet until our return.

We made sure that we showed them our appreciation by bringing them items from the U.S. – items that they cherished and that could accompany me on a plane. All I had to worry about on arrival was the Customs officer. Well, a pack of Marlboros goes a long way. I usually looked for the same agent and went right through. Friendly people.

The agent/translator that I had been assigned to by Centrotextil owned an old Volkswagen. Since Volkswagens were not made in Yugoslavia, there were no parts available, so he always needed spare parts. Each time I came, I brought spark plugs, points, carburetors, etc. In all my trips, I practically brought enough to build a new car. I drew the line when he said, "I need a new bumper."

There weren't a lot of Americans traveling to Europe on vacation in the sixties; most were going for business. The men wore suits and neckties on transatlantic flights. We were served three-course dinners on English china plates, with crystal glasses and genuine silverware. The finest cordials and wines were offered. There was only one class of service. Unfortunately, cigarette smoking was allowed. From London or Paris, connections to other European cities were sparse. To the Communist countries, there were usually two flights a day, but only three to four times a week. It was nerve racking. My work had to be completed on time. If I missed my plane, I could waste a day.

There were very few commercial hotels. People in London thought that having a new Hilton Hotel in the heart of London was scandalous. That's where I went. I got friendly with the front desk manager, a chain smoker who loved American cigarettes and desperately wanted me to bring him several cartons. I did. As a thank you, he usually gave me a suite at the minimum rate. Many times I had the Presidential suite, consisting of three bedrooms, a living room with a piano, a dining room, and a library. There were so many doors in the suite, I actually got lost in it. I had the same arrangement in the very fine hotels in Brussels, Munich, and Dusseldorf – all thanks to American cigarettes. In other countries, LEVI'S jeans were even more appreciated. For the wives of the factory managers and owners, I usually brought French perfume and Italian silk scarves.

Chapter Twelve

In **Paris-Orly Airport** on a very warm spring day in 1962, the flight to New York was delayed, as usual. European air conditioning was still in its infancy, and it was expensive to have it on, so we were pretty uncomfortable. The passengers were given coupons for snacks and drinks. I went up to the bar and requested a cold orange drink

"Un orange, s'il vous plait."

The man behind the counter smiled at me and said something that sounded like, "shit."

I knew the French didn't love Americans, but really, this was outrageous, so I said, *"Excusez-moi je new comprends pas."*

He turned around to where there were rows of shelves behind the counter and brought out a bottle that was labeled *Pschitt*.

"Wait a minute. I'll be right back."

I run down to the duty free shop and get two plastic bags, which I fill up with as much *Pschitt* as I can. The plane finally arrives, we board, and when we're about an hour out, the stewardess comes over and asks me what I've been laughing about for the past half hour.

From the overhead bin, I took down one of the bags, "I'm envisioning arriving in New York and going through Customs . . . they'll ask me what I have and I'll show them these bottles of *Pschitt*."

And that's just what happened. I collect my bags and look over the different customs inspectors. The one I choose is wearing a gold tie clip with his name on it, Sol.

"Anything to declare?" He asks

"Just *Pschitt*."

"What're you, a wise guy?"

He yells across to another inspector: "Hey Joe, I got a wise guy here."

Joe comes over.

"What's the problem?"

"The gentleman here has these two plastic bags, and when I ask what's in them, he says shit."

Joe looks at me. "Alright," he says, "let's see."

I tell him he's free to put his hands in the bags; after he shrinks back, I finally show them the bottles from France and they crack up. In fact, I give one to each of them. From then on, whenever I got to New York Customs, I always looked for Sol.

About a year later, I'm in Orly again. More Americans have started coming over, the place has been fixed up. Now there's a kiosk that sells magazines, candy, and other things, and about half a dozen women are standing at the magazine rack looking at fashion magazines. At the cash register, about 20 feet away from the magazines, I see that *Pschitt* is now being made in hard candies, like Charms in America.

Very loudly, I ask the cashier, "Madame, do you have any Pschitt?"

"Oui," she says, "beaucoup."

The women dropped their magazines. "And what flavors of Pschitt do you have?"

The cashier says, "Strawberry, orange, and lemon."

When the women approach the cashier's counter and see the candies, they break up.

At Idlewild, I go up to Sol with my plastic bags. "Now what," he says.

"Would you believe that Pschitt would come in so many flavors. . ." and I give him a handful of the candy packets. You had to see the look on the faces of the couple behind me.

Then I decide that I want to be the exclusive distributor of Pschitt in the U.S. Every home in America would have at least one bottle of Pschitt to show to friends and family. We could sell millions. I tell my agency friend Harold about it and he says that before we contact the company, he wants to make up a "Story Board" for a TV commercial, as well as for radio.

A few days went by and Harold asked me to come down to his office. He had contacted the agent for the English actress Deborah Kerr, who had been a sensation in the movie *From Here to Eternity* with Burt Lancaster. She was definitely available for commercials.

"Herb, look at these story boards. This commercial will make history. It shows Kerr at her cocktail party, talking to the camera, and saying, 'Whenever I have a cocktail party for friends, I always serve them *Pschitt*.' The same dialogue would be used for radio commercials. For the candies, she would say how delicious *Pschitt* is on the tongue."

Every leading TV and radio network turned us down. No way would they approve someone saying *Pschitt* on the air, even if it was Deborah Kerr. If we could get the distributorship, there would be no way to promote it, except in print. We dropped the whole idea, but I know we would have won every advertising award.

* * * * * *

On a few occasions, Dolores came to meet me on my trips, leaving the children in the care of her obliging parents. Usually, her junkets were planned, but sometimes they happened on the spur of the moment. Once I was in Rome with Bernie, a man I'd become friendly with after running into him many times while we were shopping European fashions every fall and spring. Bernie was a clothing manufacturer in Canada. It was his idea to call our spouses to come over and join us.

I picked Dolores up at the Rome airport a few days later. At the time, the Via Veneto was full of hookers, whom you could identify by their fashionably high boots and black capes. Dolores, not knowing about the hooker's uniform, went shopping one afternoon and bought herself some beautiful high boots and a luxurious black cape. That evening, we came out onto the street in front of the Excelsior Hotel, where we were staying. Dolores was wearing her new outfit.

"You wait here," I said, "Bernie and I have to go look at two men's shops around the corner. We won't be long."

It was a nice night, and so Dolores agreed.

From a block away, Bernie and I watched the corner where Dolores was standing. One car after another honked their horns; guys were hanging out the window, calling out to her. We were really laughing hard. When we came back to Dolores, she said, "What a great country. The people are so friendly, pulling up in their cars and greeting me. Of course I don't understand Italian, but I can tell that they were very friendly."

I looked at Bernie and he whispered, "Boy, are you in trouble. How are you going to explain that we deliberately left her standing alone, wearing a cape and high leather boots like all the hookers? You better tell her about the cars and the greetings."

I told Dolores that we made a mistake leaving her alone; I didn't say it was on purpose.

A few years later, we had another memorable escapade in Rome, except this time I was the butt of the joke. One very warm September evening, we strolled up the Via Veneto to one of Rome's finest restaurants, situated at the end of the street on the second floor of a historic building in the park. It was very romantic – a view of the park, musicians playing just below our window. The patrons were well dressed: men were in suits and ties; women were in Gucci and Pucci. I had on a crème colored suit.

We started off with a Campari and soda and ordered what the maître d' recommended. After our appetizer, out came a rolling cart, with two silver domed tureens. The waiter lifted the covers, took the tray from the burner, and walked over to me. With a slight bend, he extended his arms, presenting the chicken cacciatore simmering in a marvelous red mushroom sauce. But he extended the tray too far. It tipped and most of the steaming hot sauce fell onto my lap.

I jumped. The staff ran to our table with napkins and proceeded to blot me and my soaked pants, apologizing profusely. Dolores was laughing hysterically. "Only to you!"

A large red stain about the size of a dinner plate remained on my crème colored pants. The maître d' assured me that applying talcum powder to the stain would make it disappear. He said that the dinner was complimentary and asked if they should make another order of the chicken cacciatore. In unison, Dolores and I said, "Roast chicken, *NO SAUCE.*"

After thirty minutes, our chicken arrived, already on a plate, with no gravy and no tray presentation.

After dinner, we were invited into the Library for dessert and coffee. My pants were dry – the talcum powder had absorbed the moisture – but when I tried to stand, I couldn't. The talcum/sauce combo seemed to turn into cement. I plopped back into my seat.

Here he comes again. The maître d' had a thick-handled knife. He asked permission to scrape the patch.

"Okay, but gently."

Scraping didn't work. He suggested banging on the spot with the handle to chip away the cement so that I could stand up. No guests were left in the dining room; cement flakes were flying. I was careful not to hit my privates, but missed once. Then he asked me to take my pants off so that they could work on the stain in the kitchen. He wrapped a long tablecloth around my waist and Dolores and I proceeded to the lounge. I still had my jacket on, and the tablecloth was almost the same color. No one noticed that I wasn't wearing pants, or may have thought I was from India.

After dessert and coffee, they came out with my pants, still with an obvious stain. The restaurant offered to pick up the pants at my hotel in the morning and return them cleaned by late afternoon. They also gave us a bottle of champagne.

Now we had another problem: We couldn't take a taxi. No cars are allowed in the park or on the Via Veneto at dinner hours. The only way out of the park was along the Via Veneto. We would have to walk, with the stain on my pants, about six city streets to our hotel, while passing all the outdoor coffee shops and cafe's.

Dolores didn't know that this park was notorious for the hookers and their "Johns." I would be walking out of the park with a pretty, dark-haired, Italian-looking woman and a stain the size of a plate on the front of my pants. I mentioned this to Dolores.

"Herb, I'm not walking with you: I'm going ahead, and I'll see you at the hotel."

"Dolores, wait, problem solved."

I saw lots of Italian newspapers in the lounge. I grabbed a few, folded them strategically, and walked with the papers covering the stain. Not one glance as we strolled to our hotel.

Chapter Thirteen

IN SPITE OF THE MANY ADVENTURES I had with Dolores, or with Ed, or even alone, traveling on business was very stressful. I had to go to six to eight countries on each trip. I averaged six trips a year, each one for a minimum of two weeks, which meant I was on a very tight schedule. Jet planes didn't exist. Flying on propeller driven planes was no picnic. From New York to Europe, they were four-engine propeller planes and within Europe, only two propellers. The flight was never nonstop. From New York, we had to stop to refuel in places like Gander, Newfoundland; Goose Bay, Labrador; Shannon, Ireland; or Iceland. An average trip took nine hours going there and ten hours returning home. I had to fly to London and then catch a connecting flight the next day to the other countries I was doing business with. Sometimes, on my return, Dolores would meet me in Bermuda or Puerto Rico, where I could recover from jet lag. Even Gail, our eldest, became an international traveler, although not without some difficulty.

When Gail was in high school, she was infatuated with ballet. One summer, she wanted to go with a group of other kids to a special, month-long ballet program in France. It sounded good to Dolores and me. I offered to use my connections at Pan Am Airways to get her upgraded to first class for her trip. Gail really wanted to go with the others, even though it would mean flying tourist class on Air France, but I ultimately prevailed. Her Pan Am ticket required changing planes in London, en route to Paris, but when she got to Heathrow, lo and behold, there was an airline strike: no flights to Paris that day. She was stranded.

I had given her the name of a friend of mine in London, just in case. In the middle of a work day in New York, I got a call from my friend in London telling me that he had just heard from my panicky daughter. She wanted to come home.

What was the problem?

"She didn't have the money to buy another ticket," he said.

I realized how confused she was. She'd forgotten that not only did she have traveler's checks, she was also holding a return ticket. Too late! He had already purchased her a return flight and at that moment she was en route home.

Gail came home, having traveled alone to London and back in one day. And for the rest of the summer, she wouldn't let me forget that I had insisted on putting her in first class.

My travels continued. Part of the Europe Craft line consisted of leather jackets. Quality garments used lamb skins, the best of which came from the Middle East, where the consumption of lamb in the diet meant a tremendous availability of skins. The finishing, tanning, and curing of these skins was an ancient art in those countries. The factory that we worked with in Yugoslavia, where we did the bulk of our leather manufacturing, imported these skins until the government prohibited imports in order to develop their own mills and tanneries.

Since the skins were coming from Turkey, it seemed intelligent at the time to go there. I became friendly with an American who was married to an opera singer from Istanbul. Ted offered to help, he had good connections. In Istanbul, we were lucky to locate the tannery, and people there recommended sewing factories that specialized in leather. We visited those, leaving sketches and some Yugo-made samples for them to reproduce. It took several trips to Istanbul. On the weekends, we explored the shops and bazaars, and the souk, an ancient mall – the first of its kind to have a roof, streets, and lighting. There were hundreds of shops (mostly jewelry and carpet shops) and restaurants, some very large and air conditioned.

One of the shops was owned by a young man whom we met at the bar in the Hilton Hotel. He was educated in America and had no traceable accent. He insisted that we see his shop and raved about his collection of unique, rare, and ancient pieces of jewelry. Gold and precious stones were mined in abundance in Turkey. In his store, he showed what he was offering for sale and assured us that, of course, we would get a discount. No prices were on the pieces, so I was kind of suspicious of his "special discount" prices to us. Nevertheless, we purchased some and our wives were thrilled with what they got. They couldn't believe how little they cost. The designs were very different from what was available in the States.

After several visits, he invited us to a lower floor, where he had his personal collection. He told us the history of each piece. They were all very old and magnificent. There was a bracelet of six oblong Jade cameos connected to one another with gold ringlets. Each cameo was framed in tooled gold. It was a Russian piece, he said, more than 200 years old, originally made for the czarina. Each cameo showed her at a different stage of her life, from childhood to queen. I fell in love with it and offered to buy it. He refused. "This is my personal collection. It has been in my family for many generations and is only here to show you."

Sometime in the third year of my visits to Turkey, he gave in. This grand piece was expensive, and he let me pay in installments. We were indeed very good friends. I couldn't wait to get home and give it to Dolores. She was overwhelmed.

A few weeks later, we were invited to a party at the Pierre Hotel. We got up to dance, and as I whirled her around a few times, the bracelet went flying. I picked it up and noticed that one of the cameos had split but was still attached to the bracelet.

"Herb, why didn't you make sure there was a safety catch?"

I guess there were none in those days; maybe the czarina wasn't a dancer. I went to a jeweler in Manhattan and had him attach a safety catch, but Dolores never wore it again.

A lot of my trips were to Yugoslavia, which had become our largest source of manufacturing in both cloth and leather jackets. Late one May, Dolores met me in Belgrade for a vacation on the Adriatic coast, where we had never been. We flew to the ancient walled city of Dubrovnik on a twin-engine prop plane. The airport was just a dirt landing strip with a wooded shack for a terminal. Before landing, the pilot had to buzz the air strip in order to frighten away a few dozen sheep, some cows, and a flock of chickens. After landing, the two pilots unloaded the luggage, carted it to the shack, and put on different caps, instantly becoming the customs inspector and immigration officer. Our passports were stamped and we headed to the bus that would take us to town. Women wearing traditional peasant clothing tried to sell us local craft items. The scene was a step back in time. We boarded the bus; the driver, changing his hat again, was also the pilot/immigration officer!

We were dropped off at the hotel entrance, which was the size and height of a small shop, with a sign instructing us to ring the buzzer for the elevator. The Hotel Argentina was set into the side of a cliff. At the reception area, (which was twenty stories below the hotel entrance), we could see cascading gardens leading to the beach, 50 yards below the reception area. Since our agent, Centrotextil, had made the reservation, we were given the villa – located in the garden area away from the main hotel – which was usually reserved for Tito, the country's president. We were thrilled! It was a replica of an ancient, tiled-roof Japanese home. But there was a record-breaking heat wave and the villa didn't have air conditioning or fans, so we asked for a regular room. None were available; so much for pull.

The walled city of Dubrovnik is over 400 years old. The walls contain apartments and what should have been normal roofs are actually pedestrian walkways. The huge square is lined with shops, restaurants, churches, and one synagogue – reportedly the oldest in Europe and still active. Inside the synagogue, the *bimah* was set in the center of the square building with benches on all four sides. When the Nazis invaded, the rabbis buried the Torahs under six feet of sand covered by the wooden floor. They were never confiscated. In the following years, Dolores and I would return several times.

On another trip through Yugoslavia, we went to a hotel resort called *Sveti Stefan*. It was an island reached from the mainland by a man-made dirt road. Before World War II, the island had about sixty homes, a church, several shops, and a large boat yard. All the men from *Sveti Stefan* Island were killed in the war. When peace was declared, the government moved the surviving families to other cities and took over the island, converting it to a resort. Instead of hotel rooms there were small houses, with bedrooms, sitting areas, baths, and porches. The boatyard bordering the sea had become the reception desk leading to a grand restaurant, shops, and a small gambling casino. It was amazing. The accommodations were first class.

After dinner, Dolores and I went to the casino. It was managed and run by an Italian company, with no crap tables, only roulette and *chemin d' fer* (a version of baccarat). Bets had to be made in the local Yugoslavian currency, which was then converted into different colored chips. I was assured that if I exchanged American dollars for these chips and cashed them in when I left, I would be compensated in American dollars. We looked around for a while. We didn't spot any gambling by Americans or even Yugoslavians, only the French, Italian, and a few of the English.

Dolores said, "Let's play a little roulette."

I changed a hundred dollars and received a pile of chips in different colors and sizes. No one spoke English at our table, including the croupier. I just put down some chips. We won the first time out. The croupier pushed over a pile of square post card-sized chips, so we bet with those. We were lucky again. In fact, at each spin we had one or more chips on the winning number. The other gamblers at the table were shouting "Bravo." We started to get uncomfortable. Noticing the ever-growing pile of chips, I decided it was time to cash in.

We went to the manager's desk and slid the chips to him. He calculated and started to cash us in with Yugoslavian currency.

"Wait a minute," I interjected, "you told me that when I cashed in, I would be paid in dollars."

"Absolutely correct," he responded, "but only for the $100 U.S. that you originally changed. Winnings are not paid in dollars."

"That was not what I was told," I said, starting to get heated, "I'm with the U.S. Embassy in Belgrade, and if I'm not compensated in dollars, I will report you to the Yugoslav authorities."

He gave in. "I'm sorry sir, but I do not have enough U.S. currency here to match your winnings. I will Telex my firm and tomorrow evening you will have the full amount." He gave me a receipt for $3,400, equal today to about $12,000 or $14,000.

Knowing Dolores would scream with joy at the news, I held off telling her of our luck until we returned to our bungalow, where she did scream with joy at the news.

The next evening the gambling manager called, advising us that the money was all there in dollars. "Since there are no other secure areas in the hotel, would you like to have me lock your money in our safe?" he inquired. I said "Thanks, I'll think about it." We were sure that when we wanted our money, we'd be told that the safe had been broken into.

We were not very comfortable sleeping that night. I called Belgrade, and my office got us tickets on a flight out the next morning. We checked out three days early. About 20 years later, we returned. The place had dramatically changed for the better. It had been transformed into an island paradise. On the first night, we lost a $1,000 and never went back to the casino; we considered ourselves ahead of the game. Dubrovnik Airport had improved, as well: It now had two asphalt runways, a fence to keep out the local livestock, and a modern air conditioned terminal. The walled city, however remained the same.

Chapter Fourteen

In Belgrade, the sewing factory we used, KLUZ, was owned by the workers. They elected the president of the factory and the key executives. In addition to owning the factory, the workers owned over 100 KLUZ apparel shops throughout Yugoslavia. The profits generated by our orders went to the factory and were shared by the entire work force of over 300 workers. Since I paid in U.S. dollars, the factory used hard currency to purchase the piece goods, mostly woolens, from our suppliers in Italy and Germany. My team went to the mills in those countries and told them what would be ordered, where to ship, and that payment would be made in advance from Yugoslavia.

It all ran perfectly for a few years until the Government placed an embargo on all imported textiles, the same problem we had faced with leather hides from Turkey. The factory could not import for us, and the Yugoslav woolen mills were not producing the texture, designs, or quality that we needed. The only fabric made there that we could continue to use was cotton corduroy.

We had to find fabrics other than corduroy that was available in that country. Fortunately, Centrotextil had a warehouse filled with thousands of yards of imported material that was not being used because no one had thought of what to do with it. I looked at four or five sample yards of combed Egyptian pima cotton poplin, woven and dyed in Japan, of such exquisite quality that it could not be duplicated anywhere. We were using a lightweight poplin fabric, not as fine as this one, in the jackets that we made in Germany.

"How many yards do you have and at what price?" I inquired.

They had over 600,000 yards. The cost to KLUZ would be $1 a yard. The poplin we were using in Germany, inferior to the Japanese quality, cost us over $1.70 a yard. We would shift our German production of poplin to KLUZ and pay much less for the jackets.

It was a bonanza. With that fabric, I made lightweight spring versions of our fall styles: jackets with leather-trimmed button holes or leather piping on the collar or along the chest. These styles exploded our spring business in the North and allowed us to sell the same items as a fall and winter line to the South, where they could only use lightweight garments. They became the most important styles in our line, outdoing even the corduroy garments. Since not all of the colors were suitable for menswear, I used some of the more exciting colors for our ladies wear.

> I MADE LIGHTWEIGHT SPRING VERSIONS OF OUR FALL STYLES.

We had no competition in America on this type of leather-trimmed pima cotton jacket.

My old firm, Chief Apparel, ran an ad in our trade paper with the headline:

> **"WHY BUY IMPORTS, WHEN YOU CAN BUY FROM SHICKSHINNY, PA."**

Unbelievable. And they considered that marketing . . .

In Germany, we began to see shortages of affordable labor. Italy produced our woolen fabrics, which were then shipped to Yugoslavia for conversion to woolen jackets, but the new duty on fabrics entering from outside the country would take us out of the right price range in Yugoslavia on anything other than corduroy. We had to move on.

It was in Poland that we found a variety of available fabrics, fabrics unlike those in Yugoslavia. We ordered a few samples that came out surprisingly good, and the prices that Ed negotiated were acceptable. We put in an order. But production in Poland presented conditions far different from those to which we had become accustomed. The government told us where we could manufacture. The factories were tremendous – six floors, thousands of workers. The managers were politicians: government employees. Their operations were entirely business oriented – cash flow, production figures, etc. We were never allowed to go into the factory and we were warned to be careful about the people with whom we talked.

> PRODUCTION IN POLAND PRESENTED CONDITIONS FAR DIFFERENT FROM THOSE TO WHICH WE HAD BECOME ACCUSTOMED.

The person assigned to us as an interpreter, our go-between, didn't have any understanding of the apparel business, so we started teaching him. We were prohibited from meeting with him outside the factory or the government offices unless another monitor was present. Perhaps they felt that corrupting two factory representatives would be more difficult than corrupting just one, but our guy didn't care. He helped us a lot, and when he eventually asked for help in getting a Green Card so that he could immigrate to the United States, we managed to assist him.

In Yugoslavia, we had never received a damaged garment, but in Poland it was difficult to have quality control. Faced with inconsistent fits, mismatched colors, and stitching mistakes, our relationship with the Polish factories only lasted two years. By the time we started looking at Romania, the U.S. market was experiencing a craze for denim, especially jackets in a softer, lighter-weight fabric. Romania produced that for us, plus other cottons we could use.

In my travels, I was continually getting ideas from European magazines and learning what I could from department stores. Men's fashions were exploding during these years, especially in England, where the Carnaby Street style was all the rage. These clothes were for a very young market; they featured advanced styling and a very tight fit. In fact, the tight fit was really what was setting a new trend.

In Paris and London, I saw the younger women wearing pants with waists no higher than their belly buttons. The belts were at least two inches wide; the pant leg flared outward from the knee down, like sailor's pants; and they were tight across the thighs and seat. The pants were called "Hip Huggers." It was the sixties and very few popular-priced manufacturers in the States ever travelled to Europe. So far, no stateside company was showing Hip Huggers in their collections. Here was a chance to be first. Our only risk was the cost of making the samples.

We made our samples and they became unbelievable sellers, one of the hottest women's fashion trends in America. We made them in a variety of fabrics for both the fall and spring lines. After our second season, everybody copied them. Our European ladies import line of Hip Huggers, along with the Skinny Rib sweaters, were sensations for our new label, Elli Mode. We quickly recognized that opportunities in the ladies garment business were greater than in the traditionally reserved men's business. We were challenged.

> LET'S START A HIGH-PRICED LADIES SPORTSWEAR LINE.

My partner said, "Let's start a high-priced ladies sportswear line, completely separate from Europe Craft and Elli Mode," I thought. "Why not? We were on a roll," I answered myself. Our new firm was called *Intre Sport*. An assistant designer named Charles Suppon was then working for Calvin Klein but was interested in becoming head of design for another firm. We contacted him and were very impressed with what he showed us. We soon hired Charles, who proved to be a consummate talent.

Charles insisted that his initial line should be presented at a live fashion show. We rented a night club for the night. Charles's friend, Peter, played the piano, wearing a gold-sequined men's sports jacket that Charles had created. Buyers from all of the quality stores came, and we had a major hit. Peter, by the way, had cost us $25 for the evening's piano playing.

> *"Confidence of the collection, its imaginative design, its classic sportswear, shapes in terrific fabrics, strong color combinations and lots of workable innovative details."*
>
> - WOMEN'S WEAR DAILY

Charles Suppon helped make Intre Sport an overnight success. It was like show biz, fashion shows, and cocktail parties rolled into one. We hired an in-house chef who prepared fancy lunches in our private kitchen, and our new showroom became an open house where you could stop in, review the new clothing lines, and have turtle soup for lunch.

CHARLES SUPPON HELPED MAKE INTRE SPORT AN OVERNIGHT SUCCESS.

Then Charles offered to do me a personal favor. Our daughter Gail was about to be married, and Charles offered to create for her a one-of-a-kind wedding dress. It was a wonderful gesture, except that Charles was quite the diva and never let anyone view his original designs until finished. A week before the nightclub show of our new women's line, we hadn't seen one sample. The collection had turned out magnificently, so I was only slightly nervous when, on the Tuesday before Gail's Saturday wedding, nobody had yet seen her gown.

"Where's the dress?"

"Don't worry."

"Where's the dress?"

"You'll have it," Charles insisted. "Just leave me alone."

I aged ten years.

*At Gail's wedding, my little
Ileen at age 12.*

By Friday at noon, Gail had her dress. It was an "ooh" and "ah" dress, very sophisticated and worth all the angst, I think.

That first year, Charles won the coveted Coty Award, the Oscar for designers, and became famous industry-wide. In his second year, he said he had an original idea for menswear and we let him go with it. He made only one style, a jacket. It was a regular men's sport jacket with lapels but no front buttons or buttonholes, and we offered it in six different fabrics. That year, he won the Coty award for designing menswear.

Then, out of the blue, he was gone; he had simply disappeared. For weeks we couldn't find him. We even looked for him in night clubs and discos. Not one phone call, not one letter. Months later, I read that Charles Suppon and Peter Allen had written a musical, "Leggs Diamond," scheduled to open on Broadway.

This was the same Peter to whom I had paid $25 for playing the piano at Charles's fashion shows. Without Charles, we closed Intre Sport.

Chapter Fifteen

ONE SHIPMENT FROM ROMANIA arrived with 25% of the jackets damaged. They were unusable and our loss would amount to $400,000. The terms of our shipments included refund provisions for damages and a provision that a claim for credit would be resolved by reducing the prices on subsequent orders. We filed a claim and two people showed up in New York to check the shipment. When they agreed to the amount of damage, we asked for an official stamped document verifying that we would be getting a credit in U.S. dollars. I knew that nothing would be official without the stamp and two signatures.

Clearly, it was becoming too risky to continue production in Romania. But we wanted the money due us, not a credit against future orders. (This would be difficult, since we planned to discontinue doing business with them.) I arranged a trip to Romania with our controller, our product manager, our quality control manager, and the head of our ladies department. We rehearsed our plan in advance. We'd say that we were coming over to place several million dollars' worth of orders for the next season and, as stipulated, they would deduct our loss claim from the

> IT WAS BECOMING TOO RISKY TO CONTINUE PRODUCTION IN ROMANIA.

negotiated price. It crossed my mind that perhaps they'd sent damaged goods on purpose, to keep us coming back in order to recover our losses via the credit arrangement. Through their representative in New York, we insisted that they open a letter of credit for the $400,000, signed and stamped by a government agent, written in English, payable through an American bank, and ready for us when we arrived in Romania. I was certain they believed that I would, as was customary, tear up the claim document and take a discount on the agreed negotiated prices. Not this time. I needed to physically have this official letter of credit, leave the country with it, and redeem it in New York. No million-dollar orders were in the works. Ed couldn't go, he had to stay for one of our trade shows.

Knowing our Bucharest hotel room was bugged, we had the following rehearsed conversation:

"What is the total of our new orders?"

"Four million dollars; that's why so many of our team members are here, to make sure they can deliver."

"That will cover three months of production."

"It's a pleasure to work with such obliging people."

We said everything we knew they wanted to hear.

The next morning, before going to the factory, we went to the U.S. Embassy and told the attaché that we had scheduled a meeting at the factory that morning and that if they didn't hear from us by 5:00 p.m., they should send help.

"You're not the only ones who have ever alerted us," they warned. "It's pretty difficult doing business here. We'll be waiting for you."

At the factory, we sat around a big conference table with the head of the factory and the department managers. Next to me was my controller. I had my attaché case on the table; his was open on the floor next to me, where it was out of sight.

"I want this $400,000 letter of credit issue settled before we proceed," I bellowed. Since we would presumably be agreeing upon final prices and placing additional new orders worth millions, they fully expected that I would return the document immediately following our negotiations.

When the official document was handed over, I opened my attaché case. With the lid raised and the Romanians on the opposite side of the table they couldn't see that I actually dropped it into my controller's case, which had been deliberately left open on the floor next to my leg. We continued playing our roles, negotiating final prices, and agreeing to meet the next day at noon to finalize our new orders. I went back to the hotel with my team, called the Embassy, and told the attaché that all was okay. Just in case, I took the document with me when we all went out to dinner. We congratulated ourselves on our acting ability. Upon returning to my room, I noticed that the locks on my attaché case had been damaged and it had obviously been broken into.

The next morning, I rushed to the airport with the document and flew to Paris on a 8:30 a.m. flight. I was feeling pretty smug. I left the rest of my team to show up for the noon meeting, where they would discuss the large order we were never going to confirm. If they asked about Mr. Goldsmith, they would be told that I had an emergency call and was headed to New York. I arrived safely in Paris and went to my hotel to rest, eat, and wait for the team (they had been booked on a flight out of Bucharest to Paris via Vienna and scheduled to meet up with me by 8:00 p.m. that evening).

They didn't show up.

I started pacing, watching the clock.

By 9:00 p.m., I called the hotel in Bucharest and was told that they had all checked out.

I waited some more. Then I called the Embassy, which was closed at that hour.

I was frantic; grim thoughts ran through my mind as I paced around my hotel room.

"How could I have done this to my own people? What happened when they went back to the factory that afternoon?"

I was afraid to call Ed.

"How will I tell their families?"

At two o'clock in the morning they all trudged in. There had been a major snowstorm in Vienna, delaying all air traffic and downing all the phone lines.

The next day we explored Paris, had a celebratory gourmet dinner, and left for New York – with the document in hand. Even Ernest Hemingway couldn't top this wild adventure.

Although we cancelled all of our orders in Romania, they never stopped calling and trying to get the credit paid off by offering us lower prices; we didn't bite. They eventually had to honor our claim, and we were done; it was too risky to continue.

In Yugoslavia, we were now limited to using locally-produced fabrics, we were constantly designing and redesigning lots of poplin and corduroy garments using their fabrics. We were still using the factories in Germany and Belgium and had also begun manufacturing more expensive leather jackets in Spain. But as usual, we were stymied as to how we would keep reinventing ourselves.

Chapter Sixteen

AND THEN, AS SO OFTEN happened, we got a call. This time it was a man named Vartan, a competitor of ours. He always seemed to know where we went to do our manufacturing. The factory representatives would ask us about him because he was attempting to do business in the same places we were.

"I'm having a lot of trouble," he admitted.

His difficulty was in securing adequate financing to grow his business. But he had recently been to Hong Kong and was impressed with the possibilities there. The major factories in Hong Kong made toys and plastic raincoats but no outerwear. Labor costs in the Far East were very low. Vartan proposed becoming our agent if we would stake him for two months. He would take some of our designs and see what he could come up with in Hong Kong.

We agreed.

Two months later, Vartan came back with wonderful samples that had great workmanship, all from Hong Kong factories, offering excellent price points. We would have to visit the factories. We sent our technical production manager on ahead to Hong Kong. Ed and I would meet up with them later in the week because we were going to Japan to meet with executives of the

C. Itoh Mills in Kyoto. We needed to know whether they could remake their poplin we had been using in Yugoslavia, in order to utilize it in our Hong Kong production.

The Itoh Mill offices were a shocker. I walked into a cavernous space that felt like Grand Central Station. In the center of the room was a pillar with clocks that told the time in the U.S., Europe, and Japan. A flashing screen showed the minute-to-minute value of the Japanese yen in the U.S.A. and Europe. When a price was quoted, it was marked with the date, time, and value of the yen, fixing the price at what the clock indicated at that exact moment.

From floor to ceiling in this tremendous space were small drawers with one or two yards of fabric wound around pieces of cardboard: thousands of swatches. The labels provided information as to content and how the fabric was made. I spent most of my time filling a shopping cart with swatches and sitting in a cubicle examining the fabric with an eye loop. We were there for several days.

The Itoh Mill definitely could make the poplin we needed, so we moved on to Hong Kong. The first thing I saw was a sampan on the river, just like in the posters. The factory we visited had only 10% of the machinery we would require, which they agreed to purchase. Our costs would include the duty on bringing garments into the U.S., the freight cost, and the fee for the broker clearing it at customs, along with local trucking costs. If the factory was late on delivery and we had to ship by air, the added cost amounted to a dollar on each jacket. But the numbers were acceptable and we decided to go ahead, hiring Vartan as our agent; he moved to Hong Kong with his family.

Now, what should we make?

Since there was no import quota into Hong Kong on wool, we gave some orders for wool garments. We also developed a line around the Japanese poplin fabric that we'd been using in Yugoslavia. In addition to our European trips, Ed and I now began traveling regularly to Japan, as well as to Hong Kong.

In Osaka, an Ito functionary would meet us at the airport and take care of all the details of our trip there – perfectly. He was very well educated and spoke excellent English. Unlike in Hong Kong, where we often spent our evenings at the factory. In Japan everything was carefully regulated. We were entertained lavishly (although in neither place did we ever see the wives of the men with whom we conducted business).

My whole experience with business in Japan was memorable. I loved the cleanliness and precision of everything, including the very clean and fashionable bullet trains. Inns and smaller hotels had gardens in which to stroll, with curved bridges over trickling streams and wind chimes gently ringing. Hotels offered spas with baths and massages provided by middle aged or elderly women who were blind. In your room they would put a wood block in the doorway to keep the door open a bit, so the block acted as a *Do Not Disturb* sign, as well as protecting both customer and masseuse. The traditions supported an ease about everything, the idea of health and good food, a life meant to be lived in the best way possible. It was the one place I could relax and be relieved of pressure, if even only for a short while.

After my first year, Dolores came on a visit to Japan with me. Accompanied by traditional songs, we were treated to dinner, where a geisha in a ceremonial robe and elaborate hairdo fed us at the table – literally, from the bowl to our mouths. We were told that the geishas understood English, so Dolores had a conversation with one and complimented her on her facility with the language.

"Where did you learn to speak such proper English?" Dolores asked.

"Oh, I'm from New Jersey."

"Go figure! And with a Jersey accent."

After much back-and-forth bowing, we left. As we waited for our cars, I saw the geishas exiting the restaurant wearing, what else . . . T-shirts, short hair, and jeans!

Chapter Seventeen

BACK IN THE STATES, the general merchandise manager of the Abraham & Straus stores wanted to talk to Ed and I, which made us somewhat nervous. Was he losing his enthusiasm for carrying the Europe Craft label? "No," he said, "but its 1968 and the market's changing. Young men are being strongly influenced by the "mod" look coming out of London's Carnaby Street. When they try on Europe Craft garments," he continued, "these customers feel like they are putting on their father's clothes. Create another label," he suggested, "with designs and a slimmer fit that will appeal to the young men's market."

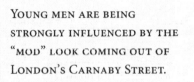

YOUNG MEN ARE BEING STRONGLY INFLUENCED BY THE "MOD" LOOK COMING OUT OF LONDON'S CARNABY STREET.

Designer names were moving into this market. Pierre Cardin, for example, was designing men's suits with extended shoulder pads, nipped waists, and vests. Some well-known American designers who had only done ladies clothes were moving into menswear. Jeans, still considered work clothes, were about to change. A whole new wholesale and retail market for young men's clothing was opening up with new retail stores and specialty chains across the country and boutiques springing up left and right.

We had to keep evolving. When we began importing from Europe in the early 60s, we had been the only American company doing so, but by now, the competition had expanded. One option for moving into this new young men's market was to license one of the new designers, but the idea didn't appeal to Ed or to me. We worried that a young designer could get caught up in the drug culture that was all around us or that he could license his name to a company or outlet that sold very down-market items. Our objective was to maintain the exclusivity and innovation we'd become known for. No, we'd have to do something on our own.

> OUR OBJECTIVE WAS TO MAINTAIN THE EXCLUSIVITY AND INNOVATION WE'D BECOME KNOWN FOR.

We met on a Friday to talk about the new line and come up with a name for it. We batted a few names around, but couldn't agree on anything. It had to be a name that suggested quality and sophistication, something unique, even exclusive. We'd think about it over the weekend and try again on Monday.

That weekend I went to my country club on Long Island, where I played tennis. I stood outside the club glancing, by habit, at two signs above the doors. One read, "No Spikes," directed at the golfers. The other sign, "Members Only."

MEMBERS ONLY . . .. That's it, I had the name!

Chapter Eighteen

BY MONDAY MORNING, I had designed a label for MEMBERS ONLY. Inspired by the Diner's Club card, which had an image of a key in the corner, for our MEMBERS ONLY label, I inserted a keyhole.

Our first MEMBERS ONLY line was small, like an exclusive collection line. We concentrated on what young people were looking for: fit. The garments had more shape, with vents in the center or on the sides, which was unheard of in outerwear. We also introduced a larger array of colors, influenced by active wear, and added stylistic touches like hoods, or hoods hidden in the collars, and new pocket ideas. We went for unusual print linings, unusual zipper placement, and metal grommets. There were no rules or restrictions; we were literally in uncharted waters.

We had moderate success with that first line until, on one of my twice-yearly shopping trips to Europe, one of those strange twists of fate sent us on a different track. I was traveling with Teo, our sketcher/designer, shopping department stores and specialty shops everywhere, always on the lookout for new ideas. We would sketch or photograph fashion details or entire garments, a practice not appreciated by those shops. Like another movie scene, this one a spy thriller, we would crouch behind clothing racks making quick drawings or snapping photos. In one store, the flash from my camera got us thrown out with only our pride wounded. We claimed that we were conducting research.

We shopped major cities for style, color, details – and in some cases, fabric. It took a lot of time to find places that created fabric designs that were difficult to reproduce at reasonable prices in the U.S. Sometimes we ordered sample yardage and brought it to our favored European mills to see if they could make a version at a more affordable price. Often, we actually purchased garments just for the fabric or the color, showing them to our suppliers so they could duplicate them perfectly.

We took in the apparel and fabric shows in London, Paris, and Dusseldorf. Marco, our Italian agent, had business cards made with our names from a store he had owned in New York. That allowed us entry to many of these shows, passing as retailers rather than competitors. Even with our proper ID, many booths denied us a peek at their line. Many firms did display in open areas where we could hide and sketch. In a lot of cases, we were able to obtain catalogues and the latest European trade magazines.

Fate opened the door in Munich at a men's store where I was a good customer and friendly with the owner.

"How come," I asked him on one of these visits, "you don't carry outerwear?"

"Let me show you something," he said.

He brought out a jacket that was selling for $150 and told me he couldn't keep them in stock. It had a Nehru-style collar instead of a typical fold-down collar.

"Do you mind if I sketch it?" I asked.

He didn't mind; I was a customer, not a competitor. Back in the hotel, Teo and I reviewed the sketch to determine why it was such a good seller. There were several distinctive features: it was the only style with epaulettes that we had ever seen; it had a knitted bottom that, in the U.S., was associated with baseball jackets; the pockets were slash pockets, three-quarter inch wide, trimmed in the same knit.

Members Only sales brochure.

"Let's fool around with it," I said. We kept the epaulettes and the Nehru collar concept and the idea of knit over fabric on the pockets. We added stitching treatments around the shoulders and a strap around the collar, to close it more tightly. Then we ordered samples in several versions of the style.

In New York, we met with an Itoh Mill executive who had traveled from Japan on a business trip. He said that he happened to have a fabric I might be interested in and showed me a shiny fabric that one of the women in our office thought was like tablecloth fabric: chintz. To me, it felt like poplin but with a different finish. Also, the fabric was available in forty different colors. Today you would say some of the colors were passé, but at the time they were shocking.

And, as luck would have it, the Itoh Mill was offering them at a great price.

The men's outerwear industry had, for decades, been locked in a boring monotonous cycle of producing in four colors only and limited variations. Why not use this fabric on that jacket we were fooling around with, and in twenty colors, not just four! Let's see what happens. Let's make an impression.

We ordered some fabric and had it shipped to our European manufacturers.

The samples looked great. We started telling our customers that they could ride this huge explosion in menswear with us and that we were offering something nobody else had. We suggested showing twenty colors. If a consumer wanted to buy a jacket in a color the store didn't offer, they should just say they ran out of that color and suggest another. We urged them to arrange the jackets on what is called a waterfall hangar so that the entire front of the jacket is what the customer sees. Normally jackets would be hung on a pipe rack, with only the side of the sleeve showing. This way, what you would see in a store was an array of unbelievable colors spread out like a deck of cards.

The jackets were not the instant success we hoped for. People were apprehensive about the unusual styling and variety of colors. We hemmed and hawed. What to do?

Our salesman in California wasn't ready to give up; he thought the garments would sell and he wanted to give it a try with the men's shop in the Beverly Hills Hotel. Our factor didn't agree and, based on the shop's credit, turned him down on the financing. Arthur, our Sales Manager, was so convinced that southern California was a market for these clothes in these colors that he convinced us to take the risk and extend credit on our own. Whatever didn't sell we would take back.

Prior to the days of fax machines and overnight mail delivery, people who did business between the two coasts did a lot of traveling back and forth, especially attorneys who worked in the movie business. A lot of those movie industry meetings took place in the Polo Lounge in the Beverly Hills Hotel, where there was a dress code: jackets were required. Because of its tailored styling and classy look, the only zippered jacket they allowed in was a MEMBERS ONLY jacket. The shop began selling our jackets in the hundreds.

Suddenly, attorneys would come back to New York from California in what was becoming a uniform: a MEMBERS ONLY jacket; an IZOD golf shirt; and LEVI'S brand jeans. New York attorneys were looking more like Hollywood executives. And when these guys wore their "uniforms" on weekends, other men wanted to know how to get them. Soon it was a uniform for anyone

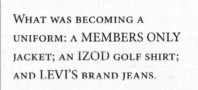

WHAT WAS BECOMING A UNIFORM: A MEMBERS ONLY JACKET; AN IZOD GOLF SHIRT; AND LEVI'S BRAND JEANS.

who had a prestigious job and could wear casual wear to work as well as at home – and for those just wanting to make that impression.

The fabric of the jackets was soft; it didn't yell at you. Some of the colors were unique – pale blue, rust, camel, wine, black, forest green, white, robin egg blue, teal, and pewter – were unique. The customary method of presenting colors to national accounts had been to show one-by-two-inch swatches, cut out with pinking scissors, mounted on cards that looked like Band Aid brand adhesives. The colors went from dark to light, there were three categories: basic, standard, and high fashion. Our *schtick* was to present the swatches in circles instead of the usual squares.

"Look," we'd tell the buyers, "we've conducted extensive research; your eyeball is round, but you've been accustomed to looking at a square sample where you can't distinguish the true color. Our new exclusive shape will reflect the true color."

We hoped they would talk about the swatches to everybody in the business, helping to spread our name. And they did.

In the seventies, the MAGIC men's trade show moved to Las Vegas because Los Angeles didn't have sufficient space to fill the growing demand. Las Vegas was ideal for the trade. It provided the retailer the opportunity to meet with current and new suppliers and have hotel accommodations only minutes away, and there were all kinds of options for dinner and entertainment in the evenings.

After dinner one evening, my partner Ed suggested that we try some gambling. His favorite game was "craps." Three of us pooled about $300; Ed bet on his own, telling us, "Now, fellas, just follow how I bet and make sure to do the same."

The game went so fast that we missed several betting opportunities. Ed was winning a lot. The tray in front of him was filled with chips. Somehow, even betting on what Ed bet on, we lost all of ours. We said goodnight and started walking away. Near a roulette table, we heard cheering. We decided to chip in $25 each and try to grab on to some of the luck that was being generated there. Within fifteen minutes we lost all the money.

As we started toward the exit, Ed caught up to us.

"Hey guys, I just cashed in; I'll go with you. But wait a minute; I have an extra $100 chip; let me put it on a number.

The wheel spun and the ball fell into the slot that Ed had bet. They paid him $3,500, and in envy we jumped on him and pounded his back as he crawled on the floor. We would never gamble with him again. We couldn't figure out what we did wrong. Cool Eddie, always a winner.

Chapter Nineteen

MEMBERS ONLY DID MORE than alright in its first years, with an array of twenty colors and a fabric nobody else would copy until at least two years after we had introduced it. By 1980, Europe Craft's wholesale billings had risen from $20 to $40 to $60 to $80 million and still climbing. But since I was always trying to keep evolving, I wanted to do more. MEMBERS ONLY was already the first men's clothing company to offer gifts with purchases sun glasses, watches, a zippered tote bag, all with the MEMBERS ONLY logo – an idea that I'd seen in the cosmetics business. And we put the MEMBERS ONLY label above the breast pocket, so you'd always know from a distance that it was a MEMBERS ONLY jacket. What we really needed, though, to take us to the next level, was the kind of thing I'd done at Chief Apparel: celebrity endorsers.

> WE PUT THE MEMBERS ONLY LABEL ABOVE THE BREAST POCKET, SO YOU'D ALWAYS KNOW FROM A DISTANCE THAT IT WAS A MEMBERS ONLY JACKET.

If anything, the public's craving for information (or gossip) about stars was greater than ever. People were mesmerized by stars, and television executives were only beginning to cater to that fascination by putting a show called *Entertainment Tonight* on the air to cater to an inexhaustible appetite for news about personalities.

Who should we get?

The idea came from my daughter, Michelle.

"Dad," she said on the phone one day, "I know you're looking for endorsements and I think you should get Anthony Geary."

"Who?"

I had no idea who he was.

Michelle explained that Geary was the star of an afternoon soap on television called General Hospital. He was a hunk, a heartthrob, his generation's version of George Clooney. In fact, videotape recorders were selling through the roof because women who worked or went to school were so nuts about Geary they would tape the show to watch it at night.

I called the key managers of our different departments together. When I mentioned Anthony Geary, everyone said, "Who's that?" We weren't exactly into daytime soap operas.

I suggested they try calling home and mentioning to their wives or daughters that they were in a room with Anthony Geary from General Hospital and give me the results. As one after another of the men in the room dialed the phone, I sat back and listened to the screaming on the other end in response.

Then I called another meeting, this one with our key customers, and they too said, "Who?" So we repeated the drill: call home, see how they react; more screaming.

I called my agency, only to be told, "You'll never get him. He's the hottest guy in showbiz."

From a clipping agency, I got copies of all his press notices and they really were terrific. I had to do it!

My advertising agency called his agent. Surprise! Anthony Geary agreed to make a commercial for us, and his fee was reasonable! I flew to California for the filming of the commercial.

With an air of confidence and self-assurance, Anthony looks into the camera and says:

Members Only National print ad featuring Anthony Geary, star of General Hospital.

> *"I never thought I'd do a commercial, but here I am doing it for MEMBERS ONLY."*

Then an attractive brunette walks in, also wearing a MEMBERS ONLY jacket. He puts his arm around her as they walk off. Then, pointing at the label, he says:

> *"It's not MEMBERS ONLY unless it says MEMBERS ONLY on the pocket."*

We followed the TV ad with color print ads in the Sunday *The New York Times* magazine section and various other publications.

The fashion experience that came out of the Hollywood motion picture industry was almost a uniform: LEVI'S jeans with the brand name on a wide leather belt loop, as though a cattle branding iron had been used; an IZOD knitted golf shirt with an alligator embroidered on the left chest, and an MEMBERS ONLY jacket with a narrow MEMBERS ONLY label sewn on the left chest pocket. All presented visual evidence of the sophistication and success of the man wearing them.

Our chintz fabric jacket appeared on many of the leading performers in television sit-coms and movies. We never paid for this.

Since thousands were emulating Hollywood, we decided to broaden the scope by using sport stars, one star athlete for each sport – baseball, golf, basketball, tennis and football. Endorsements by athletes were not common, and the cost to sign them up was nominal; this would give us more popularity with men across America. The public thought that if the product wasn't good, the stars wouldn't endorse it.

The endorsements gave us even more publicity. American men wanted to wear the MEMBERS ONLY jacket because it gave them prestige. The demand created a dilemma for department stores. Most of them sold the jacket in the Young Men's department, which was about 20% of the size of

ANTHONY GEARY FOR

MEMBERS ONLY®
(Lightweight Jacket)

COMMERCIAL TITLE: LAP DISSOLVES
LENGTH: 25 + 5 FOR STORE NAME
NUMBER: XYWQ 1213

ANTHONY GEARY: Hi, never thought I'd want to do a commercial. But here I am - for Members Only jackets.

Why? 'Cause when I put one on... something happens!

The colors are great!

And all those different styles, absolutely terrific.

They go anywhere... anytime.

But it's only authentic if it says Members Only right here.

I really believe in them. So should you.

Members Only - when you put one on something happens.

MEMBERS ONLY
When you put it on...something happens.

Available at
STORE NAME
and other fine stores.

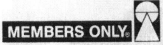

MEMBERS ONLY®

Europe Craft Imports, Inc., 390 Fifth Avenue, NY, NY 10018 (212) 594-4712

Anthony Geary commercial storyboard.

a typical men's department. The demand caused them to move the jackets into the Men's department, which allowed them to carry more jackets and a larger selection of colors. Until now, colors in men's outerwear had been limited to three, but now the jackets offered in department stores were being offered in at least seven colors.

We were the only men's company in America using a shiny chintz fabric offered in twenty colors. MEMBERS ONLY was now readily accepted by customers who wanted not only new fabrics and more variety in colors, but also a less boxy fit. We came to a decision that there was no need to continue the Europe Craft label.

Our competition picked up on new styling and new fabrics and colors, but they never came up with a successor to the MEMBERS ONLY silhouette. Eventually, many of them copied the style, fabric, and colors, offering them at a lower price. The mid- and lower-price chains offered them to their customers as well, but as Tony Geary and the sports stars would say in the commercials, "It's not MEMBERS ONLY if it doesn't have the label above the pocket." Sales of the copies were disappointing and our sales increased even more.

When the stores reordered, they didn't ask just for the usual mid to large sizes, but began requesting the smallest sizes. Ladies and girls were buying the MEMBERS ONLY jacket for themselves, shopping in the men's departments. So we added the style to our ladies line, in true ladies sizes, adding colors like baby pink, lilac, sea foam green, periwinkle blue, and even watermelon.

> LADIES AND GIRLS WERE BUYING THE MEMBERS ONLY JACKET FOR THEMSELVES, SHOPPING IN THE MEN'S DEPARTMENTS.

The MEMBERS ONLY jacket style was originally a lightweight spring jacket with a rayon lining. For Fall/Winter we added quilted linings for warmth and offered the style in other fabrics, including smooth and sueded leathers. Yet again, we needed more production. Both the fabric and the sewing had to be first class, no skimping. There was a quota on jackets allowed to be brought in to the U.S., and we soon filled our Hong Kong allotment. China would be next. As we had done in all the eastern countries, we sent our manufacturing, technical, and quality control people (along with the owners of our Hong Kong factory, because we needed their expertise in dealing with mainland China). It took time, patience, and perseverance, but in a remarkably short amount of time, we succeeded.

Another very innovative thing we were doing involved our sales meetings and the fashion shows that evolved from them. Most apparel companies conducted sales meetings in their showrooms or in hotel meeting rooms. At Europe Craft, we had always held ours, (which lasted four to five days) away from the business environment, where we could stay over, eat together, and hold company-wide athletic competitions and recreational activities. Everyone in sales, management, design, and even office personnel got to know one another, creating a camaraderie that shined throughout our company. During the sales meeting, we used professional models to showcase our new line, and the narration for these shows was conducted by members of the design team, as well as by Ed and me.

Now, with MEMBERS ONLY as a full line, we started creating shows using Broadway dancers and singers as models and the narration was provided by a professional MC. The performers wore the jackets, and each musical scene in the show related to what was being shown on the stage. For these events, we needed space. We went several times to the Concord Hotel in the Catskill Mountains, which had a large theatre with sound equipment, or to IBM's sales retreat in Scarsdale, New York, or to an Arizona hotel with its own western town that looked like a movie set.

When we started inviting key customers along with our company employees, we were mobbed. Next, we produced a broader version, with our own lyrics to well-known popular songs from Broadway musicals. Then a musical revue, open to the trade and to invited guests, which we performed in the theater at the Fashion Institute of Technology and in several of the new disco clubs opening in New York. The allure of these clubs attracted many more than we could accommodate. The trade publicity was tremendous. Twice a year for the trade, it became a bigger, more ambitious show. In

*The Members Only Sales and
Marketing Team.*

You are cordially invited to attend the
MEMBERS ONLY
Fall '82 Musical Fashion Revue

Monday, February 15, 1982 at 6:30 p.m.
Doral Country Club, Miami.
Cocktails and Hors D'Oeuvres follow.

R.S.V.P. Karen at 305-261-1339

Europe Craft Imports, 390 Fifth Avenue, New York, New York

*The Members Only
fashion show invitation.*

February 1982, we put on our first out-of-town fashion show at the Doral Country Club in Miami; the elegant invitations showed a chorus line of men in tuxedos and top hats.

These productions reignited my taste for show business and the theatrical talents I had exercised years before, when I worked in the theatre. My challenge had always been to inspire the sales force, my partners, and the company employees. "It's theater!" I would tell them. "The garments are the actors. The buyers are the audience. The showroom is the theater . . . It's show time!"

And, of course, every show had to be better than the one before. From Chief Apparel to Europe Craft to MEMBERS ONLY, I was always driven by the need for the company to succeed, to constantly impress the retailers who bought from us and the ultimate consumer, as well as motivating the people in our company to be proud of what we did. My objective was to constantly do better – to top myself, thereby enhancing the reputation and sales of the company. Some famous companies prided themselves on being consistent: the buyers always knew they were getting the same product. Not me. I wanted every show, every garment, and every ad campaign to be better than the one before. No one ever said our company was boring.

During one particular MAGIC apparel trade show in Los Angeles, we put on a fashion show/ cocktail party in the Beverly Hills hotel. We sent invitations well in advance but didn't announce our surprise MC. There was such a huge turnout (and many buyers brought their wives along), that we ran out of seats and had to accommodate several rows of standees.

When I introduced the special MC for the evening to the standing room only crowd, there was pandemonium.

Anthony Geary! He came out and actually did the first song, and he had a great time. I don't think he had any idea how hot a star he was or how much publicity he could draw. In addition to the trade press, every L.A. TV station and newspaper covered his appearance. We were off to the races. When he made personal appearances on behalf of MEMBERS ONLY in department stores, police had to set up barricades to keep the crowds in line. Often, more than 5,000 people would show up, just to see him.

So America's heartthrob launched MEMBERS ONLY into television advertising. The jacket was selling in more styles and colors than ever; we were really taking off. Although we'd always had good coverage in the trade press, we were now getting more and more public acclaim. Clara Hancox, editor of the *Daily News Record*, which catered to the menswear industry, was one of our biggest fans. When we started showing color-coordinated sweaters and jackets at the spring 1982 NAMSB show at the New York Coliseum, she sung our praises, stating:

> *"Every color in that rich and vividly colored knit line was related to the company's enormous color palette for outerwear."*

She named MEMBERS ONLY as being a leader in the eye-opening, positioning, and niche-filling going on in the market among the most fashion-aware folks.

We were getting even bigger play in the general interest press. That summer, the *Los Angeles Herald Examiner* did a huge feature story on "The Biggest Little Jacket Around L.A."

THE BIGGEST LITTLE JACKET
AROUND L.A.

"Among the thousands who are sporting this high-fashion outerwear," they reported, "were Johnny Carson, Donald Sutherland, Frank Sinatra, Robert Wagner, Tony Geary, and Angie Dickinson." (We had just introduced a women's collection.) The paper noted Tony Geary's ad campaign as contributing to the:

> *"Sex appeal of the colorful outerwear, whether it's purchasing a jacket for herself or the man who is buying his own, she has a say,"*

... the *Examiner* concluded.

And this underscored our idea that women were an important part of our market. Couples were coming in to buy a jacket for the man, and they were walking out with one for the woman also. Some male customers bought a jacket and came back shortly afterward to pick up the same style in other colors. The regional supervisor for one chain said that he hadn't seen anything to match the popularity of MEMBERS ONLY in the 15 years he'd been in retailing, and an L.A. buyer called us:

> *"The best thing since sliced bread."*

What could we do to top that? Our theatrical presentations became even more ambitious. We not only introduced the new season's line but began writing parodies of well-known songs to tell our latest fashion and color story.

The spring 1983 show started with a takeoff on *I've Got Rhythm*:
"We got color,"
"We got fashion,"
"We got status,"
"Who could ask for anything more?"

Although our shows were professionally scripted and carefully rehearsed, sometimes chance presented us an exciting addition. We were on a break during rehearsal for a New York City show. Standing on the sidewalk outside the building, I noticed six kids performing in the street. They were break dancing, a really new and amazing urban craze at the time, very acrobatic and agile. It was about noon and our show was that evening. I went up and asked the kids if they'd like to be in the show.

"Yeah, sure, man, sure."

I wasn't so sure but gave each kid $10. They came inside to rehearse with the rest of the cast and the musicians, and then we locked them into the rehearsal room until show time. I paid them each an additional $10 and we gave each one a MEMBERS ONLY jacket because their impromptu performance helped put the show over the top.

Now what could we do? We needed to broaden the demographic that Geary's TV ads were reaching. We opened our musical trade show featuring the 1983 line of fall outerwear to the tune of *Winter Wonderland*. Our all-white wool jacket collection appeared while the singers performed *IT'S ALL WHITE WITH ME* to the tune of *It's Alright With Me*. We presented our leather garments with a series of parodies of songs from *West Side Story*, including a favorite of mine, *Maria*:

> *"Korea,*
>
> *They're cut and they're sewn in Korea. A land of pure delight, that's where they do it right, you see . . . Korea."*

After a year of using the sports stars, we knew that we needed to have new celebrities. When we introduced our new spokesman, it was not one spokesman, but three. At the time, Country Western Music was very popular and growing. We discussed which star to contact. It was decided that in order to show more styles and colors in our advertising, we should concentrate on getting a Country Western group. The Gatlin Brothers were three rising stars, clean cut and young. We met with them and their agent and showed them mock ups of the ads that we planned to create. We also brought along the actual jackets that they would be wearing in the ads. No problem, they loved what we were creating. They loved the jackets so much that we had to give them to them. The Gatlin Brothers were very enthusiastic. In fact, they suggested that for their first ad, we should photograph them in Memphis, the home of Country Music, and we did.

At our next fashion show, the MC said:

> **"With their ranches, private airplanes, sports cars, and active athletic style, and their performances on records and television, they represent a way of life every American aspires to, riding the crest of the wave."**

The Gatlin Brothers ad.

The Gatlin Brothers for...

MEMBERS ONLY.

TITLE: NEW ORLEANS FALL '84
LENGTH: 30 SECOND
NO: QEAE-9013

Hey, hey have you tried it,

Put it on you're...

gonna like what you see,

Members Only,

When you join the club...

you're in great company.

Members Only,

When only the best will do...

Members Only, Members Only

When you put it on...

something happens to you.

© Europe Craft Imports, Inc., 390 Fifth Avenue, N.Y., NY 10018 (212) 594-4712

MEMBERS ONLY.

We played the video tape of our new TV commercial – the Gatlin Brothers, dressed in different colored MEMBERS ONLY jackets, singing the song they had written especially for us, which gave us a tag line we used for years to come:

> *"MEMBERS ONLY, MEMBERS ONLY, when you put it on,*
> *something happens to you."*

For the next two years, the Gatlin Brothers were our spokesmen. MEMBERS ONLY underwrote a cross-country tour for the group and we used them in both print and television ads. Ed supervised the shoot of our TV commercial in New Orleans, where the Gatlins created a street parade and ended up cruising away on a Mississippi steamboat. When we filmed that commercial, more than 1,000 people lined the streets, all the way down to the pier; it reminded me of the crowd's enthusiasm for Anthony Geary.

The Gatlins sang the National Anthem at the U.S. Tennis championships; at Knicks basketball games, which were televised from Madison Square Garden; and at Yankees and Mets baseball games – always wearing their MEMBERS ONLY jackets.

The Gatlin Brothers were there in early 1984 when we took on our first major athletic endeavor: we were a major sponsor of the Volvo Master's Tennis Tournament at Madison Square Garden, which we kicked off with a cocktail party at the Garden's Penn Plaza Club. That sponsorship proved so successful that a few months later, in April, MEMBERS ONLY presented the "Paine Webber Tennis Classic." The finals were to be aired nationally on NBC, featuring the top men's players at the time – Borg, Connors, McEnroe, Geralitis – on the grounds of Boca West, a gated community in Boca Raton, Florida. A giant banner hung over the gatehouse, visible from as far away as I-95:

PAINE WEBBER CLASSIC - MEMBERS ONLY.

We couldn't understand why, with all the top names in tennis on the schedule, initial sales for the event were so embarrassingly low. Then we

Members Only presents the Paine Webber Classic.

learned that people were driving up to the gatehouse to purchase tickets, only to turn away when they saw the sign, MEMBERS ONLY, understanding that to mean that entry was restricted to residents of Boca West. We quickly changed the banner to read: presented by MEMBERS ONLY. It looked like our label. We were sold out.

At the time, my mother lived in nearby Miami Beach. She was still vibrant, still looked great, and still danced. Her husband had died and she now lived alone. When I called to ask if she would like to come to the tournament, she said she didn't like tennis, but she would watch it on TV.

Well, I said, she might get a chance to see me giving out one of the winning checks. NBC was broadcasting the whole tournament, and I was scheduled to present the check to the runner-up. But, according to the NBC schedule, if the final match ended close to the half hour, only the presentation to the winner by a Paine Webber executive would actually be televised.

My brother Billy also lived in Miami Beach. After graduating from the University of Miami, he opened a retail men's store in Manhattan, but he never liked living in New York City and eventually we came up with a plan for him to open MEMBERS ONLY stores in Florida. But it was a seasonal business; no one in Florida needed a jacket from April till October. Billy, for whom horseracing had always been a hobby, decided to become involved in it full time.

He and I would take mom to dinner that night.

I was lucky. The final match ended with Jimmy Connors as runner-up and it was only a quarter after the hour. There was plenty of TV time for me to present the trophy and a blown-up check from MEMBERS ONLY. I was introduced on center court and picked up the microphone, thanking the people of Boca Raton and looking around for Connors. He was not on the court.

The Stage Manager gave me the signal to stretch, so I kept talking. I thought they must have liked the way I talked, so I kept talking until Connors came running out. He'd needed a bathroom break! He'd taken so long that there was no time, after I presented the check, for the Paine

Members Only and the
Paine Webber Classic with
Jimmy Connors.

Webber president to award the winner's trophy. NBC went to station break. We were off the air.

"Mom, did you see me on TV?"

I'd been on for almost ten minutes. That's a long time on TV.

"I'm not talking to you ever again," she said.

"What? What did I do wrong?"

"You know."

"Mom, I don't know what you're talking about."

"Yes, you do; you know very well what I'm mad about."

And then she told me, "I waved at you and you didn't wave back at me."

When I protested, she said, "Listen, young man. In this age of electronics, you're gonna tell me I can see you, but you can't see me!"

And she hung up on me.

Something was not right. This was an intelligent, articulate woman who did crossword puzzles and read at least one book a day. I stood with the phone in my hand, and when my brother asked me what was wrong, what had happened, I said, "Call mom and ask her why she will never talk to me again." He went to a phone booth, made a call, and came back, saying, "We're in big trouble."

We go to pick her up for dinner. My mother opens the door and she's all dressed up in a cocktail dress, her hair and makeup immaculate.

"I'm so glad to see you again," she says, "you're a bit early for my cocktail party. Walter Cronkite and Dan Rather will be here shortly, and I'm expecting Ed Murrow."

Inside, there's nobody, and nothing is set up. We take her to dinner, perplexed.

My brother's girlfriend later suggests that my mother sounds like her mother, who was diagnosed with Alz . . . something or other, and gives us the name of the doctor who's treating her. We should call for more information. Perhaps he can check her out.

The next day, back in New York, I call the doctor, telling him exactly what we experienced with my mother and how anxious we are about the Alz . . . something. He says that it sounds like I'm referring to Alzheimer's, a recently diagnosed disease.

"I can't diagnose anyone by talking on the phone, Mr. Goldsmith; I need to see her and to have her tested."

We confirmed an appointment. "What's Mrs. Goldsmith's first name?"

I say that her married name is Ethel Sandberg. Dead silence on the line.

"Doctor, are you there?"

"There's nothing wrong with your mother," he finally says.

"How do you know? You just said that you can't diagnose a patient by talking on the phone."

"I've been dating your mother, but she keeps me out until one in the morning. I can't keep up with her, and I can't stay out dancing 'til one in the morning, much longer."

Not knowing what to do, I called my brother and we tried to arrange Meals on Wheels for her, but she wouldn't take them. My Aunt Dotty began visiting every day. Billy drove her to interviews at two assisted living facilities, but they said she needed more care than they could give her. A few weeks later, as Thanksgiving approached, we found somebody to stay with her full time, and I booked flights for Dolores and the girls to come with me to visit my mother. Billy made arrangements for all of us to meet for Thanksgiving dinner at a hotel restaurant.

My mother, who was eighty, was already seated at a large table in the restaurant when we arrived.

"Oh, what a very nice looking young man you are," she said. And, turning to Dolores, "Who's this charming young lady?"

A week later, she passed away in her apartment. I found a note dated years before, in which she asked to be buried in a cemetery near the Miami Airport because, she had written, "I always loved to travel and I'll be near the planes."

Picture wih Joe (mom's hus-
band) and Billy (my brother),
taken 1962.

Chapter Twenty

IN AUGUST 1984, we really topped ourselves by putting on a MEMBERS ONLY tennis tournament in Monte Carlo. Major movie, TV, and sport stars were invited to play. Prince Rainier's Grace Kelly Charity would be the beneficiary, and the Prince himself would participate. The tournament would be taped and shown in the States on cable TV in the fall. Our contract guaranteed that participants would only wear MEMBERS ONLY garments and that we had the right to use the players in our advertising, as long as we mentioned Monte Carlo and the tournament.

Among the stars who signed on were John Forsyth, Dina Merrill, Charlton Heston, Robert Duvall, Erik Estrada, Bernie Kopell, and Don Budge. For the three day affair, we were booked into the luxurious Hotel De Paris, which thrilled our wives and children. My daughter Gail suggested that we make a baby size MEMBERS ONLY jacket for Princess Stephanie's new daughter, Pauline, personalized with her name embroidered in gold. On the first day, Prince Albert arrived with the news that his father could not participate because of a cold. Instead, *he* would participate.

The players drew lots and, to my amazement and concern, I was picked to play against Prince Albert. He was pretty good, but my serves were better than his. At one of the breaks, the promoter came over:

*At the Monte Carlo Tennis
Championship.*

"Are you crazy? It'll be embarrassing to all of us, if you win."

In the interest of maintaining diplomatic relations, I made sure that I lost. The Prince was very happy; I was the runner up, but I coulda been a contender!

In the evening, dressed in formal clothing, we were escorted to the Palace. I carried the baby's jacket in a box, but it was taken from me by security, with the assurance that it would be returned during cocktails in order for me to make a formal presentation. Cocktails were served on the palace roof. The Prince took the jacket out and smiled; then he shook my hand and said, "Thank you." The Prince was no *schnorrer*; he never asked for a MEMBERS ONLY jacket for himself!

At one point during the evening, he put his arm around my shoulder, walked me to the edge of the roof, pointed down at the harbor, and said, "See that boat? That's the only love I have."

Spotting a majestic yacht moored near shore, I remarked at how large it was.

"No, not that motor yacht," he interrupted, "the little sail boat to the right." Pointing to a two-seater skiff with a single mast, he quietly added, "I go out early. No one recognizes me, and I spend most of the day at sea."

He looked terribly sad.

At the Monte Carlo Tennis Championship.
Gail, Michelle, Ileen, Dolores, me.

Chapter Twenty-one

ALTHOUGH BUILDING AND RUNNING a large commercial enterprise consumed a great deal of time, it was my family life that provided the richest and most memorable moments. Looking back to the late 50s and early 60s, we, along with a few other families, always set aside time for a week-long winter holiday in the Catskill Mountains at the Concord, Grossinger's, or Laurels in the Pines hotels. My two daughters, Gail and Michelle, loved sleigh riding, ice skating on the lake, or swimming in the indoor pool. Ileen wasn't born yet.

In the evening, after the kids went to bed, supervised by a sitter, we would go dancing and see a show at the casino.

One year, when my daughters got older, we all decided one afternoon to go to the Concord's ski area, where instructions were offered and skis were complimentary. It was very popular, too much so, because the lower part of the ski trail was packed with beginners and instructors helping both the kids and the beginning adults. Since I'd had the luxury of spending weekends in ski areas outside of Munich during my many business trips to Germany, and I'd had lessons in mountain skiing, I considered myself an accomplished skier.

At the Concord, the only way to the top was by a rope tow . . . then, another wait for our turn among about 50 others before skiing down the hill. Near the

Laurels HOTEL and COUNTRY CLUB

*Enjoying time with my
daughters in the 60s.*

bottom, we had to stop above the beginner's section and "ski walk" down, about 50 yards to the bottom. We had to wait in line again before being pulled up. One time, I was with our friend Sid at the top of the trail, waiting our turn to head down. To my left, I saw a heavily snow-covered trail. There was a rope blocking the entrance and a sign that read, "DO NOT ENTER."

Sid said, "It's so crowded over there; let's just go here – it's empty. We'll have it all to ourselves." We skied over to the crest of the slope. No one was there. About halfway down, there was a hump blocking the view of the bottom of the trail. Since I was much more advanced, I said, "I'll go first, and if there's any problem, I'll yell back to you when I get to the bottom. Wait till you hear my okay."

I got into a crouch and pushed off. The trail was about ten yards wide and totally clear of trees. All I needed to do was go straight. There was nothing to avoid; this was a cinch.

Gaining speed, I approached what appeared from the distance to be a hump and rocketed up and over it. From the air, I could see the bottom a long way off. I was on the ski jump course; no wonder it was closed. I crouched and grabbed onto my calves. Luckily, I hit bottom while still in the crouch, with my backside hitting at the same time. I got up and yelled to Sid, cautioning him not to go.

It was too late. He tumbled when he hit the ground and rolled about thirty yards.

Neither of us was hurt, having been saved by ten inches of snow accumulation. We swore that we wouldn't tell our wives. If we did, we would never hear the end of it: "You coulda been killed!"

Three years after I had purchased Europe Craft, we moved to Roslyn, Long Island. Dolores was pregnant with Ileen, and we would need more room. Our new house was much larger than our first in Uniondale, and the Roslyn school system had been a major factor in our decision to move. Graduating from high school with decent grades would easily get you accepted to many of the top colleges. There were several country clubs close by, and we joined the Old Westbury Country Club, where many of our new neighbors already belonged. It had a 27-hole golf course, plenty of Har-Tru-surfaced tennis courts, and three pools, including a wading pool for infants. It gave us an opportunity to experience a new lifestyle. Originally a tennis player, after a while I took up golf, too. Our lives were full, with all the social activities, sports, and new friends.

The rear of our house had a family room, with sliding glass doors leading to our outside patio. Behind our property was a 50-acre estate, owned by the Whitneys. In the morning, we would scatter small pieces of bread on the patio and then go inside. About ten minutes later, we watched as a few squirrels would come and take the bread. One in particular would wait there on the patio, and if we hadn't yet put out some bread, it would bang on the glass door. Out came the bread. We named it Chippy.

This went on for two years. In our third year, although Chippy showed up during the spring, she had not shown up during the previous summer. We thought an animal must have killed it. The next year, in the early spring, we were having breakfast in the kitchen and heard a continuous knocking from the family room. We went to investigate. The sliding glass door was closed, and there was Chippy, on her hind legs, knocking; alongside her were two baby squirrels. We got some bread, broke it into small pieces, and watched as they ate it all.

When they were finished, they walked to the far end of our patio, stopped, turned around to look at us for a moment, and then disappeared into the wooded property across the road. They never returned. After that, spring and summer were never the same!

Back in the 1960s, when I was taking those long trips to Europe in the spring, I'd come back glad to be home with Dolores and my daughters. But the truth is that if I came home on a Friday, I'd be playing tennis at the club on Saturday morning and golf on Sunday morning. When Monday came, I'd drive to the Long Island Railroad station, leave my car, and take the train into Manhattan. After a day at the office, I'd drive home to Roslyn at around 7:00 p.m. and have dinner by myself, the family having eaten long before then. Finally, Dolores was fed up.

"This is not going well," she said. "The only time this family can be together is in the summer, and that's not good enough; you're going to have to change."

What Dolores said wasn't quite true. After our times in the Catskills, Christmas time had become an important season for our family to be together. We'd started to go to the magnificent Hollywood Beach Hotel in Florida, situated on the beach with extensive gardens and walking paths. The hotel had a fabulous reputation for catering to young children, including a special building and beach area only for them. My kids had breakfast and dinner with us in the main dining room and lunches at the day camp. For the adults, there was golf, deep water fishing and lounging at the hotel's pool. In the evening, there was entertainment. It felt like a hotel in the Catskill Mountains, only with an ocean. We met many of the same guests year after year, and we remained friends with some of them for more than 50 years.

During the winter my grandpa, Abe, would close up his bungalow colony in the Catskill's and move to his small house in Florida. Even at 85 years of age he was healthy and bright and always with a sense of humor. Knowing how he loved fishing, I insisted that he go out with us on a fishing boat that I would hire for the day. His only experience on a boat was on his row boat on Swan Lake in the Catskills. I picked him up and on the way to the Marina, I explained to him that the boat will constantly be moving and the fishing line is made of steel because of the large sizes of fish that we expected to catch. I had him sit in the "Fighting Chair" and the captain explained how to use the reel and what to expect if we hooked a fish. My Zayde was smiling as we pulled out from the Marina. I explained that we won't be using bait or worms, that he was used to. We only use "LURES." The fish we expected to catch would be weigh anywhere from 20 to 50 pounds.

The Mate applied the lures and dropped the lines into the sea. Zayde started to laugh. "What are you laughing about?". He smiled and said," We're never going to catch a fish." Why do you say that Zayde? "Because, those shiny things you put on the line look like mirrors." Yes, I said, that's what's going to attract the fish and since there's a hook on each lure, we're sure to

A picture of me and my grandfather, Abe "Zadea."

catch plenty of them." Listen, I know you're a college graduate, but you don't understand, when the fish gets near this shiny thing that looks like a mirror, he'll see his ugly face, get scared and swim away."

We were out for four hours and never caught a fish. "See, I told you". Zayde was smiling all the way home. The captain apologized and said that this was the first time that he never caught anything.

As soon as we docked, Zayde said that we'll get in trouble with grandma if we don't come home with a fish. She'll think we did something else and didn't want her to go with us. He solved the problem. On the way back to his house, we stopped at a fish store, and bought two of the largest fish, wrapped them in newspaper and proudly handed them to grandma.

Each year, the hotel set up a large tent on the grounds for a free, two-night circus starring the famous clown, Emmet Kelly. There were animals, trapeze and clown acts, and lots of organ music. One of the daytime activities was the annual children's fashion show, performed at the pool area. Try to picture dozens of four- to seven-year-olds, walking down a runway wearing the most contrived and garish outfits. It was pure delight.

After a few years, we decided that Acapulco, Mexico was the place to go. Inexpensive, brand new hotels were popping up, offering fabulous facilities at lower prices than in Florida. And unlike Florida, sunshine was guaranteed every day. At night, the adults enjoyed the new throbbing discos, staying out until two in the morning. We hired baby sitters who would stay overnight, sleeping on the convertible couch. Getting paid in dollars was worth their effort.

By the early 70s, southern Florida was changing. The hotel scene was done with; it was the age of condominiums. For a reasonable sum, it was possible to purchase a two- or three-bedroom apartment in a gated community, with a club house, several restaurants, a golf course, tennis courts, and pool areas. Some even had small groceries and convenience stores. We chose Inverrary in Ft. Lauderdale. It had all the facilities that we needed, even a separate tennis club house. Owning our own place meant we could go to Florida more often. Dolores and I were avid tennis players and were able to fit in with a large group of our contemporaries. Again, lasting friendships were established. From time to time we would fly down on the spur of the moment, even with the kids. It was home; at least for a while.

It was a phone call from our friend Charles, inviting us to join him for a picnic on the 20-foot runabout he kept on the south shore of Long Island that resulted in our next big change.

My initial reaction was, "I'm too old for picnics." But we went anyway, and it was delightful. We anchored in a cove, swam, ate and laughed. At the end of the afternoon, I said to Dolores, "Why don't we buy a boat?"

Dolores thought that was a great idea and we ended up buying a 28-foot Egg Harbor brand motorboat. Our kids really loved to steer the boat and delighted in occasionally taking their friends along on our outings. Soon I had no time for golf. I'd get up Saturday morning and play tennis at eight, change, and go down to the boat. The three beauties, as I called them, would show up later with a picnic lunch, and we'd be out on the Long Island Sound by noon. The highlight was anchoring in a secluded cove and swimming off the boat and picnicking. Somehow, food of any kind always tastes better when you're on a boat. Little by little, we got braver and braver and decided to buy a larger boat with a stronger engine. Then we could go as far as Newport, Rhode Island or Block Island.

By the late 70s, I was braver and more confident in boat handling. We both could navigate by using our Coast Guard charts. We needed more room, especially a galley with a refrigerator/freezer and cooking stove. We'd been bringing plastic containers filled with ice to keep the food fresh. A stove would give us the luxury of a hot cup of coffee on those chilly trips back to our marina at the end of the day. Our new 38-footer could only sleep two, but our next boat, a 40-foot Egg Harbor, slept six, had two toilets, a living room and dining area, and a full kitchen. Now we could venture as far as we desired, even make overnight trips to Cape Cod and Nantucket.

By this time, our daughters Gail and Michelle were older and were going to sleep away camp with their friends. Ileen was still attending a local day camp, but on some weekends she would join us on the boat. She was an excellent navigator, following the course plotted on the charts, and quickly

An enjoyable day on our
boat "SCHNOOKY"

learned how to maneuver the boat in rough seas. Eventually I lost my first mate, and she too went to sleep away camp.

Dolores and I formed friendships with other boat owners. After we considered ourselves experienced and brave enough, we charted a course to Nantucket – cruising around Long Island and then North to Massachusetts with a first stop at Martha's Vineyard. Although the marina was packed, we had made reservations well in advance. Compared to other boats and yachts moored in the bay, we looked like a dinghy. Boating can be very humbling; no matter how large your boat is, there's always another larger than yours. When it comes to boating, size matters.

Nantucket is an appealing island only about 13-miles long and five-miles wide. Most of the homes are over 200 years old, with renovated interiors but exteriors retaining the original look. Many of the streets are still surfaced with cobble-stones. There aren't any traffic lights, and pedestrians always have the right of way. No McDonalds, Burger King, Walmart, or any of the national chains; only the A&P and ShopRite groceries. It is a calm place; no one is rushing.

For two summers we went to Nantucket, spending two weeks hooked up at the marina. We vowed that someday we would buy a house on the island.

Two of our friends in Roslyn had moved to Old Westbury, Long Island. When we saw their new place, with its own pool and tennis court, Dolores and I couldn't stop talking about it. We considered what they had paid for the house to be a lot of money; there was no way we could afford such extravagance. So we stopped talking about it, until our next-door neighbors sold their house for exactly what my friends had paid for theirs in Old Westbury. At that point, I yelled, "Sell this house, if we can get that amount of money, I'm moving tomorrow!"

It wasn't exactly the next day, but we did put our house up for sale and started looking in Old Westbury, where old estates were being divided up into two-acre lots and developers were building custom homes on those lots. We found a beautiful two-acre piece of land with magnificent old trees. Dolores got in touch with John Saladino, a famous design consultant who was so hard to reach that you had to know the Pope to get an introduction. Saladino looked at the builder's plans and said that he'd like to not only *decorate* the house we would build, but also *design* it.

After all our years of planning and moving in order to accommodate family life, Dolores and I decided to build a home just for the two of us. By the time we moved in, Gail and Michelle would already be away at college and Ileen would be in her senior year at Friends Academy. Done. We sold in Roslyn and bought in Old Westbury!

At the end of August 1982, Dolores and I recognized that building a custom house in Old Westbury, plus landscaping and furnishing it, would require all of our time and that we would no longer have time for boating. Instead, why not consider buying a small house in Nantucket? It would be a great summer vacation spot. So we started looking at houses. The realtor showed us a great place, an old weathered-wood *GRAY LADY*, a typical Nantucket house with a widow's walk, sitting on one acre down a private dirt road. Furthermore, it came totally equipped. The owners were leaving everything – pots, pans, dishes, rugs, towels, even a housekeeper. The agent who owned the house was getting divorced and it was available if we could close on it fast. We bought it.

On our last boat trip home from Nantucket, we were caught in a massive thick fog. I put the motor in neutral and every few seconds rang a bell to prevent any moving vessels from crashing into us. The biggest danger was sailboats: no engine, no noise. The fog was so thick that we only had about three feet of visibility. While in idle, we heard a putt-putt sound. It had to be an old boat. I immediately clanged our bell so that they knew we were there.

What happened next seemed just like a scene out of an old-time movie. This small, shabby old boat proceeded to slowly come alongside us. Through the fog, we could just make out two middle-aged ladies wearing large, feathered hats and flowing chiffon dresses, each daintily holding a cup and saucer with pinky fingers delicately poised. Not a man in sight. They were facing forward in their boat, when one of them, noticing our presence, moved her head ever so slightly to face us, never setting down her tea cup, and asked, "Do you, perchance, know where we are?"

I replied that we were ten feet from the Connecticut shore. No response, no thank you as their boat serenely drifted past, this time without even a putt-putt of an engine. No sound whatsoever. Looking at each other, Dolores and I both realized that it was time to get out of boating.

We moved into Old Westbury on April Fool's Day, 1983.

Ileen attended high school at Friends Academy in Locust Valley, Long Island, where, in addition to being a good student, she showed great acting and musical talent, playing guitar, piano, and clarinet. Dolores decided that Ileen would make a wonderful commercial model; with her mother's help, Ileen built a career in commercials (Burger King, Good & Plenty candy) and then moved into acting. She was actually in an episode of Kojak. I never let Telly know that the girl he had spoken to in one of his Kojak scenes was actually my daughter. Eventually, she moved to California where she wrote and sang her own songs, performed in clubs, formed her own band and recorded three DVDs. When she had a baby, she took early retirement from show business.

After finishing college, Gail and Michelle worked for me. Gail started off in our men's wear office and showrooms, eventually running the ladies MEMBERS ONLY division with great success from our showroom at 1407 Broadway. Michelle had also worked in the ladies division, but I brought her back to the men's division of MEMBERS ONLY because, as we grew, we needed someone to be in charge of organizing the trade shows, which took place twice a year in California and New York City. Michele designed what amounted to a design set for our garments and hired and trained the local people who helped create our displays. One of her innovations was to convert the second story of these displays, usually used only for storage, into a lounge and selling area. It was a comfortable place for our buyers to relax. She was also responsible for setting up our fashion shows and sales meetings. A true asset to the company.

As rapidly as MEMBERS ONLY was evolving and changing, so was our family life. Suddenly, our condo in Florida didn't have enough room for the grown up daughters and their friends who wanted to use it for their winter getaways. Eventually, we had to find a bigger house and ended up in a gated community called Frenchman's Creek in Palm Beach Gardens. We had thought of buying a parcel of land in that community and having a house built by an outside builder, I knew that with my makeup, I'd have to keep running down there to make sure everything about the house was right. Luckily, the developer offered to sell us a model house, where we could make whatever interior alterations we wanted, although we had to leave the exterior unchanged. He built it. Eventually, we moved into that house, which was situated next to a lake and had a lovely pool and deck; it became a place where our grandchildren would come and have a ball. Part of the interior change we made was creating a tremendous children's play room. One of the grandchildren's favorites was riding and sometimes steering my golf cart around the neighborhood. We had plenty of room for all.

Chapter Twenty-two

FOR MOST OF MY PROFESSIONAL CAREER, I was in the men's apparel or fashion business. Philosophically, I differed greatly from most people in the industry. It was my belief that selling apparel was no different from selling soap; there was no great mystique involved. The goal was simply to capture space in the store and generate consumer sales.

In my opinion, there are no greater marketers than those who sell soap powder. To put their products on the middle shelf, they have to turn a simple box into a package of success and dreams. In the fashion industry, there are many new styles to sell each season; in the soap powder business, the product remains the same. It is only the creative marketing approach that changes.

> THERE ARE NO GREATER MARKETERS THAN THOSE WHO SELL SOAP POWDER.

I respected the intelligence of my competitors; I knew that our sources of information were the same. Therefore, it followed that if our information was the same, I would have to take a lesson from the success of soap powder marketers. My advertising had to offer that one special creative element that would separate my products from those of my competitors. My company had to present advertising that would appeal to the consumer but also motivate retailers. I lived by the same rule: "You can't look like everyone else."

Forty years ago, MEMBERS ONLY was a $100 million (in today's dollars $500 million company) and I was never afraid to try new marketing approaches.

The one thing that distinguishes men's apparel manufacturing from all other industries is its singular lack of interest and expertise in marketing. In a billion-dollar industry that sells sophistication and style, many companies lack the know-how to correctly market their product.

The single most important factor in planning my advertising and marketing strategies was the realization that fashion is show business. The presentation of the product and the advertising are the players in the show; the buyers and consumers are the audience. They have to feel good about the product and be ready to pay the price of admission: The sale!

> THE CONSUMER BELIEVES THAT AN ADVERTISED PRODUCT IS BETTER THAN ONE THAT IS NOT ADVERTISED.

Although fashion is important, advertising, promotion, and publicity are essential. Right or wrong, the consumer believes that an advertised product is better than one that is not advertised.

By the mid-1980s, the brand name MEMBERS ONLY had become part of the national vocabulary. The press was having a field day with our rags to riches story:

> *"Ed Wachtel and Herb Goldsmith had been running Europe Craft Imports, Inc. in New York City for 17 years without setting the sportswear industry on fire . . . Annual sales are now about $100 million, compared with $19 million in the year they introduced the MEMBERS ONLY jacket."*
> - NATION'S BUSINESS, August 1984.

> *"Their Overnight Success Took 18 Years: By the time*
> *MEMBERS ONLY finally propelled them onto the fast track,*
> *Wachtel and Goldsmith had acquired the know-how to control it..."*
> — *NEW YOUR CITY BUSINESS, August 1985*

Although consumers are aware that the personality is paid to endorse a product, they still believe that a celebrity would not recommend something he or she did not believe in.

Before we advertised, we did some research and discovered that 70-75% of all men's apparel purchases were controlled or influenced by women.

Recognizing that women were so important to our sales, we sought out a personality for our first major advertising effort who could make a major impact on that particular segment of the market.

Most people in our industry thought we had lost our senses when we launched in 1981 our initial campaign. Not only did we break tradition by using television as a medium, but our advertising featured Anthony Geary, the star of the daytime soap opera "General Hospital."

Store buyers didn't know who Geary was: male consumers weren't aware of him at all. However, he not only appeared in our TV commercials, but also made personal appearances in retail stores. Women flocked in droves to the stores to see him. There he was wearing his Members Only jacket, and sales boomed, their boyfriends and husbands had to wear it. They had no choice!

In the next phase of our advertising in the early 80s, we wanted to reach a larger segment of Middle America. In 1982, we retained the Gatlin Brothers.

It was important that we continued to motivate the male in the family. We knew that sports stars would appeal to them. It would be best if we chose a "star" from each of the most popular sports.

We contacted the agents and found a warm reception. Often we were told that they and their clients owned a Members Only jacket.

Members Only Sporting Team.

In 1985, our "sporting team" consisted of Lou Piniella of the New York Yankees, Buck Williams of the New Jersey Nets, Boomer Esiason of the Cincinnati Bengals, Payne Stewart, PGA golf champion and Vincent VanPatten, tennis pro.

These guys wouldn't jeopardize their reputation if they didn't believe in our product.

> THESE GUYS WOULDN'T JEOPARDIZE THEIR REPUTATION.

The male consumer had a sense of pride. "Hey, look at what I'm wearing." Soon their friends, neighbors and relatives were wearing a Members Only jacket. "If it's good enough for the pros, it's good enough for me."

I thought, "How do we top this?" Do we risk becoming boring through repetition of using "stars"? Is it time to make a new statement? To quote Yul Brynner in "The King and I" – "Is a puzzlement!"

Just when others thought we had reached the top, a small change led to even bigger things – things we could never have predicted. The advertising agency we were associated with decided to break up. Two of the partners retired, and the third, who had a passion for cooking, opened a bed and breakfast. Ed and I felt that we weren't getting enough new energy from the agency anyway, so this was an opportunity to change.

We looked around; the large agencies wouldn't talk to us – even one whose vice-president was a member of my country club. He said, quite honestly, that we were too small. The amount we were spending on advertising might be unique to us and to our industry, but as he told us, it didn't make business sense for him to take it on.

New offices and showrooms at 440 Fifth Avenue gave us the additional space we now needed. There we met with Lois Korey and Alan Kay, owners of the Korey Kay advertising agency. Alan had made his name by creating an ad for XEROX that featured an elderly monk in the year 50 A.D. The ad showed the monk turning the color pages of a giant bible and asking

The Members Only sports team: Boomer Esiason, Lou Pinniella, Ed, Buck Williams, Herb, Vince VanPatten amd Payne Stewart.

another monk how many years it would take to make 500 color copies of it. After a short interval, the second monk came back with the copies. The solution: XEROX! This ad was one of the biggest hits aired on television during the Super Bowl.

We explained our dilemma to Lois and Alan: MEMBERS ONLY was so successful that we were getting boring. Our sales force was blasé – business was so good that they didn't even need to personally call on stores anymore; their answering machines took the orders while they were playing golf or socializing. They mainly concentrated on a style that what was, by now, a classic – the strap collar MEMBERS ONLY jacket. But what should be done about all the other styles in our line? We needed to remind both retailers and consumers that MEMBERS ONLY made other styles. We accomplished this by creating ads featuring several celebrities together: one star wore the original basic style and the others wore other MEMBERS ONLY styles. We had already featured the TV star Anthony Geary, country western stars, the Gatlin Brothers, and famous athletes from every sport. How could we top that?

The next day, Alan called and said he wanted to meet with us immediately. They took no longer than one night to come up with our next advertising campaign. Alan and Lois arrived at our

> NO BIG BOARDS, NO ATTACHÉ CASES; ALL THEY HAD WAS THE *NEW YORK TIMES*.

office without any of the usual presentation materials – no big boards, no attaché cases; all they had was *The New York Times*, which was flung onto the conference table.

"There's your campaign," he said.

*Billy Martin, George Steinbrenner
and Lou Pinnela. George is in
a Members Only jacket made
especially for him in
Yankee stripes.*

Chapter Twenty-three

THE NEWSPAPER THAT ALAN KOREY FLUNG on our conference table featured President Ronald Reagan's announcement of the government's 1986 campaign against illegal drug use, which was at unprecedented levels. Estimates were that at least 150,000 people a year died from drug-related deaths and that at least 5,000 people a day tried drugs for the first time. A new lethal epidemic of crack cocaine had been sweeping through the cities. In June 1986, the death of a promising young athlete not only horrified the world, but brought home the idea that young black men were particularly at risk. Len Bias, an All-American college basketball player, was about to begin his first season with the Boston Celtics when he was found dead of a heart attack, brought on, the coroner said, by cocaine use.

Alan and Lois's idea was that MEMBERS ONLY should support the national anti-drug campaign by being the first national brand to advertise public service announcements in prime time, on television and radio. We could use famous spokespeople wearing MEMBERS ONLY jackets, but there would be no mention of the clothing or the company, except for a written tagline at the end saying:

> *"This public service announcement is brought to you by MEMBERS ONLY."*

At first, it was hard to grasp the concept. The only public service announcements that existed on television were aired between two and four in the morning, surrounded by ads for truck driving schools, tools, and old movies. How would this help us? Would some of our colleagues in the apparel industry raise their eyebrows at the idea of our committing a large chunk of advertising dollars to something that did not obviously "push" our product? Eventually, they persuaded us to take what amounted to a huge gamble, and to start right away. "Do it before some other company does." We did, and in Primetime. (6:00 p.m. to 11:00 p.m.)

> DO IT BEFORE SOME OTHER COMPANY DOES. WE DID.

Our trade newspaper, the *Daily News Record* reported:

> *"Even for a firmly entrenched market leader like MEMBERS ONLY, it was a risky move in an outerwear market where heavy promotions and cut-throat marketing strategies are a way of life."*

The athletes who made up our sports advisory team were eager to volunteer for the new campaign. To produce and direct the TV spots, we got Bob Giraldi, one of the best television professionals of that time. Generally credited with transforming music videos into an art form and directing Michael Jackson's mega-hit *Thriller* video, Giraldi rearranged his schedule to meet our deadlines and waived his fee. Larry Gatlin, himself a recovering addict, was eager to participate, also pro bono.

We filmed our first four 30-second ads. One featured New York Yankees Manager Lou Piniella, New Jersey Nets basketball star Buck Williams, Cincinnati Bengals quarterback Boomer Esiason, and Larry Gatlin. Many others would follow. That summer, we found our greatest ally, the governor of New York State, Mario Cuomo.

Governor Cuomo had been crusading against the rising use of crack cocaine for some time and when we contacted him about our *Education through Communication* program, urging people not to try these drugs even once, he was enthusiastic. To introduce the campaign to the public and give it the prestige of the Governor's support, his staff arranged a major press conference at the state offices on the 57th floor of the World Trade Center. On the morning of August 12, 1986, we assembled there, along with 50 reporters representing the national press, and rows of video cameras from all the TV networks.

Ed and I announced that we had committed our company's entire $6 million advertising and promotional budget for the coming year to this campaign, aimed at persuading people not to try drugs. Starting in September, we would buy national commercial time on prime TV and radio, and also advertise in newspapers, magazines, and billboards.

Governor Cuomo announced that he had volunteered to participate in an ad himself, and then he added, "I've said many times that if we are to beat the scourge of crack and drugs, we must work together; MEMBERS ONLY has heard our call and I am pleased that a New York-based company is making such a timely and effective commitment to the fight against drugs." He then called on other private sector companies to join the effort.

He also headed off any possible criticism that we were taking advantage of the drug crisis by saying, with a smile, ". . . and if these two guys make a couple of bucks on it, that's great."

We played two ads for the assembled press: First, Yankees manager Lou Piniella,

> *". . . If you're dumb enough to take drugs, you'll never be a member of my club."*

Second, New Jersey Nets star Buck Williams,

> *". . . You want to wreck your life with cocaine? Then I got news for you, buddy, you're a loser."*

STATE OF NEW YORK
EXECUTIVE CHAMBER
TWO WORLD TRADE CENTER
NEW YORK, NY 10047

Press Office
518-474-8418
212-587-2126

FOR RELEASE:
IMMEDIATE, THURSDAY
AUGUST 7, 1986

PRESS ADVISORY

Governor Mario M. Cuomo and executives from Members Only apparel will announce on Tuesday, August 12, a multimillion-dollar program which will impact on the drug crisis.

Participating in the announcement will be Buck Williams of the New Jersey Nets and Lou Piniella of the New York Yankees.

Date: Tuesday, August 12, 1986

Time: 11:30 a.m.

Location: Governor's Office
            2 World Trade Center, 57th Floor

\#

*Governor Cuomo and
Members Only Press
conference.*

------ 302

*With Governor Cuomo at
the Members Only Press
conference.*

Members Only Continues Anti-Drug Campaign

By STUART B. CHIRLS

NEW YORK — In 1986, Members Only/Europe Craft shocked corporate America by publicly announcing that the outerwear and sportswear giant would devote its entire advertising budget for the coming year — some $6 million — to the fight against drugs.

The resultant television, radio and print ads, which featured sports and music celebrities espousing anti-drug messages, featured no direct product exposure save for a discreet Members Only credit at the end of each announcement. Even for a firmly entrenched market leader like

Members Only, it was a risky move in an outerwear market where heavy promotions and cutthroat marketing strategies are a way of life.

The gamble has paid off. Company executives told DNR that total sales in 1987 of Members

Only merchandise (outerwear and sportswear) increased 15 percent over year-ago figures, an impressive rise in a lean outerwear market. And, according to a random independent marketing study, unaided brand awareness of the Members Only label among

consumers checked in at 21 percent during 1986, up from 15 percent in 1984, the last time such a survey was conducted.

The goodwill aspect of the campaign has other media organizations eager to participate, to the tune of $60 million in gratis airtime and advertising space donated to the cause, according to MaiaHauser, director of promotion and event marketing for Members Only, who has worked on the project since its inception.

But even more difficult, Hauser said, was getting retailers involved. "They were apprehensive at the beginning, particularly where co-op ads were concerned. Many felt that they just didn't have the money for advertising that didn't show merchandise."

Sports marketing has always played a large part in promoting the company's lifestyle image, so Members Only used its pull as an official sponsor of the National Football League to answer retailers' doubts. "In-store appearances of NFL players were arranged in Tampa, St. Louis, New Jersey, Dallas and Los Angeles area malls. The players were also made available for local TV and radio spots, as well as models for newspaper ads," says Hauser. "The appearances are great traffic builders, and because the mall picks up a percentage of the expenses, every store benefits." The appearances also tie in anti-drug messages, as well as point-of-purchase strategies like sweepstakes giveaways and gift-with-purchase promotions. "Everything can be individually tailored for each retailer, whether it is a department store or specialty store," she pointed out, adding that specialty stores are a tremendous part of Members' business.

"DRUGS ALMOST RUINED MY LIFE. DON'T LET THEM RUIN YOURS. JUST SAY NO."
—Larry Gatlin—

Larry Gatlin delivers his message

Larry Gatlin continues the anti-drug campaign with Members Only.

Both wore MEMBERS ONLY jackets. The commercial ends with the printed words:

"This Public Service Announcement is
brought to you by Members Only."

Then we introduced Piniella and Williams, who both commented to the press on why they had volunteered to participate in the MEMBERS ONLY campaign. The coverage by the networks that followed, gave us free publicity worth millions. Even before the first paid commercial hit the air, they showed them on their newscast.

GAVE US FREE PUBLICITY WORTH MILLIONS, EVEN BEFORE THE FIRST PAID COMMERCIAL HIT THE AIR.

Los Angeles Mayor Tom Bradley and U.S. Senator Alphonse D'Amato, head of the Senate caucus on narcotics control, became active supporters. National and local media outlets donated an additional $70 million (in today's dollars, over $200 million) worth of space and air time in print, broadcasts, and billboards to the MEMBERS ONLY campaign. Over the following two years, we expanded the program with more ads and extended the message from, "Don't try Drugs," to offering help to those who were already hooked. Larry Gatlin made a spot in which he looked straight into the camera and announced,

"Drugs almost ruined my life. Don't let them ruin yours.
Just say no."

We used our position as sponsors of the National Football League to arrange in-store appearances with players who carried the anti-drug message and, of course, always sporting a MEMBERS ONLY jacket. After some initial resistance to advertising that didn't show merchandise, local retailers began to join us. They added their own tag lines to our spots or created their own ads, featuring hometown heroes and athletes. They hosted drug abuse symposiums with local sports figures and celebrities describing the dangers of using drugs.

THE WHITE HOUSE

June 1, 1987

Dear Mr. Goldsmith:

I was so happy to learn of the fine work your
company is doing to help rid our country of
the horror of drugs. Your advertising campaign
against drug abuse is a powerful and effective
tool, and I applaud your fine work.

As you know, I have been deeply involved in
the fight against substance abuse for some
time. And only when more people like you
become involved will we make this problem a
thing of the past. I hope others are wise
enough to follow the courageous example you
are setting.

Again, thank you for caring. Please continue
doing all you can to stem the tide of drug
abuse. If you can help save just one life,
all your efforts have been worthwhile.

                    Sincerely,

                    Nancy Reagan

Mr. Herb Goldsmith
Members Only
445 Fifth Avenue
New York, NY 10016

A congratulatory White House
letter from Nancy Regan.

As we and Governor Cuomo hoped, MEMBERS ONLY did, in fact, benefit from the goodwill generated by these activities. We were the talk of our industry, and more important, the talk of America. In June 1987, we received a congratulatory White House letter from Nancy Regan. The plaudits from the press, consumers, and customers was more than one could expect. Our sales dramatically improved; department stores reported an 82% increase. Consumers rated the program, "Very effective in terms of communicating a positive social message and association with MEMBERS ONLY."

> SALES DRAMATICALLY IMPROVED; DEPARTMENT STORES REPORTED AN 82% INCREASE.

We received hundreds of letters from families and anti-drug organizations throughout the country congratulating us on this campaign. Daily, we received requests for copies of our print ads and video tapes of our television commercials, which local TV stations wanted to run at no cost to us. This momentum and positive reaction continued. Fortunately, the factories making our jackets were able to supply us as the demand increased.

Behind all of this demand for our products was a changing consumer lifestyle. The cost to travel was reasonable, employment was at its peak, and salaries were at new highs. Even though MEMBERS ONLY made many different styles of jackets for each season, we decided that there should be distinct styling for a special lifestyle customer. All styles would have a new identifying label, included below the new label, with the words: by MEMBERS ONLY. We created an active line called Stadium Club, an outdoor country look called Great Horizon Express, a high fashion look for disco enthusiasts called Studio. Although initial sales were modest for these new lines, we were able to demonstrate to our customers that we were not complacent, but rather, innovative, just as we were in our products and our advertising.

Like all companies, our need for growth was constant, we responded.

THE COMMISSIONER OF CUSTOMS

October 2, 1991   WASHINGTON, D.C.

Mr. Herb Goldsmith
President
Members Only
441 Fifth Avenue
New York, New York 10016

Dear Mr. Goldsmith:

  I would like to commend you for your corporate
policy of dedicating Members Only's advertising budget to
fighting drug abuse.

  I became aware of this policy through a Chemical
Bank advertisement in <u>Women's Wear Daily</u>, and while I have
seen your ads - and thought them very effective - I was
deeply impressed to learn that they are much more than a
token nod to the anti-drug bandwagon.

  The agents and inspectors of the U.S. Customs
Service are especially appreciative of your message that
"Drugs Don't Just Kill Addicts."

  Virtually one hundred percent of the two most
deadly drugs threatening our country - cocaine and heroin -
must be smuggled through U.S. borders on their way to our
streets. Because those borders form the front line of
America's war on drugs, our employees work daily, knowing
that they could be the casualty of a drug smuggler's
ruthlessness.

  The demand for drugs in this country has given
rise to a wave of crime that endangers not only users and
dealers, but those who serve this country in an attempt to
stop it. Pairing a trendy product such as yours with the
message that drugs are bad, is an excellent way to undermine
the glamourous image of casual drug abuse. I wish to thank
you for your dedication to this cause.

        Sincerely,

        Carol Hallett
        Carol Hallett
        Commissioner

REPORT SMUGGLING TO UNITED STATES CUSTOMS SERVICE 1-800-BE-ALERT

*Commerissioner of Customs
Carol Hallett, commends us on
our fight against drug abuse.*

Congressional Record

United States
of America

PROCEEDINGS AND DEBATES OF THE 101st CONGRESS, FIRST SESSION

| Vol. 135 | WASHINGTON, TUESDAY, SEPTEMBER 26, 1989 | No. 125 |

Senate

HERBERT GOLDSMITH, LEADER IN WAR ON DRUGS

Mr. D'AMATO. Mr. President, I rise to call my colleagues' attention to the leadership being provided by Herbert Goldsmith, president and CEO of Members Only, in the war on drugs.

Since 1986, Members Only has committed its advertising budget, worth some $18 million to date, to the war against drugs and, in the process, has persuaded the media to donate an additional $70 million in space and air time.

Mr. Goldsmith's antidrug efforts began in 1986 when New York's Gov. Mario Cuomo joined Mr. Goldsmith in unveiling an antidrug ad campaign, which featured Lou Piniella, Buck Williams, Boomer Esiason, and Payne Steward, wearing Members Only attire, and warning of the dangers of drugs.

The next year, a Members Only percent-of-sale program to help infants who are born addicted to drugs was announced by Larry Gatlin and Payne Steward. It raised $150,000 for a wing at Clara Hale House in New York and for the ICAN Program in Los Angeles.

Mr. Goldsmith is a public spirited citizen with an impressive track record. In 1988, an election year, he joined the League of Women Voters in tackling voter apathy. He launched a 3-week, $3 million campaign involving hardhitting commercials and a nationwide voter registration drive in department stores.

The campaign was awarded a Clio, the prestigious advertising honor, and a Spire for sales promotion excellence. This year, Herb Goldsmith was named an all-star of the year by Crain's New York Business.

Mr. Goldsmith is extending his antidrug campaign to include a focus on dangers to police officers. "Drugs don't just kill addicts" will be the theme, highlighted in a new national advertising and retail promotion campaign. In addition, Members Only is conducting a national grassroots basketball program with the Police Athletic League to foster positive relationships between young people and police and to keep young people off the streets and off drugs.

Mr. President, Herb Goldsmith is to be commended for channeling his business acumen toward public service. The war against drugs is not just the Government's war. It is a war most effectively waged by all Americans, corporate and individual alike. Herb's leadership in this regard stands as a challenge to the rest of corporate America to join in similarly dedicating their corporate resources to the national effort against drugs.

Congressional Record

GEORGE BUSH

August 8, 1988

Mr. Herb Goldsmith
Members Only - League of Women Voters
"There's No Excuse Not To Vote"
445 Fifth Avenue
New York, New York 10016

Dear Mr. Goldsmith,

        Congratulations to <u>Members Only</u> and <u>The League of</u>
<u>Women Voters</u> on your efforts to focus attention on the
importance of every American exercising their right--and duty-
-to vote.

        The result of the 1988 election will effect future
generations as well as today's voters. Solutions to many key
issues--economic and social, will be charted by the next
President. But a democracy cannot reach its potential for
fair and responsive government by the people without the
active participation of all of her citizens.

        Voting is not just a right; voting is a
responsibility. Criticizing our country's ills does no good
without a willingness to get involved, contribute and
sacrifice. Every citizen's first contribution should be the
informed use of their vote for that is what sets the United
States apart from so many nations of the world. Only the
active involvement of people like yourselves will keep our
government strong and responsive. Thank you for your hard
work on behalf of all citizens.

        Barbara joins me in congratulating you on your
dedication to encouraging more Americans to meet the challenge
of democracy and participate in the political process
established by our Constitution.

                Sincerely,

                George Bush

A congratulatory letter from
George Bush.

*Our anti-drug campaign
billboards.*

Chapter Twenty-four

ED AND I HAD COMPLETELY different personalities. He was a very easygoing, charming guy. Respected and admired by our customers. Over the years, he invested in race horses, and most of his passion outside of business lay in that area. I, on the other hand, didn't have an outside interest other than my family. I loved the challenge that each new season brought.

We were riding high, on top of the world, the prime outerwear label in the U.S. By the mid-80s, Ed wanted to take it easy; I didn't. He suggested that he and I alternate, each working only six months out of the year, and delegate more responsibility to our executives. To me, it didn't make sense; we still needed to grow. If we didn't, somebody else would become more popular and replace us. We had to keep promoting and diversifying the line.

"This is your life, Herb," Ed responded. "You love it. Why don't you just buy me out?"

That hit me like a ton of bricks.

"We're partners," I stammered, "I can't replace you. And I couldn't possibly take on your responsibilities."

"Well then, why don't we think about selling?"

I was reeling, but I was also committed to what we had built together. A friend suggested that I talk to an investment firm he knew in California, a company specializing in corporate acquisitions using junk bonds. He arranged the meeting. They were interested and were already familiar with our brand. After I advised them that I intended to remain and Ed would be leaving, they asked for our last three years' financial statements and my business plan covering the next three years. A few days after I had sent the figures and business plan, a written offer came back. They offered to buy the company, but in stages and take it public. On the condition that I stay, they wrote a preliminary letter of understanding, with which I was satisfied.

> THEY OFFERED TO BUY THE COMPANY.

Before I could act on the proposal, another friend from Long Island came to talk to me. Howard was a very smart venture capitalist with a lot of success in a variety of businesses and acquisitions. When he came to see me, he had no idea about the negotiations already in the works. He sat down and said, "Herb, I feel a little embarrassed asking this, but would you ever consider selling your company?"

Without providing any details or the name of the California firm, I told him what was happening, and he asked if I could postpone the other deal.

"Let me make you an offer," he said, "just let me see the last three years of your financial statements."

I sent him the figures. A few days later, we were meeting again. Howard put his hand inside his jacket pocket and pulled out an envelope. On the outside of the envelope, written in pencil was his offer.

I could hardly read his hand writing. "Are you kidding?" That was my response to his presentation. It was an all cash deal, with a cash incentive based on profits.

The California investment firms, offer was unbelievable, but unlike Howard's, it offered little cash up front. The import business, as I well knew, was always a dangerous business with lots of uncertainties, especially the changing quotas for bringing goods in from the Far East. And Ed was clearly leaving.

I sat down with my legal team and accountant and we did some calculations about where we thought I would be financially in five years with each of the offers on the table. The all cash offer was agreed to be the wisest choice. Dolores agreed that the money that we would get would provide a great future for us and for our kids. When we discussed the provisions of my new contract, which included not only my staying on at a salary and percentage based on profits, but also searching out a new president for MEMBERS ONLY and training him before I left. Dolores was very supportive – just as she had been when I resigned from Chief Apparel 27 years before.

> SEARCHING OUT A NEW PRESIDENT FOR MEMBERS ONLY AND TRAINING HIM BEFORE I LEFT.

"This is what you really want to do," she said, "running the company with no one to report to or approve your ideas. It's your ship to steer. I know you can do it."

Once the deal was done, I assembled all of the executives to reassure them that although we were, in effect, taking on a new business partner, our new partner agreed to a hands-off policy. Their promise to me was, "You built it, you run it. MEMBERS ONLY doesn't change. The company continues as it is; there are no new corporate suits coming in." I also took the opportunity to look back a bit, reminding everyone that during our first year in business, one of our accounts had said, "One day you'll be doing one million dollars in business." At the time we thought he was crazy. Now, of course, we were well beyond that financial mark; but even more important, I said, we had still not reached our company's potential. "The reputation and backing of our new partners would help us continue to grow. We know the potential . . . we know our motivation . . . we have our pride . . . and we've done things that have never been done before – let's do it again!"

1989/1990 Drugs Don't Just Kill Addicts

The company unveils a breakthrough extension of its anti-drug abuse campaign. The campaign goes beyond the "publicized" victims of drugs -- the addict and his/her family -- and focuses on the damage and death forced upon the nation's police force. This spring, the company in conjunction with its retail stores, will launch a multi-city grassroots basketball program with the Police Athletic League: The Members Only "Big Shot" Tournament.

Members Only strengthens its lead as the number one men's outerwear company in the country. It accounts for over one-quarter of total department store sales, outselling its top four competitors combined. In the short time since its introduction, Members Only sportswear has a number five ranking in overall department store sales, while its position in knitwear is still expanding with a broader sportswear offering.

Members Only's 1988 Vote Campaign receives CLIO and SPIRE awards for advertising and promotion excellence.

1988   "There's No Excuse Not To Vote" Breaks New Ground

In yet another innovative program, Members Only works with its department store outlets in urging Americans to vote in the 1988 Presidential election. In a joint effort with the League of Women Voters, the company also registers thousands of voters in department stores nationwide.

1987   Making a Difference

Members Only establishes a special fund to aid infants born drug-addicted. Advertising campaigns raise money for a Members Only wing at Clara Hale House in New York and the ICAN program in Los Angeles.

1986   The First Cause-Related Advertising

Members Only takes the lead by devoting its entire advertising budget for the year to an anti-drug abuse program campaign. The hard-hitting "Education through Communication" ads use celebrities such as Boomer Esiason, Buck Williams and Larry Gatlin to communicate a strong anti-drug message. New York State Governor Mario Cuomo unveils the campaign.

In addition to spending its entire $12 million budget on the anti-drug campaign, Members Only works with national and local media outlets to donate an additional $70 million worth of space and air time in print, billboards and broadcast.

1985   The All-Star Team Helps Sales Climb Further

Members Only creates its own "Sporting Team" of stars including Buck Williams, Payne Stewart and Lou Pinella to endorse and advertise its products.

1983-1984   "Changing The Way America Looks"

The company launches its "Changing The Way America Looks" campaign featuring the country western group the Gatlin Brothers.

1982   A First With Celebrity Advertising

The Members Only racing jacket breaks the $20 million sales barrier and becomes a favorite of the rich and famous -- publicly donned by celebrities such as Frank Sinatra, Johnny Carson, and Presidents Jimmy Carter and George Bush.

Members Only is one of the first companies to use celebrity endorsements to sell its products. One of TV's hottest stars, Tony Geary of General Hospital, conveys the advertising message, "When you put it on, something happens..."

Members Only launches a line of licensed products, including luggage, gloves, children's wear, toiletries, dress shirts, underwear, eyeglass frames and automotive accessories.

1980   Members Only Is Born!

The Members Only name is created. Its flagship product, the racing jacket, breaks ground in men's apparel. The latch throat collar design and choice of 28 colors is an instant success, becoming one of the best-selling clothing items ever produced.

1961   The Beginning

Europe Craft Imports Inc., manufacturers of men's and ladies' outwear, coats and rainwear, is purchased by Herb Goldsmith and Ed Wachtel.

When Ed retired in 1987, we held a huge party at the conference center in Tarrytown, New York, which we'd often used for sales conferences. All the attending sales managers and staff were told to secretly bring formal wear, tuxedos, and evening dresses. We arranged a separate room, other than the usual dining room, for the surprise dinner. Ed's wife, Norma, brought Ed's formal wear, along with some of Ed's close friends. Since Ed would be coming to the dinner in his casual meeting clothes, he would change after he was surprised. In recognition of Ed's love of gambling in Las Vegas, we hired a firm that supplied a room full of games of chance, including Black Jack dealers and roulette wheels. All the play money we used had Ed's picture on it. On behalf of the company, our final gift to Ed was a race horse named – what else – MEMBERS ONLY. It was the first time I had ever seen tears in Ed's eyes.

Dolores and I decided to celebrate the sale of the company with our entire family by going to Davos, Switzerland during the Christmas holiday. I booked flights on the British Airways Concorde, which made it from New York to London in three and a half hours. In Long Island, we purchased the clothing and ski wear that we would need – down parkas, heavy sweaters, ski boots, gloves, long silk underwear. Skis could be rented at the ski lodge. We were advised that formal wear would be required at dinner on Christmas and New Year. We arrived with plenty of luggage.

The hotel accommodations were quite elegant; the setting in the mountains was breathtaking. We were surprised at the lack of snow; perhaps tomorrow. After all, we're in the Swiss Alps and its December. We got up early the next morning, put on our new ski outfits, and after breakfast we were taken to the hotel's ski area. Sure enough, there was snow on the lower slope. They had sprayed it during the night and it looked more like shaved ice than packed snow. No wonder – the temperature was 62 degrees.

The only ski trails open were at the very top of the mountain. My son-in-law, also named Herb, was an accomplished skier, but I hadn't skied in 20 years. We left my daughters and grandchildren to the small slope and arranged for my grandchildren to have their first ski lessons. Herb and I

*Dolores and I celebrating
the sale!*

took the funicular to the top of the mountain, where there was snow, even though it was only about 10 degrees cooler. I was in a sweat. I took off my parka and wrapped it around my waist. Herb had on a white one-piece jump suit, similar to what the instructors were wearing, except theirs were black. We rented our skis and hired a ski instructor to help us acclimate to the trail. He started us off and said we should stop at the rope-tow at the bottom of the trail. He would follow behind.

"How do I know if I'm going in the right direction?" I protested.

He said he would shout out if I went wrong. I felt as if I'd been drafted into the German Army.

Off I went, with Herb and the instructor staying behind me. This wasn't snow, it was packed ice. I felt like I was ice skating with skis. Several times, the instructor called out that I should turn or slow down. Ahead, I could see the area with the rope-tow that we would use to get back to the top. Twenty yards to go; I twisted my body around toward them, waved, and proudly yelled out, "I made it."

I made it alright . . . right smack into a five-foot-high solid boulder. Later I learned that I had been unconscious for a few minutes, but when I started to awaken, my vision was blurred. I felt no pain; I felt as though I were floating upward. My son-in-law Herb was standing over me. "Herb," I moaned, "What are you doing here?" In his white suite I thought he was an angel. I had hit the boulder face-first and there had been a lot of blood, but no pain. At the tow, there was an attendant trained to do first aid. An emergency motorized snow sled had to come up from the very bottom. They wrapped me in blankets and said that I had to be taken to the hospital. The only way down was by the original funicular. After we got there, we had to wait until it came up from below and the arriving passengers exited. They bandaged half my face and forehead, and propped the stretcher in a vertical position. I looked like Hannibal Lecter. I was facing the door of the funicular as the passengers got off. I greeted them with, "WELCOME TO SWITZERLAND!" Some not-so-brave skiers got back on with me for the ride back down.

At the hospital, the doctors did some tests and told me that I had a slight concussion and that I must stay overnight to be observed, in case I had dizziness or nausea and further bleeding. I asked for a mirror. There were scabs of blood above both eyes and on my nose and chin.

Our hotel was right across the street and Christmas Eve was that night, with a special costume party planned for the adults and kids. It was late afternoon, and I didn't want my family to worry about me in the hospital. Herb was at my side and promised to watch me for signs of any problem. They agreed to let me go to the hotel. I was ready to leave, but they hadn't cleaned up my face. My scabs, they said, would help me heal faster.

We had been told in advance to bring costumes for the hotel party, but we had only brought masks. I could hide my bloody scabs by wearing a mask!

It was late in the afternoon when we got back to the hotel. The kids were playing in one of the rooms.

"Grandpa, you look silly." Knowing me, they thought I was made up with fright makeup. After we told my daughters what happened, they exclaimed, "Oh my God!" I wore a mask to dinner and we all had a great time, scabs and all.

The next few days the weather got warmer. The beginner's ski trail was shut down, and skiing at the top was too hazardous – all ice. The hotel offered the children hayrides, and later a sightseeing tour. Everything was complimentary. We didn't have the right clothes for those types of activities, and local stores were not equipped to provide them. We decided to leave three days before New Year, as did many of the other guests. Unfortunately, I had to pay for the unused days. But the hotel did credit us for the uneaten meals. Whenever we talk about that family celebration, my nose and eyes begin to ache and I imagine my face again covered with scabs.

1989 NOMINEES

Leaders
Cesar Chavez
Jesse Jackson
Nelson Mandela
Ronald Reagan

Music
Marvin Hamlisch
Willie Nelson
Lou Rawls
Bruce Springsteen
Stevie Wonder

Sports
Kareem Abdul-Jabbar
Jimmy Connors
Greg Louganis
Bob Wieland
Mookie Wilson

Lifesavers & Crusaders
Dr. Robert Gale
Harry J. Gaynor
Dr. Michael Gottlieb
Dith Pran
Robert Schornstheimer

Business
Herb Goldsmith
Eugene Lang
Ralph Nader
Edward H. Rensi
Ted Turner

Kids
Richard Belanger
Trevor Ferrell
Jason Gaes
Rocky Lyons
Brent Meldrum

Arts & Entertainment
Michael Crawford
Jim Henson
Joseph Papp
George Plimpton
Oliver Stone

Legendary
Walt Disney
John F. Kennedy
Martin Luther King, Jr.
Babe Ruth
John Wayne

The National Hero Awards have been created to salute our nation's choice of its greatest hero figures. Americans from coast-to-coast have cast their votes and selected the winners based on criteria of heroic ideals, demonstrated excellence, a deep moral conscience and a shimmering example.

Chapter Twenty-five

WITH ED GONE, the responsibility for all aspects of MEMBERS ONLY – styling, manufacturing, and now sales, was totally mine. Fortunately, Ed had built a solid sales organization over the years. With our national and regional sales managers, I set up an incentive program, which included sales quotas and bonuses based on profits. Even though computer software was in its infancy, our in-house system manager was able to write programs that gave us profit projections on all sales made prior to shipments to the store, as well as on the potential profit on garments not yet sold. Each regional sales manager knew what the profit was on the orders his team wrote.

The manufacturing division had to keep orders flowing to our factories. I gave more responsibility to the people in the styling and manufacturing departments. I had a right-hand man, Ronnie, whom I was grooming to take my place when my contract was up. Everyone in the company referred to him as my clone, "Little Herbie."

> I GAVE MORE RESPONSIBILITY TO THE PEOPLE IN THE STYLING AND MANUFACTURING DEPARTMENTS.

Like the fashion business, advertising always has to change. The purchaser needs to be stimulated and the product name must be reinforced in their minds. What could be as powerful and successful as our unique drug campaign? We had continued our long association with sports and celebrities. In addition to celebrity spokesmen, we sponsored many sports events and had radio and T.V. commercials during football, basketball, hockey, and baseball games. On some, the announcer would say, "And now, the MEMBERS ONLY scoreboard . . ." We sponsored the Volvo Classic Tennis Tournament at Madison Square Garden and several of our own tennis tournaments. At the U.S. Tennis Open in Queens, N.Y., the Gatlins, wearing their MEMBERS ONLY Jackets, sang the National Anthem. We sponsored The Final Four college basketball tournaments and much more. Even if we didn't sponsor a sporting event, sometimes when the camera panned onto the announcer, he was wearing a MEMBERS ONLY jacket. Many TV actors wore them.

Our jackets were even mentioned in fiction. In one crime novel, the perpetrator was caught because someone described him as wearing a strawberry-colored MEMBERS ONLY jacket. Strawberry was not one of our best-selling colors.

We had achieved a kind of brand identification that was rare in our business. IZOD had it with their alligator logo shirt, LEVI'S Jeans with their leather branded belt loop, Wrangler's embroidered a "W" on the rear pockets of their jeans, and Ralph Lauren had the well-known Polo Pony embroidered shirt. To the consumer who wore them, these identifications conferred stature and exclusiveness. They in effect, said "Look at me, I know what class means." We were in the company of these giants, but how would we stay there?

> WE HAD ACHIEVED A KIND OF BRAND IDENTIFICATION THAT WAS RARE IN OUR BUSINESS.

How do we continue to motivate and stay creative? We'd started the anti-drug campaign in 1986. By 1988, I was starting to feel like we'd been doing the same campaign for a pretty long time. We needed another miracle. Something struck me one day while I was reading the *New York Times*. I called Alan at our ad agency and asked him to come to our office.

"Alan," I said, "I've a crazy idea." "Herb," he replied, "crazy is what we need." We met in the same conference room where he and Lois had dropped

The New York Times on the table with the headline disclosing that President Reagan wanted the private sector to help in the fight against drugs. I had the *Times* spread out on the table, four pages of stories about the election in November. Voter apathy, I had read, was a huge problem. In 1984, nearly 81 million citizens eligible to vote had stayed away from the polls.

Alan, how about MEMBERS ONLY ads urging Americans to vote?"

Alan, together with Bob, our publicist, really nailed it. They got the League of Women Voters to endorse and support our campaign.

This is the trade ad we ran initially:

AN ADVERTISING CAMPAIGN SO IMPORTANT IT COULD CHANGE THE COURSE OF AMERICAN HISTORY

This fall, MEMBERS ONLY will launch its biggest advertising campaign ever. We've joined with the League of Women Voters to increase voter turnout. We'll be running television commercials and radio ads all across the country, as well as print ads in top consumer magazines, and even billboards – a campaign so widespread it will reach over 210 million Americans. And with your help, even more. We want our campaign to be so effective that we won't have to run it again in 1992.

The first print ad in *People Magazine* and on billboards around the country showed an illustration of the signing of the *Declaration of Independence*. Our message at the top read:

50% voter turnout isn't exactly what they had in mind.

Then came the illustration, followed by these words:

There is no excuse not to vote
A public service message provided by MEMBERS ONLY and the League of Women Voters.

An advertising campaign so important it could change the course of American history.

This fall Members Only will launch its biggest advertising campaign ever.

We've joined with the League of Women Voters to increase voter turnout.

We'll be running television commercials all across the country. As well as radio. And print ads in top consumer magazines. Even billboards.

A campaign so wide-spread it will reach over 210 million Americans.

And with your help, even more. To find out how your company can get involved, call Maia Hauser at (212) 686-5050.

We want our campaign to be so effective, we won't have to run it again in 1992.

There is no excuse not to vote.
MEMBERS ONLY

*Daily News Record -
September '88*

As a result of this new campaign, we were again the talk of the industry. In conjunction with the League of Women Voters, stores across the country set up tables where the public could register to vote. Macy's in New York City, staffed by the League volunteers, actually registered close to a thousand eligible voters. Other major stores across the country successfully emulated Macy's.

> AS A RESULT OF THIS NEW CAMPAIGN, WE WERE AGAIN THE TALK OF THE INDUSTRY.

Our dramatic public service advertisements not only continued, but got even more exposure and more attention than before. To the press, we were now described as one of the most widely recognized brand names in America.

We spent $3 million during the three weeks leading up to the national election, bringing our new ads to the public. The program was introduced by two hard-hitting 30-second television commercials. The first, "Idiots," showed old footage of Hitler, Stalin, and Mussolini screaming propaganda while the voiceover announced:

"Two hundred years ago, the drafters of the Constitution of the United States suggested a way to keep idiots like these out of our government."

Fade to black. The words.

"There is no excuse not to vote"
A public service message provided by MEMBERS ONLY and the League of Women Voters.

The second commercial showed crowds and soldiers from World War II, followed by shots of fenced in, emaciated concentration camp inmates. The voice-over said:

"We'd like to take this opportunity to remind you of why so many of us came to this country in the first place. On November 8, vote . . . for all the people who didn't make it."

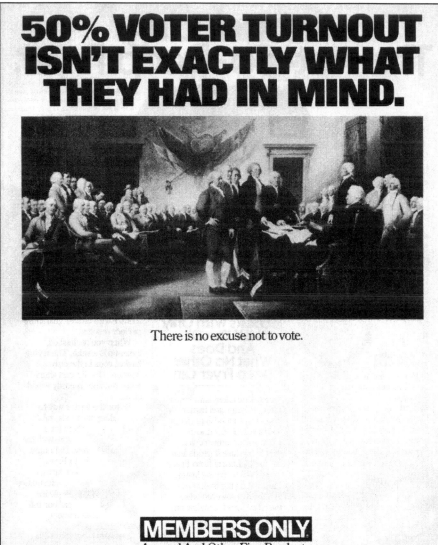

There is no excuse not to vote.

MEMBERS ONLY.
Apparel And Other Fine Products.

A public service message provided by Members Only and The League of Women Voters.

*Our new campaign on
Voter apathy.*

Some stations considered this ominous commercial too controversial to air.

SOME STATIONS CONSIDERED THIS OMINOUS COMMERCIAL TOO CONTROVERSIAL TO AIR.

Throughout the country, stores with MEMBERS ONLY departments became on-the-spot voter registration sites. By then, we had become a sponsor of the National Football League, so we recruited local football players to aid in the effort. We also ran a sweepstakes where the prize was a trip for two to Inauguration Week in Washington D.C.

This time, we made certain that our commercials did not show a single piece of MEMBERS ONLY clothing. Our philosophy was to associate the brand name with a company that cared about critical issues. The results proved that we were right. Again we were flooded with mail, even more than before, and we got more and more national attention in the press. The campaign won CLIO and SPIRE awards for advertising and promotion excellence.

Of the many awards and letters that MEMBERS ONLY received each day, a surprising number came from police departments across the country. I received an especially moving letter from the National Organization of Chiefs of Police, who presented us with a commendation for promoting anti-drug programs in a productive and selfless manner. Accompanying the letter was a note from the editor-in-chief of that organization's magazine.

"Having worn MEMBERS ONLY shirts and jackets for several years by personal choice, it was refreshing to learn that the company was the first commercial enterprise to devote its entire advertising budget to public service campaigns for anti-drug awareness."

They urged local stations to run our anti-drug ads because, among other things, the numbers of police officers killed in the battle against drugs was staggering. Still, more had to be done.

I discussed all of this with Alan Kaye. MEMBERS ONLY, I was happy to say, was firmly associated with public service. The consumer had responded by purchasing our products. Our business had grown each year. But again, just as after all of the other campaigns, I worried that we were back to square one. What's our new ad campaign? What will be fresh, innovative, and exciting? What will once again make our employees proud of their company? What's the new excitement?

I told Alan that I kept thinking about the police officers being killed in the drug wars and how drug addiction was not a victimless crime. I said, "What would represent police everywhere? Guns, uniforms, hand cuffs. The police badge!

"For our next commercial," Alan said, "why not show a police badge being shot up by bullets?"

It would be the talk of the nation if we could pull it off in a way that would not disturb too many viewers."

This was a gutsy decision, committing to such a shocking campaign.

"Let's do it!" Alan expanded on the idea about the badge, building a more ambitious campaign around the idea that "Drugs don't just kill addicts." We would film the badge being shot up, with the sounds of sirens and police radio messages in the background. Then we would do an even more harrowing ad, showing a crack-addicted baby crying and twitching in a crib, and we would go on to do a third, featuring a funeral for a police officer brought down in a drug arrest. Just as we had done during the vote campaign, we avoided showing MEMBERS ONLY clothing in any of the ads.

Instead:

> *"Drugs don't just kill addicts"*

faded out to:

> *"This public service announcement is brought to you by MEMBERS ONLY.*

MEMBERS ONLY

Apparel And Other Fine Products.

"BADGE" :30

(SFX: GUNSHOTS) DISPATCH: (VO)
All units, code 33! Code 33!!
OFFICER:(VO) Headquarters, this is
unit six. My partner's been shot! My
partner's been shot! I need an ambulance!

(SFX: GUNSHOTS CONTINUE)
DISPATCH: (VO) Location Unit six and
condition of your officer. OFFICER:
(VO) Main street by the park! He's hit in
the chest! Get me back up!

DISPATCH: (VO) Help is on the way.
Repeat condition of your partner.
OFFICER: (VO) I need help here.
(SFX: GUNSHOTS CONTINUE)
DISPATCH: (VO) Hang in there. Units
responding now.

OFFICER: (VO) Step on it, will ya'?!!

SUPER: Drugs Don't Just Kill Addicts.
OFFICER: (VO) Step on it!

ANNCR: (VO) This message was brought
to you by Members Only.
SUPERS: Members Only Logo.
A public service message paid for by
Members Only.

Our storyboard for our anti-
drug campaign commercial.

As these new commercials were being developed, I received a slightly disconcerting Telex from the U.S. Senate Judiciary Committee. Senator Joseph Biden, Committee Chair, was convening a hearing on drug abuse prevention programs, and I was summoned to appear before them to testify on October 31, 1989.

Feeling both excited and apprehensive, Dolores and I flew to Washington D.C. the day before the hearing and checked into the Mayflower Hotel. I didn't sleep more than four hours. At 11:00 a.m., the hearing began in a room on the second floor of the Dirksen Senate Office Building. Whatever your feelings may be about politics and politicians, walking the halls of government is both humbling and empowering. I was humbled by the history and achievements of our country, yet felt empowered in that even I, a simple guy from Brooklyn, could impact a nation with such consequence. As I sat at a long table beside the three others who would testify that day – New York Yankees outfielder Dave Winfield, whose foundation, supported by the Yankee organization, sponsored a grassroots campaign against drug abuse; Darrell Green, a Washington Redskins player who was actively involved with drug prevention programs in junior high schools; and Shelley List, CBS scriptwriter and producer, cited for promoting responsible depiction of drug use on television. After Senator Biden introduced the panel and made some initial remarks, I was called first to address the committee.

In my allotted time, I described the efforts of MEMBERS ONLY to combat drug abuse: our 1986 "Just Say No" campaign; a second campaign, highlighting the desperate plight of babies who were born addicted and our fundraising efforts to build a wing in a New York hospital where these babies and their mothers would be treated; and the campaign we were about to launch, and for which we were once again committing our entire advertising budget: ***Drugs Don't Just Kill Addicts.*** I described the grim reality of the link between the drug crisis and violent crime – nearly four out of five people arrested for violence against police were under the influence of drugs at the time.

JOSEPH R. BIDEN, JR., DELAWARE, CHAIRMAN

EDWARD M. KENNEDY, MASSACHUSETTS   STROM THURMOND, SOUTH CAROLINA
HOWARD M. METZENBAUM, OHIO   ORRIN G. HATCH, UTAH
DENNIS DeCONCINI, ARIZONA   ALAN K. SIMPSON, WYOMING
PATRICK J. LEAHY, VERMONT   CHARLES E. GRASSLEY, IOWA
HOWELL HEFLIN, ALABAMA   ARLEN SPECTER, PENNSYLVANIA
PAUL SIMON, ILLINOIS   GORDON J. HUMPHREY, NEW HAMPSHIRE
HERBERT KOHL, WISCONSIN

RONALD A. KLAIN, CHIEF COUNSEL
DIANA HUFFMAN, STAFF DIRECTOR
JEFFREY J. PECK, GENERAL COUNSEL
TERRY L. WOOTEN, MINORITY CHIEF COUNSEL
AND STAFF DIRECTOR

United States Senate

COMMITTEE ON THE JUDICIARY
WASHINGTON, DC 20510-6275

October 26, 1989

FOR RELEASE: IMMEDIATELY   CONTACT: KEN DREXLER
202/224-8050

PRESS ADVISORY

BIDEN TO CHAIR HEARING ON DRUG ABUSE PREVENTION PROGRAMS

Senator Joseph R. Biden, Jr. (D-Delaware), Chairman of the Senate Judiciary Committee, announced today that the Committee will hold a hearing on Tuesday, October 31, to hear testimony from four sports, entertainment and corporate leaders who are active in promoting drug abuse prevention programs. The hearing will begin at 11:00 AM in Room 226 of the Dirksen Senate Office Building.

Testifying at the hearing will be:

DAVE WINFIELD -- The New York Yankees' outfielder is president of the Winfield Foundation, an organization that operates a nationwide, grassroots campaign against substance abuse, including training workshops and early intervention programs. A $3 million commitment by the Yankees organization and an annual $100,000 contribution by Winfield fund the bulk of the foundation's activities.

DARRELL GREEN -- A three-time all-pro defensive back with the Washington Redskins, Green is actively involved with drug prevention programs in junior high schools in the Washington area. Green has also participated in the Drug Enforcement Administration prevention programs and has established the Darrell Green Foundation to focus largely on children's issues.

SHELLEY LIST -- As a scriptwriter and producer for the CBS television series "Cagney and Lacey," List has been active in promoting responsible depiction of drug use on television. She won an award in the New England Press Association Competition for a nine-part series she wrote on drug addiction.

HERBERT M. GOLDSMITH -- As president of the Members Only Corporation, Goldsmith instituted a policy of devoting the apparel firm's entire advertising budget to anti-drug messages. He will preview a new line of television commercials that depict the risk taken by police officers who fight drugs on the streets. Goldsmith sponsors a basketball program for youth in conjunction with the Police Athletic League.

-30-

United States Senate drug
hearing.

The heart of my testimony emphasized that very few sectors of our society were as well poised as the business community to address these issues.

"If corporations have the power to influence the choices people make in buying their clothes, food, homes, and cars, I believe we have a responsibility to use that power in a much more important arena, the public good."

"We can mobilize substantial material resources to assist in the anti-drug cause. Sports equipment manufacturers can provide equipment and personnel to inner city schools; computer manufacturers could donate computers and employee hours. Electronics manufacturers, publishers, carmakers, architects, builders, furniture makers – the list is endless."

I closed with, "As the president of MEMBERS ONLY, I feel deeply that if we can save one person from taking drugs, thereby saving his or her life, then the millions of dollars we have spent will have been worth it."

It was the kind of imposing public setting that would make anyone nervous, so I was surprised that I hadn't felt uneasy in the least. But then again, I had so much early experience on stage and radio, and from 1987 on, I had become quite literally the face of MEMBERS ONLY. Our company was phenomenally successful. More than one fourth of all men's outerwear sales were made by MEMBERS ONLY. We were so much in the public eye that my new job as president kept me constantly in the spotlight, accepting awards, making speeches, and even appearing in some advertisements, like the ones for Chemical Bank, (now J.P. Morgan Chase) who had backed us for years. Chemical had been our banker from the beginning, when they first extended us a loan and issued letters of credit to our factories. All those years, we dealt with only one individual – our liaison – who attended our sales meetings and trade shows and was an integral part of our financial/ management team. Now the bank ran a full page ad, using a photograph of

How Chemical Bank helped Members Only make more than a fashion statement.

When you see the words Members Only,® you think of two things. Trend-setting jackets and advertising that has a strong public service message.

Members Only is not just the country's leading men's outer-wear manufacturer. It's the first corporation to devote its entire advertising budget to fighting drug abuse.

To make this and other important projects possible, Herb Goldsmith, President of Members Only, needed the backing of an equally innovative bank.

He went straight to Chemical. At Chemical Bank he found financial advice perfectly tailored to his needs. Chemical's letters of credit helped Members Only do business overseas. And Chemical's investment services have aided the growth of the company's assets considerably.

We have financing that can help you expand your operations, buy a fleet of trucks, or acquire a new business. Our investment banking services offer innovative ways to build your business. And one of our many cash management services can help you achieve greater control over your cash flow.

No wonder Chemical Bank is the leading bank for small and medium-sized businesses in the tri-state area. Call us at **1-800-243-6226 (Ext. 7)** and give us a chance to help you. Before you know it, we'll be running an ad about your success story.

Success Stories Start Here.

CHEMICALBANK

Herb Goldsmith
President, Members Only

Chemical Bank's ad campaign.

me wearing a MEMBERS ONLY jacket, under the headline: "How Chemical Bank helped MEMBERS ONLY make more than a fashion statement." I also did some of their radio commercials.

And the awards had begun to arrive at a pace that was almost dizzying. Korey Kay was honored with Clio Awards, the Oscars of the advertising industry for the "No Excuse," print ad campaign and the "Idiots," TV ads in 1988 and 1989. These were followed by Clios for the "Badge/Funeral" in 1990. I was honored at a black tie dinner in the Grand Ballroom of the Plaza Hotel as one of *People* magazine's National Heroes. My name appeared on the program in the Business Category along with Ralph Nader and Ted Turner. A few weeks later I was honored by *Crain's* magazine as one of their New York Business All-Stars, and received their Man of the Year Award.

I believe it was all that exposure and practice and experience that made me feel so comfortable sitting in the hallowed halls of the U.S. Senate in the fall of 1989. As I read my statement, I felt a great deal of pride in my company, more so than in myself. We really had made a difference.

Then off I went for the next award, which was scheduled a half hour later. The Order of Michael the Archangel, comprised of police chiefs from all over the country, made me a Grand Knight of the Order. Their ribbon and medal were draped around my neck as I was politely asked to kneel. Thanks to today's internet technology, most of our distinguished, and not-so-distinguished, MEMBERS ONLY ads can still be found on places like *YouTube* and *Facebook*.

We kept our anti-drug campaign going by joining with the Police Athletic League for a huge event in the summer of 1990, just as the commercials were appearing on TV, radio, in print, and on billboards. The "BIG SHOT" Tournaments were designed to strengthen the links between community kids and their local police. Across the country, in high school gymnasiums or department store lobbies or malls, we, along with 55 Chapters of the PAL, sponsored a basketball shooting competition. Registration was free. Patterned after the schoolyard game of "H-O-R-S-E," participants shot at a basket from points around the court that spelled out MEMBERS ONLY.

★THE CRAIN'S ALL-STARS

Dressing a drug message in $12 million ads

HERBERT M. GOLDSMITH
CONSUMER PRODUCTS

Picking the right jacket can be important—but for Herbert M. Goldsmith, it changed his life.

After 25 years in the men's outerwear business, Mr. Goldsmith turned his world around in 1978 when he created a racing jacket in a chintz fabric. It was the first and only design for his brand new label—Members Only.

Young record and film execs immediately made it their uniform. In just two years, $20 million worth of those hip jackets—emblazoned with Members Only above the breast pocket—were also sold to the likes of Frank Sinatra and George Bush. Today, Members Only, with sales of $100 million, is the leading brand of men's outerwear sold in department stores.

In the past few years, 61-year-old Mr. Goldsmith has used that same marketing flair to develop a unique advertising campaign for Members Only that not only bolsters his company's sales but serves the public good. For unlike other fashion companies that seem to promote sexual decadence in their ads, Members Only has devoted $12 million—its entire advertising budget since 1987—to publicize a strong anti-drug message.

Celebrities like Lou Pinella, clad in Members Only attire, have warned of the dangers of drugs in the company's ads. This spring a new $3 million campaign will focus on drug-addicted babies.

"It was an opportunity to give back," says Mr. Goldsmith, whose lavender silk pocket scarf bespeaks his love for show biz. "We may be losing a generation to drugs. You can't do business without that generation." It was a stroke of marketing genius on Mr. Goldsmith's part to see that the same recording stars and sports heroes who gave Members Only a slick image of exclusivity were the perfect celebrities to reach potential drug abusers.

Mr. Goldsmith is the first to admit that the company's anti-drug campaign had ulterior motives. By 1986, he decided the celebrity-endorsement format that had boosted Members Only was growing stale.

When Manhattan-based Korey, Kay & Partners suggested TV commercials featuring well-known personalities speaking out against drugs (with only a tagline mentioning the company's name), Mr. Goldsmith immediately gave the go-ahead.

"It's very easy to use part of your ad budget for public service if you are a Coca-Cola," says Lois Korey, who helped devise the anti-drug concept. "But Herb is one of the few who has the guts to put his whole budget behind fighting drugs."

Mr. Goldsmith's skills in reaching customers go back to the 1950s, when he developed advertising campaigns for his father's nel Apparel Co. He conceived one of the first major promotional tie-ins with a movie when the menswear company sold snowflake-design jackets in conjunction with Bing Crosby's *White Christmas.*

Mr. Goldsmith went out on his own in 1961 with partner Ed Wachtel to operate Europe Craft, also a men's outerwear company. The business had minor successes until it devised Members Only to compete with designer brands like Pierre Cardin.

"We knew we needed a snob-appeal label," says Mr. Goldsmith. "Walking into my country club one day, I saw the sign 'Members Only' and knew that was the name."

Members Only still sells the racing jacket, along with a complete line of men's sportswear and a dozen licensed products, including eyewear and auto accessories. Two years ago, for access to more capital, Members Only was sold to Jersey City-based Marcade Group Inc., with Mr. Goldsmith remaining as its president. The company hopes to make an acquisition that would help regain some of its licenses.

Mr. Goldsmith admits to one major failure in reading consumers over the years in the apparel trade. A velcro-closing jacket—slightly ahead of its time in the 1950s—was a colossal flop. ■ *Cynthia Rigg*

An article on our anti-drug campaign.

The Order of Michael the Archangel

This will attest that

Herbert M. Goldsmith

has been designated a Knight of the Order of Michael the Archangel
with all the rights, privileges, titles and honors that pertain to this office as

Grand Knight of the Order

and is inducted into the Knighthood by reason of an act of bravery or service to his or her
community so outstanding that it merits the respect and admiration of the honorable
Order of Michael the Archangel Police and Fire Legion. That through this act as a
Good Samaritan the Knight designated shall enjoy the respect and admiration of the honors
bestowed upon said person by all those who shall read this document.

Supreme Grand Knight of the
Order of Michael the Archangel.

Issued the 31st day of October 1989
at New Orleans, Louisiana, United States of America.

*"Beat the Big Shot" campaign
with NBA star Walt Frazier.*

Each shooter had 90 seconds to make as many shots as possible. As before, top athletes were eager to join us. NBA legends John Havlicek and Rick Barry co-chaired the program, and New York Knicks star Walt Frazier was the center of attention at our introductory press conference at City Hall in Manhattan. Local retailers got a lot of media exposure, especially when the basketball stars did in-person promotions for the tournament. All the way through, the emphasis was on "Don't do Drugs."

Our advertisements appeared during the tournament, and we were once again deluged with letters of gratitude from police and civic organizations and the public, all of whom agreed that we had done more than save individual kids from the horrors of drug addiction – we had probably saved many, as well as keeping the message in the public consciousness.

1000 Connecticut Ave. N.W.
Suite 9
Washington, D.C. 20036
(202) 293-9088

National Association of Chiefs of Police

17th October 1989

Cindy Spunger
FLEISHMAN HILLARD, INC.
1301 Connecticut Avenue NW
Washington DC 20036

Dear Ms. Sprunger:

This is in follow-up to your correspondence with our Executive Director, Gerald S. Arenberg with reference to our organization's decision to present *Members Only* and Fleishman Hillard with our "E-Flag", which is representative of individuals and companies that have used their resources to promote anti-drug programs in a productive and selfless manner.

As Editor-In-Chief of THE CHIEF OF POLICE, which is the official publication of The National Association of Chiefs of Police, I did want to take this opportunity to send you a complimentary copy of our publication, in which the story of the "E-Flag" and a photo presentation of same appears on pages 6 and 7 of this enclosed issue.

On a personal note, having worn *Members Only* shirts and jackets for several years by personal choice, it was refreshing to learn that the company you represent was the first commercial enterprise to devote its' entire advertising budget to a public service campaign to such diverse areas of anti-drug awareness. Be assured of my personal commitment as Editor-In-Chief to make our readership aware of your contributions in this area, and that of your client, *Members Only*.

Sincerely,

JIM GORDON
Editor-In-Chief

J:bm

cc: Gerald S. Arenberg, Executive Director
    Severin L. Sorensen, Co-Chairman NACOP Demand Drug
    Reduction Program, Washington, D.C.

My "Honor Award for Distinguished Public Service"

NATIONAL PAL UPDATE

Creating A Bond Between Cops and Kids

Non Profit Org.
U.S. Postage
PAID
West Palm Beach, FL
Permit No. 776

VOL. 6, NO. 3 **Official Publication of National Police Athletic League** SUMMER 1990

National Conference Catches The Spirit...

REACH OUT TO MAKE A FRIEND

"Italy" took home the O-Limp-Cop gold medals at the 1990 National PAL Conference and Training Seminar Theme Party.

Colorado Springs, Colorado was the site of the National Police Athletic League's 46th Annual Conference and Training Seminar, held May 19-26.

The most successful conference thus far, the week had much to do with it Colorado Springs laid out the carpet. The hospitality was outstanding. The variety of natural and man-made recreation is hard to match. Colorado is America's most colorful state.

The opening ceremonies were held poolside in a lovely garden atrium area at the Sheraton Colorado Springs Hotel. The conference was called to order by President Reuddy Dowd. The Chaplain of Colorado Springs Police Department delivered a thoughtful invocation.

The Colorado Springs Honor Guard impressively performed the presentation of colors and Mike Mirelle, First Vice President, led the group to the pledge of allegiance to the flag of the United States.

Conference attendees were welcomed to Colorado Springs by Colorado Springs Chief of Police James Munger, George Waldtmeier, 2nd Vice President delivered the response.

President Dowd presented the conference rules and a delightful luncheon

was hosted by Sunmark, Inc. followed also enjoyed by all.

Dr. Orv Owens, of Orv Owens and Associates, Marco Island, Florida, delivered an outstanding keynote address. He addressed "Today's Issues, Tomorrow's Solution," focusing on developing leadership qualities in the youth of America.

Dr. Owens believes that bringing out the leadership in our youth, with the help of Police Officers as role models, will curtail current problems faced by youth, such as drug and alcohol abuse.

Leadership can be acquired by increasing self-worth of young people by positive feedback and helping each child realize that they are unique individuals and special in their own right.

Dr. Orv Owens was presented with a plaque of appreciation for his keynote address by Joseph Johnson, National PAL's Executive Director.

Following the luncheon and opening ceremonies, the conference attendees spent time speaking with exhibitors also attending the conference and viewing their wares.

The annual trade show exhibition continues to provide an opportunity for suppliers to show their products first hand to key decision makers of local chapters. It's a one-on-one contact that builds the necessary support for good business.

The Exhibit Hall also provides the advantage for attendees to see, touch and feel a product, negotiate in person, in some instances sample the product, ask questions and receive answers, and on the spot shopping. **Continued on p.4**

PAL Gives Thanks To Its 'Big Shot' Pal 'Members Only'

Although the Members Only/National PAL Big Shot Tournaments are over — thanks to Members Only and their retail stores — the anti-drug message they promoted through the program will be a lasting memory to all of the young Big Shot participants.

The Big Shot Tournament was a basketball shooting competition in which the participants shoot from various points on the

basketball court that spelled out MEMBERS ONLY. Each shooter had 90 seconds to make as many shots as possible.

The Big Shot competition was a part of a national anti-drug program sponsored by Members Only and National PAL. The Cranford, NJ PAL was one of 55 PAL Chapters to take advantage of this program.

"We're taking the anti-drug message to the streets," said Detective Charles Archdeacon, Director of the Cranford PAL.

"We hope that this PAL program will strengthen the link between kids and community and the police, and at the same time make a strong statement against drug abuse," continued Archdeacon.

The Cranford PAL had 118 participants in their Big Shot Tournament and at the end set up an additional contest between the parents of the participants. Archdeacon added, "It added a nice flavor to the tournament watching the kids root for their parents."

Many of the PAL Chapters who participated in the program teamed up with

a Members Only retailer in their area to make their tournament more memorable.

Hector Tavarez, Director of the Egg Harbor Twp., NJ PAL says, "By joining efforts with Burton's Department Store, a Members Only retailer) we were able to generate more media exposure and witness the number of kids involved in the program than we would have been capable of doing in our own."

Retailers donating prizes for the tournament, Burton's helped recruit the assistance of former Washington General's basketball great Al Siebold to speak to Big Shot participants and spectators about his "Hugs Not Drugs" program.

Egg Harbor's PAL was not alone in asking for the assistance of the NBA and its "stars" to help promote the Big Shot tournament. John Havlicek and Rick Barry, two NBA legends, were Members Only Big Shot Co-Chairpersons offering their time to make appearances at Big Shot tournaments. **Continued on p. 7**

Cops and kids working and playing together as a key to a happy, healthy youth.

Procedes from "Big Shot" go to PAL.

* * * * *

The most surprising celebrity experience that occurred to MEMBERS ONLY was a telephone call from the manager of the then current Heavy Weight Boxing Champion, Evander Holyfield. He said that Evander was so thank full and impressed with what we were doing with our Anti Drug campaign and fostering a relationship with the youth and the Police Athletic League. He volunteered his service at no cost to us. We told his manager that we were not using celebrities in our current advertising campaign, but give us a few days to come up with something. "Please tell Evander how much we appreciate his offer."

I called our ad agency and our publicist and told them about the offer. I reminded them that Holyfield was scheduled to box, Buster Douglas three weeks from today. Why not try to get the MEMBERS ONLY label sewn on his boxing short. The exposure would be great. It would be seen on TV during the match. I called the manager and asked if Evander would agree to have the MEMBERS ONLY label sewn on the front of his boxing short. "No, we can't do it because we have a contract with the Everlast Company that specifies that only the EVERLAST label can be displayed on the front." I asked if sewing the label on the rear of his shorts would be okay. He laughed and said that he'll get back to us. The next day he called and said it was okay and asked us to send a messenger to pick up Evander's shorts and make sure they were returned in one week.

Our label that is sewn above the front pocket of our jacket is much too small to be seen on TV. If we made a larger one, which rear cheek should we put it on? Having our label on his rear end didn't bode well with us. EXCEPT! What if we made the label the size of the back of his waistband? That would really photograph well. The problem for us was that sewing a larger label on the elastic waistband meant it would have to be legible after he puts it on and it stretches out. We experimented, and came up with the perfect solution. The short was returned and what we did worked perfectly. All throughout the fight, each time his back was to the camera, there it was, very clear, MEMBERS ONLY.

Sports Pages

The New York Times

Holyfield Flattens Douglas and Takes the Title

Holyfield wearing his Members Only label. Photo in "The New York Times."

The next day our trade ad.

The real surprise and payoff was the photo that was used in every newspaper in America, including *The New York Times*, showing the back of Holyfield leaning over the knocked down, Buster Douglas. We sure lucked out… again!

In order to capitalize on this spectacular publicity, our advertising agency created an ad that we ran in our trade paper. It showed the photo that *The New York Times* ran and the only printed words were:

MEMBERS ONLY STILL A KNOCKOUT!

There are no statistics available to detail the additional voter awareness we created, or the number of drug-related deaths we may have prevented. How do you measure the positive reactions we received from the retail community? How do you weigh the letters of praise we received? The average American did more than pass along tributes to our company. They registered their approval at the cash register.

Lending advertising support to community responsibility can be more than a supplement to the soul. It can supplement responsiveness to your product.

As per my contract, I had insisted that my agreed term of employment would conclude at the end of 1992, I wanted to make sure that the company's reputation as the leader in the outerwear industry remained intact. Ever so slowly, at the start of the year, I slowly shifted my responsibilities to my executive staff. The system and controls had been put in place long before. Nevertheless, on my last day, I felt strange. We celebrated with the annual Christmas party. The always-present cake was there. The pride that my staff, executives, and employees had in the company was evident. The salutations, speeches, and good wishes were honest and some, very emotional. We all found it hard to say goodbye.

This was my life, my passion. How does one replace such success, recognition, and fame?

I insisted on waiting for all of them to leave. It was very quiet! This was it! The last time.

I blew a kiss, GOOD BYE. I smiled as I locked the door, and left.

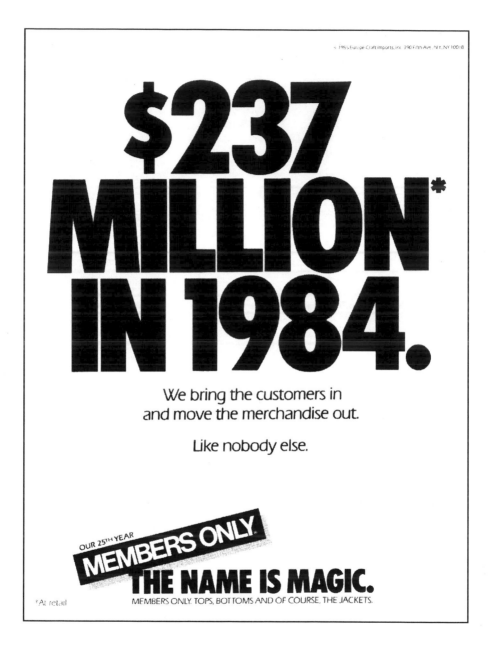

$237 MILLION* IN 1984.

We bring the customers in
and move the merchandise out.

Like nobody else.

OUR 25TH YEAR

MEMBERS ONLY

THE NAME IS MAGIC.

MEMBERS ONLY. TOPS, BOTTOMS AND OF COURSE, THE JACKETS.

*At retail

Epilogue

HOW OFTEN DO WE HEAR PEOPLE SAY, "Those were the good old days." To me, the years in which I grew up were a very different time and style of living than now. I'd leave home in the morning and play all day long. We played together in the streets . . . boy's games like ring-a-levio, stick ball, stoop ball, and marbles. The girls played games like hop-scotch, potsy, or Double Dutch jump rope. No one was able to reach any of us all day; cell phones hadn't been invented. There were no Play Stations, Nintendo's or X-boxes. There were no video games and we didn't have 150 video cable channels. There were no DVDs or CDs or personal computers. No Internet, Facebook and no chat rooms . . . WHAT WE HAD WAS FRIENDS!!!

The past generations have produced some of the best risk takers, problem solvers, and inventors ever. The past 83 years have seen an explosion of innovation and ideas. As with every one of my generation, there was freedom, failure, success, disappointment, and responsibility. Somehow we learned how to deal with it all.

Yes, some lived in a better house or apartment. Some parents had better paying jobs. Some had larger or smaller families. Even so, essentially we all did the same things day in and day out, living and working in the same neighborhood. Circumstances beyond our control, like war and depression, influenced our lives. New highways, railroad modernization, and communication exposed us to new cities and towns that weren't in our reach or imagination. There were new places to go, new things to see and do. Our lifestyle constantly evolved.

This new exposure and growth influenced our daily lives. Publications wrote about and showed how other people lived. Influenced by those, many of us were able to achieve a better lifestyle than our parents. The explosion of suburbia was perhaps the most influential. Ex G.I.s were able to get a government loan that enabled them to purchase a brand new home for between $7,500 and $13,000. The monthly mortgage cost less than paying rent in an apartment. From the mid-50s and on, most every family had a car (unless you lived in "the City"). The economy was thriving. Business and employment opportunities were plentiful. Transportation was inexpensive and readily available. Those living in the cities and suburbs had trains and buses. Commuters didn't use a car to go to work. The car was used by wives during the day, for car-pooling the kids to school and for shopping at the local stores.

Circumstances, economic situations, and opportunities changed our ways of life. Many of us took advantage of them and others were content with their current situation. Time changes everything.

In the suburbs, the daily newspaper was delivered to your door. New schools with grassy playgrounds were used for all kinds of outdoor sports. On weekends, in the spring, summer, and fall, families would watch and cheer for their kids at play. In the winter, there was ice skating, bowling, and other indoor sports, either to participate in or simply to observe. There was even time on weekends to visit relatives or take a daily car trip to places not seen before. It was an exciting time.

The extraordinary circumstances and opportunities that occurred in my life were there to be taken. There was not much to lose. I could always go back to what I had been doing before.

Success is achieved by determination, innovation, motivation, and a bit of luck. It cannot be achieved without the support of family and colleagues.

In business, one also needs a motivated staff and colleagues who have respect and pride in the company and its executives. We are all steering the ship. Each is needed to help keep the course true and steady. I am extremely proud of each and every person I worked with along the way. My former partner and still my friend, Ed Wachtel, helped to make the journey with MEMBERS ONLY smooth, exciting, profitable, and memorable. Our mutual dedication and business acumen was truly a partnership made in Heaven. We created a national brand name! It was the best of times.

Of great import was the love and support of my family.

I'll always remember the people I met along the way, famous and infamous. Some remain friends and some helped me when I needed their intellect, talent, and support.

After MEMBERS ONLY . . . thanks to my friends and associates in the theatrical industry, who have enabled me to win two TONY awards and four Drama Desk awards so far. But that's a whole other story!

I would like to end "my story" with the most incredible accomplishment – my daughters, Gail, Michelle and Ileen.

*My daughters, Ileen, Michelle
and Gail*